Wales Says Yes

Devolution and the 2011 Welsh Referendum

Richard Wyn Jones and Roger Scully

UNIVERSITY OF WALES
CARDIFF
2012

www.uwp.co.uk

British Library CIP Data
A catalogue record for this book is available from the British Library.

ISBN   978-0-7083-2485-1
e-ISBN   978-0-7083-2486-8

The right of Richard Wyn Jones and Roger Scully to be identified as authors of this work has been asserted in accordance with sections 77 and 79 of the Copyright, Designs and Patents Act 1988.

Typeset by Mark Heslington Ltd, Scarborough, North Yorkshire
Printed by CPI Antony Rowe, Chippenham, Wiltshire

i Gwenan Creunant
Cyfaill, cefn, Cymraes

Contents

Figures

Tables

Preface

The referendum that took place in Wales on 3 March 2011 was a curious event. As we discuss here, there are good reasons to argue that it should never have happened. And when the referendum did occur, the clear majority of the Welsh electorate chose not to bother participating. Yet, underwhelming as it was in many respects, the referendum was also an event of signal importance to Wales.

The referendum was important because the process by which this rather bizarre vote came to occur encapsulates so much about characteristic pathologies of Welsh political life. The referendum was also important because the way in which the campaign was fought, and the result that the vote produced, crystallized deeper and broader changes in Welsh politics over the previous decade. The referendum mattered because of the direct consequences that the result would bring over subsequent years for the policies of the Welsh Government and the responsibilities of the National Assembly for Wales. The referendum was also important because of the further consequences, for how Wales and the other nations of these islands are governed, that may well follow from the result.

For all these reasons, the 2011 Welsh referendum deserves serious, sustained analysis. In this book, we attempt to provide that: focusing not only on the vote itself, and the immediate campaign preceding it, but also trying to place this vote in its broader historical, institutional and political context. The referendum was an important event, but as we have come to understand all too well in Wales, devolution is a process.

The research on which this study was based has received support from a number of quarters. We gratefully acknowledge financial support from the Economic and Social Research Council (grant RES-000-22-4496) to conduct the 2011 Welsh Referendum Study (WRS), which provides the bulk of the data used in chapter six. WRS was conducted in collaboration with the survey company YouGov: at various stages of their work on this project, Laurence

Janta-Lipinski, Joe Twyman, Coralie Pring and Kate Davies at YouGov all distinguished themselves for their professionalism and their determination to help us deliver the best surveys possible. We are also very grateful for the helpful suggestions on the content of the surveys made by Robert Johns of the University of Essex, and by participants in a seminar at Cardiff University in January 2011.

We are also happy to thank the McDougall Trust for a small grant which supported the conduct and transcription of the interviews with those involved in the referendum campaign that provide much of the evidence discussed in chapter four. We are very grateful to our interviewees: Leighton Andrews, Rachel Banner, John Broughton, Nigel Bull, Meilyr Ceredig, Cynog Dafis, James Davies, Nigel Dix, Mark Drakeford, Lisa Francis, Len Gibbs, Daran Hill, Rob Humphreys, Roger Lewis, Cathy Owens, Lee Waters and Rebecca Williams, as well as some who spoke to us on condition of anonymity. They were, without exception, generous with their time and their insights. Given that some of the events discussed in the book are so recent and politically contentious, there have inevitably been some instances in which we had to rely on the testimony of our anonymous sources. Where we have been unable for this reason to supply a named source we have in each case sought to verify the claims made with two different (if anonymous) sources. We also thank Einion Dafydd and Catrin Wyn Edwards for their assistance in conducting the interviews, and Laura Considine and Lorrae Wright for help with transcription. Such is the richness of the material supplied in many of these interviews that we will be depositing edited copies with the Welsh Political Archive at the National Library of Wales in Aberystwyth, in order that they be available to future researchers. Some of the archival and interview material utilized in chapters one and two was collected as part of an earlier research project undertaken by Richard Wyn Jones on behalf of the University of Wales Board of Celtic Studies. We would like to thank both the Board and project researcher Bethan Lewis for their support. A final note on sources: all the website URLs referred to were current as of August 2011.

Aspects of the research reported here were presented in draft form at the annual conference of the Political Studies Association in London, April 2011; at breakfast seminars in Cardiff and Aberystwyth in June 2011; and at the annual conference of the Elections, Public Opinion and Parties specialist group in Exeter,

September 2011. We thank participants in all those events for helpful comments and criticisms. We also thank Dafydd Trystan Davies, Lee Waters, Joanne Foster and an anonymous reviewer for their detailed comments on individual chapters. We are wholly responsible for any errors or inadequacies that remain.

We also gratefully acknowledge support and assistance from our home institutions, Aberystwyth University and Cardiff Universy, and particularly our colleagues in the Institute of Welsh Politics at Aberystwyth and Cardiff's Wales Governance Centre. And we thank Sarah Lewis and the rest of the team at the University of Wales Press for all their assistance.

Last, but certainly not least, we thank our families for their consistent support, encouragement and love.

Roger Scully
Aberystwyth

Richard Wyn Jones
Treganna, Caerdydd

The road to the referendum

In April 2009, the House of Lords Select Committee on the Constitution published a report entitled *Referendums in the United Kingdom*.[1] A key issue for the committee – a group of genuine distinction – was the question of when it is appropriate for referendums to be held.[2] This is a question of relevance to many political systems, and one worthy of serious consideration.

Referendums have traditionally been regarded as foreign to the 'Westminster model' of parliamentary democracy. This model is one based on indirect democracy. It is characterized by the election of representatives who campaign on the basis of party manifestos. Once returned to parliament it is the task of members of the majority party to form a government to implement the platform on which it was elected. While the role played by the electors is fundamental to the democratic legitimacy of the system, it is nonetheless limited. Beyond their infrequent visits to the polling booth, the people delegate the task of government to others. They are not invited to pick and choose between different elements of any party's platform. Rather, the governing party is regarded as enjoying a mandate to implement its programme as a whole.

It is obvious that referendums sit uneasily within such a model. Referendums confer on the electorate direct power of decision on a specific issue: one that is deliberately, some might say artificially, isolated from other concerns. When implemented within a Westminster-style parliamentary democracy, referendums also operate outside the broader context and culture of civic engagement and direct democracy that characterizes a system such as Switzerland, where referendums are a regular occurrence.[3] It is little wonder, then, that in the UK and its fellow Westminster-type democracies, referendums have traditionally been viewed with suspicion, and they have remained rarely used. The 1975 vote on continuing membership of the 'Common Market' (as it was then dubbed) was the first ever UK-wide referendum. Only one further such referendum has since occurred: that on the adoption of the Alternative Vote (AV) electoral system for UK general elections, some thirty-six years later. Moreover, the latter came about through highly exceptional circumstances: the formation of the first UK peacetime coalition government since the days of Ramsay MacDonald, and concerning a policy that had not featured in the manifestos of either coalition partner in the preceding general election. Thus, one might reasonably regard the AV ballot as an exception proving the general rule: that referendums do not fit comfortably within, and are not normally a prominent part of, a Westminster democracy.

Wales has greater experience of referendums than the rest of the UK. Local referendums on Sunday drinking were an intermittent feature of Welsh life from the time of the 1961 Licensing Act (which repealed the uniform provisions of the 1881 Sunday Closing (Wales) Act) until the requirement for such votes was finally abandoned in 2003.[4] More relevant to our concerns are the two nation-wide referendums on devolution held in 1979 and 1997. These votes, which we discuss in much greater detail below, were part of the evidence considered by the Lords' Committee as they examined previous experience with referendums in the UK, and the prospect that referendums might become more frequent. Their Lordships' overall conclusion was clear:

> The balance of the evidence that we have heard leads us to the conclusion that there are significant drawbacks to the use of referendums. In particular, we regret the ad hoc manner in which referendums have been used, often as a tactical device, by the government of the day. Referendums may become a part of the UK's political and constitutional practice. Where possible, cross-party agreement should be sought as to the circumstances in which it is appropriate for referendums to be used.

> Notwithstanding our view that there are significant drawbacks to the use of referendums, we acknowledge arguments that, if referendums are to be used, they are most appropriately used in relation to fundamental constitutional issues.

The committee did not believe it possible to give a precise definition of a 'fundamental constitutional issue'. But they did provide illustrative examples, including abolition of the monarchy, secession from the Union and the abolition of either House of Parliament.[5]

One of the central arguments of this book is that the referendum held in Wales on 3 March 2011 illustrates almost perfectly many of the problems that the House of Lords Select Committee identified. The referendums of 1979 and 1997 concerned the fundamental question of whether or not Wales should have devolution. By stark contrast, the subject of the 2011 vote – a choice between two systems of granting primary law-making powers to the National Assembly for Wales – cannot remotely be considered as constituting a fundamental constitutional issue. Moreover, the referendum itself resulted from tactical manoeuvring, made to overcome internal divisions within one party, rather than following any all-party agreement or consensus. Perhaps predictably, far from being a shining example of participative democracy in action, the resulting campaign was generally uninspiring and at times dispiriting. And the referendum result left important questions unanswered; some even unasked.

In this opening chapter, we set the context for the 2011 Welsh referendum. We begin in very general terms, by reviewing briefly how referendums are understood as a form of democratic decision making. In particular, we discuss how the apparent simplicity of a straight Yes/No vote on a single issue is often complicated by apparently extraneous factors, thus leading many people to vote for reasons other than their views on what is ostensibly at stake.

Our focus then moves more specifically to Wales. We begin by examining the 1979 referendum. We consider the circumstances that led to the holding of a vote on devolution. We also draw attention to the broader political and social context in which the vote was eventually held, the nature of the opposing campaigns and the overwhelming final result.

In the next section of the chapter, we move on to consider the 1997 referendum. We again spend some time considering the peculiar circumstances that led to the decision to hold a referendum. We also review the nature of the respective campaigns, and the context in which the vote was held, before explaining the very different result that transpired from eighteen years previously.

The final section of the chapter addresses the 2006 Government of Wales Act and its aftermath. In particular, we explore the gestation of the 2006 Government of Wales Act and the decision to include within its provisions a referendum on a move to extended legislative powers as provided by Part IV of the Act. We conclude by discussing how the referendum provision of the 2006 Act became central to coalition negotiations between Labour and Plaid Cymru after the 2007 National Assembly election, and thus helped pave the way for a referendum to be held in 2011.

Referendums across the world

While the political systems of the contemporary world can be classified according to many criteria, probably the most common distinction is that drawn between democracies and non-democracies. Democratic political systems supposedly embody the principle of government by the demos, the people. In practice, the defining characteristic of these systems is usually understood to be that those who hold major political offices are chosen via free and fair elections in which the great majority of the people are able to participate. The system is democratic not because the people directly make the major decisions themselves, but because they get to choose the decision-makers. Non-democratic systems differ because the rulers are not elected at all, or because the elections supposedly used to select them are significantly lacking in freedom and/or fairness. Of course, in practice, all democracies fall short of the ideal. The conduct of elections will usually be imperfect to some degree. And much power in a society is typically wielded by people who are not elected: those who lead powerful private-sector economic organizations and those occupying significant public roles that are not filled via election (such as senior judicial roles, or the headship of central banks). But the regular conduct of reasonably free and fair elections to fill at least some key political offices usually suffices for a political system to be regarded by analysts, and by its own people, as being broadly democratic.

Making free and fair elections the defining characteristic of a democratic political system implies an understanding of democracy as an indirect process. The people are not expected to decide for themselves; they choose those they wish to make the major decisions on their behalf. At subsequent elections, they may then pass judgement on the decisions and behaviour of those previously chosen as their representatives. The use of referendums does not obviously fit easily within this understanding. A referendum takes the power of

4

decision over a specific question back from the elected representatives and returns it to the people, who decide a matter directly.

The use of direct democracy within political systems founded upon indirect democracy raises numerous questions. To give the people direct power of decision over one particular issue, out of the multitude that a political system may be grappling with at the time, suggests that the issue is in some way special or distinct. Analysts and citizens are likely to ask why this specific matter should be isolated from the normal procedures of indirect democracy and given to the people to decide. What is different about this issue from others?

A second set of questions may be raised about the specific nature of the choice that a referendum offers the people. While some issues may present two very obvious alternatives between which the people can be asked to choose, in many cases there will be considerably more room for discretion about the number of alternatives to be placed on the ballot, which particular options these will be, and how they will be phrased. As scholars of politics have long understood, considerable influence can be wielded by those with agenda-setting power: the ability to shape the nature of the options between which people must choose.

Many other questions can be asked about referendums as a form of democratic decision making. Should the referendum outcome constitute a legally binding decision for the political community, or merely be something for holders of political power to take into account? If a referendum result is binding, for how long should it remain so? Under what circumstances might the people legitimately be asked to reconsider their original verdict in a second vote? And if it is accepted that some issues should be given to the people to decide directly, then what remains the proper realm of representative democracy? And what, if any, role should representatives have in direct democracy?

Although their use can be seen to raise these and other fundamental questions, referendums have become increasingly prevalent within the democratic world.[6] Very few of the established major democracies have never held a nation-wide referendum;[7] among those that have not, the United States has made frequent use of referendums in many of its states. Nonetheless, the frequency with which referendums are held continues to vary substantially across political systems. In most democracies they remain much less common than representative elections.

5

There are a very small number of instances – of which Switzerland is by far the most well-known example – of plebiscitary democracies, where the frequent use of referendums to make many major political decisions, both at the national and sub-national level, has been built into the design of the political system. Elsewhere, referendums are used less frequently, and most commonly in particular types of situations. Referendums will often be used to approve or reject a new constitution for a political system, or for proposed constitutional amendments. Constitutions may also require them to be held to approve certain types of decision: for instance, provisions in the Irish constitution have necessitated a series of public votes over European Union treaty revisions in recent decades. Some political systems provide for citizen-led referendums to be held: usually requiring a certain number of validated signatures supporting a particular 'initiative' for it to be placed on the ballot paper. California is perhaps the most well-known example where such initiatives are frequently used, and have had major political consequences.[8] In many other political systems there are few requirements to hold popular votes to decide major political issues. But referendums have often been used by political leaders as a means of resolving otherwise intractable political disputes: a governing political party that is deeply divided over an issue may find it highly convenient to 'let the people decide' rather than having to come to an agreement internally.[9]

How people vote in referendums remains rather less well understood than voting in elections. In some contexts, voting choices appear to be little more than a reflection of group identities. In the March 2011 South Sudanese referendum that overwhelmingly endorsed independence from the rest of Sudan, voting patterns appeared primarily driven by the fundamental rejection of Sudanese identity by nearly all the southern people. But such factors can be important not only in supposedly 'tribal' societies: national identities and broader national sentiments were highly influential on voting in the 1992 Canadian and the 1980 and 1995 Quebec referendums.[10] Similarly, those with a more Welsh identity were substantially more likely to have voted in favour of devolution for Wales in 1997 than those with a British identity.[11]

Although parties are not 'on the ballot' in referendums, the obviously political nature of many referendum questions means that parties often take stances on many referendum issues. And voters often appear to heed such stances. The cues offered by parties to voters are central to many explanations of referendum voting decisions.[12] The willingness of many voters to be guided by the positions taken by major parties and political leaders often appears to function as a cognitive short cut, compensating for voters' lack of knowledge on the issue ostensibly at stake.[13] However, the type of cue followed may vary. Popular parties and leaders can attract support to causes that they endorse: such a process seemingly shaped the outcome of the UK's 1975 referendum on European Community membership.[14] But the electorate may also use a referendum to register discontent with an unpopular party or leader, as with President Mitterrand and the French Socialists in the 1992 French referendum on the Maastricht Treaty.[15] Voters can even use referendums to indicate unhappiness with an entire political class, as occurred in the 1992/1993 New Zealand referendums on electoral reform.[16]

Finally, how people vote in a referendum may, of course, be driven by their views on the question on the ballot paper. The extent to which many people will have settled or deeply rooted views on the matter at hand will likely depend heavily on the nature and history of the issue. Does the referendum concern a matter that has been the subject of public debate for many years? If this is so, or to an even greater extent if the referendum relates to one of the defining cleavages in a society, then large proportions of people can be expected to have deeply rooted and well-developed opinions about the matter. If the referendum concerns a rather more esoteric issue, or one about which there is little tradition of widespread public debate, then few beyond some of the most highly educated and politically engaged can be expected to have thought much about the question. We certainly cannot assume that the votes cast in referendums will always reflect the settled will of the people on the question placed before them.

The 1979 devolution referendum

The Labour Party emerged from the February 1974 UK general election as a minority government, but with a clear commitment in its Welsh manifesto to establish an elected Welsh Assembly.[17] In stark and obviously unsustainable contrast, at this point Labour was still formally opposed to Scottish devolution, pledging rather that meetings of the Scottish Grand Committee would take place in Edinburgh. The Scottish and Welsh Grand Committees are the proverbial knacker's-yard ponies of the devolution debate: their fate has been to be wheeled out periodically, after years of neglect, for further flogging by opponents of reform every time devolution-ists appear to be threatening progress. Not until several months after February's inconclusive election was the Scottish Labour Party forced (by the crudest of organizational fixes) to accept that it must also embrace devolution, after intervention from a British leader-ship alarmed by the dramatic election breakthrough of the SNP.[18] To the consternation of some Welsh Labour devolutionists, Scotland now leapfrogged Wales. Labour entered that year's second general election campaign pledging legislative devolution for Scotland and only executive devolution for Wales. Indeed, writing in 1980, Drucker and (future prime minister, Gordon) Brown claimed that, as a result of this episode, 'devolutionists within the Welsh Labour Party ... never regained the initiative'.[19]

Though they offer a beguilingly simple explanation for the travails suffered by Welsh devolutionists during the remainder of the decade, Drucker and Brown overlook the extent to which Labour's position on devolution for Wales had actually been consistent for several years prior to the machinations of 1974. As we review in much greater detail in chapter two, following a major internal party dispute in the summer of 1969, Labour had recom-mended to the Royal Commission on the Constitution that an elected assembly with executive powers be established in Wales. This remained the position in Labour's 1970 general election mani-festo, and was restated regularly by the party leadership in Wales, not least after the publication of the Royal Commission's rather convoluted recommendations in the autumn of 1973, and again in the February 1974 election. Although the Wales TUC briefly attempted to resurrect the case for legislative devolution for Wales during the summer of 1974, there was never a realistic prospect of the argument making headway. It was precisely because the commit-ment to executive devolution was so relatively well established and had been so regularly restated that it gave supporters the best hope of securing any kind of devolution at all.

In addition to consistently supporting an elected assembly with executive powers, Labour had been equally consistent in rejecting the idea that its plans should be subject to a referendum.[20] This position was wholly consistent with long-standing traditions within the Labour movement that regarded plebiscites as a means of vetoing radical reform. These traditions contended that, provided the (first past the post) election was fairly won, the elected party had the moral right to implement its manifesto. Parliamentary sovereignty was thus a crucial mechanism for achieving 'democratic socialism'.

Referendums, however, had become a central part of British political discourse in the 1970s, mainly due to ongoing controversies and divisions surrounding UK membership of the European Community. It is hardly surprising, therefore, that sections of the Welsh Labour Party opposed to their own party's devolution policy began to advocate that this, too, should be subject to popular vote. At a June 1974 delegate conference in Llandrindod Wells, convened to reiterate support for an elected assembly based on 'the principle and points which the party made to the [Royal] Commission in 1969', three Caerphilly delegates staged a walkout in protest at the conference not being allowed to vote on calls for a devolution referendum.[21] Their actions were little noticed at the time. But they were a harbinger of the future. By the end of 1974, several Labour MPs – Neil Kinnock and Leo Abse most prominently – were publicly advocating a referendum. The momentum behind this call soon became unstoppable.

The idea of using a referendum to block moves towards some form of 'home rule' was not new. A. V. Dicey is the name most prominently associated with the very notion of parliamentary sovereignty. Yet, such was his opposition to Irish home rule that in 1890 he was willing to abandon the position to which he has become irredeemably linked in order to call for a (UK-wide) referendum on the issue, precisely as a means of overriding any parliamentary majority in its favour.[22] Indeed, so deep and unyielding was Dicey's animosity that he offered active advice and support to those Unionist conspirators at the heart of the UK state who were willing to stop at nothing – even army mutiny – to thwart the government of the day.[23] Parliamentary sovereignty and the rule of law formed the twin foundation stones of the thought of the English constitution's chief ideologist. But in order to oppose home rule, Dicey was willing to turn his back on both.[24]

The passions aroused over half a century later by Scottish and Welsh home rule were rather less heated. One point of similarity,

9

however, is that advocates of a referendum again seem to have been drawn to this position for instrumental, rather than principled, reasons. Many proponents of a referendum on Welsh devolution displayed striking inconsistency in their advocacy of direct democracy. Across sections of the Labour left, in particular, the doctrine of parliamentary sovereignty was regarded as providing more than sufficient mandate to allow the profound socio-economic transformation that would be required to emancipate the working class – or indeed to facilitate the progressive social reforms associated with Leo Abse. Yet, by contrast, even explicit manifesto commitments to Welsh devolution were deemed insufficient mandate, requiring instead additional confirmation in a popular plebiscite. Indeed, despite the class-laden rhetoric, intensive cooperation with the Conservative opposition was regarded as justified if it could lead to the defeat of the government's proposals.[25] Once residual Conservative support for some form of Scottish devolution was abandoned, Labour opponents of devolution regularly joined the official opposition in parliamentary votes designed to halt the devolution proposals before the people were ever given a say. As was the case for Dicey and Irish home rule, the referendum was not valued for its own sake – as a means of popular participation or legitimation – but rather as a last line of defence for the territorial status quo if parliamentary opposition failed.

After they had secured only a narrow majority in the October 1974 general election, defections and by-election defeats thereafter rapidly eroded Labour's position in the House of Commons. This left the Labour government in general, and its devolution proposals in particular, in a highly vulnerable position. In an abject humiliation for the government, rebel Labour MPs (including several Welsh Labour MPs) joined the Conservatives in successfully opposing a government 'guillotine' motion on the original Scotland and Wales Bill. This defeat, which had opened up the possibility of almost limitless parliamentary 'trench-warfare' over the bill, directly prompted the withdrawal of the legislation.[26] The vote, it should be noted, took place several months after the government had conceded that post-legislative referendums would have to take place in both Scotland and Wales before either nation's assembly could be established.[27]

Yet, while devolution faced substantial opposition from outside the government, and while senior members of the government also lacked enthusiasm for the project,[28] the survival of the Labour government depended on the support, or at least acquiescence, of pro-devolution minor parties. Thus, devolution could not simply be abandoned. But when separate Wales and Scotland Bills were reintroduced to Parliament in November 1977, both contained provisions to require popular affirmation in post-legislative referendums before devolution could be enacted. Yet, this concession remained insufficient for opponents. In January 1978, the Labour MP George Cunningham secured majority support in the House of Commons for an amendment requiring that a 'Yes' vote in the referendum would also have to secure the support of 40 per cent or more of the electorate before it could be considered properly valid.[29] As supporters of devolution pointed out at the time, no UK government elected since the Second World War had won the support of 40 per cent of the electorate. (Nor has any government done so in subsequent years: even the combined Conservative and Liberal Democrat vote in 2010 falls short.) No intellectually convincing argument was advanced as to why 40 per cent represented a 'legitimate' majority for constitutional change. But the politics was clear: the Cunningham amendment raised the bar for devolutionists to an unfeasibly high level. It was a wrecking amendment. That the government failed in subsequent attempts to overturn this amendment demonstrated that it had, by now, lost all authority around the issue.

The lack of government control was further demonstrated in the referendum campaign in Wales. This was nothing less than an unmitigated disaster for devolutionists. The Devolution Bill, the outcome of messy and unhappy compromises, had few admirers. Indeed, Mari James and Peter D. Lindley observed that there were 'few (and probably none who were not on the government payroll) who were willing and able to defend its details'.[30] Perhaps unsurprisingly, then, the arguments deployed in favour of devolution were generally weak and defensive, sometimes even contradictory.[31] With the Labour Party bitterly divided over even the general principle of devolution, and amidst a wider collapse in the party's popularity across the UK, there was a notably hesitant and even apologetic quality to the government's campaigning. Though a long-term advocate of devolution, Secretary of State John Morris remained curiously detached, leaving leadership of the Labour–Wales TUC Yes campaign to Elystan Morgan. Despite the latter's huge talents as an orator, he lacked credibility in this role. Not only had the former MP been rejected by the electors of Cardiganshire in the 1974 elections, but as a former prominent member of Plaid Cymru, Morgan's presence at the head of the campaign served merely to confirm Labour dissidents in their suspicion that devolution was a nationalist plot.

Despite deep reservations from many of his own party activists, the Plaid Cymru leader Gwynfor Evans had manoeuvred his party into supporting the government's proposals.[32] Yet, while Plaid provided many of the foot-soldiers for the Yes campaign on the ground, the linking of devolution to the nationalists in the public mind also greatly inhibited the gaining of wider support. Though Plaid had enjoyed its best ever result (in terms of MPs elected) at the October 1974 election, much of the Welsh population continued to view the party as 'extremist'.[33] The party's activists channelled their referendum efforts through the all-party 'Yes for Wales' campaign, of which they were by far the most important element. But this failed to insulate the Yes cause from guilt by nationalist association.

Meanwhile, in line with the old adage that it is easier to oppose than to propose (and Marx's observation that plebiscites tend to favour the status quo), opponents of devolution made hay. The government's proposals were assailed from all sides, and on various grounds. Some of the arguments deployed against devolution were patently contradictory – after all, the proposed assembly could hardly have been simultaneously dominated, as No campaigners vehemently claimed to different audiences that it would be, both by hard-line south-Wales socialists and by middle-class Welsh-speaking extremists from Gwynedd. But fighting against such a weak and unconvincing opponent, the contradictions in the No campaign's arguments did them little harm. Indeed, the fact that the umbrella 'No Assembly Campaign' (which in practice was Conservative-dominated) remained organizationally and ideologically distinct from the 'Labour No Assembly Campaign' that was marshalled by the so-called 'Gang of Six' Labour backbench dissidents, proved ultimately to be a great tactical advantage for the No side.[34] It gave the No side great flexibility to attack from all directions, and they exploited this to the full.

A victory for the Yes side was always unlikely. As we review in more detail in chapter three, at no stage in the years leading up to the

March 1979 referendum was the Yes side ever ahead in any opinion poll. But the lop-sided nature of the campaign almost certainly contributed to the scale of the defeat for the government's devolution proposals. A further contributor was the government itself. As we discussed in the previous section, votes in referendums are often cast for reasons unconnected to what is actually on the ballot. In particular, referendums are often used by voters as an opportunity to cast a 'protest vote' against an unpopular government. And by March 1979, there was much for many people to protest about. The UK had just passed through the now-infamous 'winter of discontent'; in Wales the evening news programmes had regularly featured the same kinds of horror stories familiar during those months, from unburied bodies being held at a chapel in Newport to rubbish piling up uncollected outside a Cardiff hospital. The devolution referendum provided discontented voters with the perfect opportunity to display their discontent with the government; the presence in the No camp of prominent Labour stalwarts reassured many voters that they could do so without endorsing a wholly Conservative cause.

The fact of defeat was little surprise to Yes campaigners. But the scale of the rebuff meted out by the Welsh electorate on St David's Day was shocking. For Secretary of State John Morris, the four-to-one rejection represented the proverbial 'elephant on the doorstep' that could not be ignored. Many Welsh poets and literary figures interpreted the outcome in wholly apocalyptic terms. The dream of some form of home rule appeared dead; even the very existence of Wales could no longer be taken for granted.[35] In the event, however, it was the more sober reading provided by historian K. O. Morgan that proved nearest the mark. Writing in 1982, he emphasized that,

> the idea of Welsh devolution did not disappear from history in March 1979. Nor have its champions yielded the field ... The political administration of Wales, and its relationship to the other nations of the United Kingdom, will remain on the public agenda and within the public consciousness.[36]

Morgan's words proved prophetic. Yet, as we will see, even when new champions emerged to ensure a renewed position for devolution on the public agenda, they did so in the shadow of the 1979 experience.[37] Indeed, it was perhaps only in March 2011 that Wales finally escaped from that shadow.

The 1997 devolution referendum

Reports of the death of Wales turned out to be greatly exaggerated. And the idea of devolution also proved more durable than its defeated supporters had feared or jubilant opponents had hoped in March 1979. Many, often interlinked, factors encouraged the gradual re-emergence of devolution on to the political agenda in the late 1980s and early 1990s.[38] Among these factors were moves within the Labour Party in the early 1980s to promote English regionalism as a vehicle for economic regeneration; increasingly determined agitation for a Scottish parliament following the 1988 Claim of Right and the subsequent establishment of the Scottish Constitutional Convention; growing dissatisfaction with the Welsh 'quango state'; the 'normalization' of Plaid Cymru and many of the political demands associated with it;[39] the consequences of the local government reform of 1993;[40] the replacement of Neil Kinnock (who initially made his name through his opposition to devolution) as Labour leader by John Smith, the 'motive force' behind the 1970s proposals;[41] and, certainly not least, John Redwood (the highly unpopular Secretary of State for Wales from 1993–5).

The 1984–5 Miners' Strike was also consequential. Not only did it encourage increased trust and cooperation between some sections of the labour and national movements in Wales,[42] but arguably even more fundamental was the way in which the failure of the strike was to herald the final collapse of that version of traditional class politics that had been strikingly prevalent in the rhetoric of Labour anti-devolutionists in the late 1970s. Over time, a new generation of centre-left activists would emerge who viewed devolution as part of a broader project of progressive politics – indeed, as an enabling condition for such a project – rather than some reactionary or atavistic throwback.

Nonetheless, while personalizing history is almost always a mistake, in the case of the revival of Welsh devolution, particular and even primary influence must be accorded to two people: Margaret Thatcher, on the one hand, and Ron Davies on the other. Mrs Thatcher's (wholly inadvertent) contribution to forcing devolution back on to the agenda was her determination to pursue her radical policies and her apparent indifference to their disproportionately negative effects in Wales. This ultimately convinced many in Wales that, no matter how bitter the divisions of the 1970s, more united than divided them. The continued pursuit of this agenda, despite the Welsh Conservatives' rapidly declining support after 1983, created the perception of a 'democratic deficit': as colloquially expressed by one graffiti writer, 'We Voted Labour We Got Thatcher'.[43]

The response in Wales to the Thatcher period created the 'political opportunity structure' within which devolution proposals that had been comprehensively defeated in 1979 could be revived. But it required agency to ensure that this opportunity was seized. It was Ron Davies who provided such agency. In retrospect, his appointment as shadow Secretary of State for Wales in 1992 can be identified as a key moment in Wales's modern history. Davies had voted No to devolution in 1979 but by around 1987 had revised his views. Now, with the zeal and commitment of the convert, enjoying strong support from the new Labour leader John Smith and possessing a detailed understanding of the internal culture of the Labour Party both in Wales and Westminster, Davies skilfully marshalled and manoeuvred his forces to ensure that his party committed itself to devolution without reopening the divisions of the 1970s.[44]

The evolution of Labour's devolution policy is discussed in more detail in the following chapter. What is important for now is to observe that it was only in 1996 that Labour acknowledged the possible need for a referendum on the matter. Hitherto, policy statements had been vehemently emphatic in their opposition.[45] It is doubtful whether this position could have been sustained. Given the 1979 result, would an Assembly have ever been considered legitimate without conclusive evidence that the public had changed its mind? But the circumstances in which Labour reversed its stance on a referendum say much about the status accorded to Welsh devolution by the party leadership in London.

In June 1996, Labour leader Tony Blair informed Ron Davies that a decision had been taken to promise a referendum on the party's proposals for Scottish devolution.[46] The broader aim was to neutralize some of the Conservatives' most potent lines of attack against Labour in the forthcoming general election. Given the great play that John Major had made of 'defending the Union' in the 1992 election, Labour sought to take both devolution and the prospect of UK membership of the Euro out of the electoral debate by promising post-election referendums on both matters.[47] But Wales did not feature in the original decision. Blair seems to have believed that Welsh devolution was fundamentally different from

Scottish devolution, given the much more limited powers envisaged for the Welsh Assembly. He was not, therefore, minded to insist on a Welsh referendum. But Davies immediately recognized that this was simply not a sustainable position. Any Scottish referendum would necessitate a Welsh equivalent. Thus, Labour's position on a second devolution referendum for Wales was reversed.

This reversal posed a new, and substantial, problem for Ron Davies. Hitherto, his entire strategy for reviving devolution had focused on winning the debate within the Labour Party, and particularly the upper echelons of the party. Davies had consciously eschewed entanglements in cross-party fora similar to the Scottish Constitutional Convention for fear that this would reopen divisions within his own party. But now he had been left with a new mountain to climb. A referendum would now have to be fought: one for which no preparatory work had yet been conducted, and for which little or no preparation could be carried out until the forthcoming general election had been safely disposed of. However, this 'hospital pass' decision was ameliorated, for Davies, by three important details.

First, recognizing that support from other opposition parties would be required to organize a credible Yes campaign, Blair authorized a change in the voting system for the proposed Assembly. Instead of a plurality system (first past the post), a semi-proportional additional member system (similar to that already proposed for the Scottish Parliament) would be used in Wales too. As we discuss in the next chapter, this key concession – which has been highly consequential for the country's subsequent political development – represented the only substantive change between the proposals that would be voted on 1997 from those rejected in 1979. It is most unlikely that the Labour Party in Wales would have supported such a change but for the new context created by the referendum decision.

Secondly, in sharp contrast to 1979 when the referendum had been post-legislative, following years of parliamentary wrangling, now the proposal was for pre-legislative votes in Scotland and Wales. With the referendums planned to occur as soon as practicably possible after a general election victory, this would encourage a short campaign focusing on the general outlines of the scheme, rather than the prolonged war of attrition of the late 1970s. It was even subsequently agreed that the Scottish vote could take place a week before the Welsh: a decision whose only credible explanation was a desire to ensure that a 'Scottish bounce' would boost the chances of victory in Wales.

Finally, there was to be no 40 per cent threshold: a majority of any kind would suffice. Even so, with a four-to-one No majority from 1979 to be overcome, the auguries for Davies and devolution were far from propitious.

The referendum campaign itself can be summarized briefly. In contrast to 1979, in 1997 the Secretary of State led energetically from the front. Ron Davies staked his political career on a successful outcome. While a separate Labour Yes campaign was organized, it was the all-party Yes for Wales group that provided much of the public face of the campaign. Behind the scenes, the 1997 referendum was also characterized by intensive cooperation between Labour and Plaid Cymru. The close cooperative relationships that had developed in the early 1990s between Ron Davies and his Welsh opposition counterparts, in particular Plaid Cymru leader Dafydd Wigley, proved vital in this regard. Devolutionists of all parties were also blessed by the almost unprecedented popularity of the new prime minister, then enjoying the most ardent of honeymoon relationships with the British electorate. Indeed, the extent to which the Yes campaign relied on Blair's popularity can hardly be exaggerated. 'Tony Blair says vote Yes' was the loudspeaker message from the campaign battle bus, while a banner trailed behind a light aircraft flying over parts of south Wales summed up the case in favour as 'Vote Blair, Vote Yes'.

Devolutionists also benefited from the relative weakness of the No campaign. In contrast to the late 1970s, when rebel Labour MPs had lined up with dissident constituency Labour parties and unions to provide vocal opposition to their own government's proposals, in 1997 only a handful of Labour supporters publicly broke ranks to denounce the plans. And while 1979 had seen the Welsh Conservatives in the ascendant, 1997 was without doubt one of the lowest points in their history. Having failed to return a single MP at the general election, the Welsh Tories were in no fit state to offer much support to a No campaign. Indeed, they were aware that to associate themselves too closely with the No campaign would be deeply damaging to the latter. The 'Just Say No' campaign itself remained a ramshackle affair, pulled together as much as anything by broadcasters who needed voices from both sides of the debate to ensure balance in their coverage. In stark contrast to 1979, in 1997 the Yes side outpunched their opponents.

Yet, victory still required a vast swing from 1979. And holding the referendum in mid-September meant that campaigners were forced to work through the summer, when much of their target audience was away on holiday and the media was in non-political, 'silly season' mode. Furthermore, the death of Princess Diana at the end of August led to a temporary halt in campaigning just when it should have been stepping up a gear.

The high drama of the 1997 result contrasted sharply with a campaign almost completely devoid of memorable moments. In contrast to the thumping majorities in Scotland, the Welsh electorate approved devolution by a tiny margin. The outcome remained in doubt until the very final declaration, which left the Yes campaign with a margin of victory of 6,721 votes (a mere 0.3 per cent of the Welsh electorate), on a turnout of just over half those eligible to vote. Greeting the result, a visibly relieved Ron Davies modestly claimed that it represented 'a very good morning' for Wales. He was wise to eschew greater triumphalism. Although the pro-devolution swing from 1979 had been a gargantuan 30.0 percentage points (even greater than the pro-devolution swing over the same time period in Scotland), it was evident that Welsh voters remained to be convinced of the merits of home rule.

Tri chynnig i Gymro? The 2006 Act and the referendum provision

As we have seen, the 1979 devolution referendum in Wales did not occur due to some sense of principled commitment. Those demanding a referendum seem to have viewed this merely as one potential means by which they could halt a change of which they disapproved. Few, if any, proponents of a referendum did much to indicate that they viewed it as part of a coherent and consistent approach towards fundamental political reform. They championed direct democracy when it seemed as if the parliamentary majority might deliver results of which they disapproved. But they also sought to use every parliamentary means necessary to achieve the same ultimate objective: stopping devolution.

As for the government, there had been no intention of calling a referendum on Labour's devolution proposals when the party initially committed itself to them in the late 1960s. Nor did a referendum appear in any of the three subsequent election manifestos. The referendum concession was made when the parliamentary arithmetic demanded it. It was a 'tactical' decision, in the terms of the House of Lords Constitutional Committee: a means to secure parliamentary passage of the legislation. Though given that the government had no other realistic option, it might perhaps be best understood as reflecting *force majeure*.

Whatever the complex combination of motivations and circumstance that led to its calling, it is nonetheless clear that the referendum did focus on an issue of 'fundamental constitutional importance'. Whatever their other differences, opponents and proponents of devolution always agreed on that. Indeed, if referendums are to have any place at all in parliamentary democracies then establishing devolved legislatures would seem an obvious example of an issue on which a referendum is appropriate.

Tony Blair's decision to hold a pre-legislative referendum on devolution was certainly not the result of *force majeure*. Nor was it occasioned by a sense of constitutional propriety. After all, the early years of New Labour government saw other momentous constitutional changes, such as independence for the Bank of England and the incorporation of the European Convention on Human Rights into UK law, take place without resort to a referendum. Mr Blair's decision was a matter of electoral strategy: neutralizing the potentially contentious parts of Labour's constitutional reform agenda as election issues by allowing the electorate the power of decision in future referendums. But Wales, as we saw, did not feature at all in these calculations: Wales was included only because Ron Davies realized that calling a referendum in Scotland without one in Wales was politically unsustainable. Thus, referendums on Scottish and Welsh devolution joined referendums on electoral reform, on English regional government, the creation of a London mayoralty and on the European single currency as pledges in Labour's 1997 manifesto.

The 1997 Welsh devolution referendum was thus, once more, tactical rather than principled in motivation. And as a tactical device, it worked very well. Despite John Major's best efforts, devolution was not a major issue in the 1997 election campaign. And following the pulverizing Conservative defeat at that election, opponents of devolution failed to mobilize effectively for the subsequent referendums. This, in turn, helped ensure the narrow Yes vote in

Wales. Nonetheless, one basic point remained as true for 1997 as it was for 1979: the referendum focused on an issue of fundamental constitutional importance.

The 2011 Welsh referendum offers a greatly contrasting case. It is impossible to discern any issue of fundamental constitutional importance that was at stake. Even if one accepted that a move from 'executive' to 'legislative' devolution should have required popular assent – a proposition of which we are doubtful – the fact is that this move had already been approved in principle by parliament, and at least partly taken place in practice, before 2011.[48] The requirement for a referendum on enhancing the law-making powers of the Assembly seems particularly dubious given that no similar vote was required to approve the provisions (contained in Parts I and II of the 2006 Government of Wales Act) establishing the *de jure* distinction between the National Assembly for Wales and the Welsh Assembly Government (since 2011, the Welsh Government): a change that overturned the basic local government model of internal organization that had been at least implicit in all Labour's devolution proposals since the late 1960s.

But if the subject of the vote was rather different, one commonality between 2011 and the two previous referendums was that the decision to hold the vote was a tactical one, reflecting the political circumstances of Wales's dominant political party. On the basis of a devastating critique of the original 1998 Government of Wales Act, the 2004 Richard Commission Report had recommended far-reaching changes to the internal organization, the electoral arrangements and the powers of the National Assembly for Wales. Richard's recommendation that Assembly and Government be formally separated from each other was constitutionally momentous but also uncontroversial, being accepted by all major political actors. Far more controversial were Richard's recommendations regarding the size and electoral arrangements of the Assembly. The proposal for an eighty-seat National Assembly elected by the single transferable vote system was rejected by the Labour government, with no serious consideration given to putting this issue to a public vote. It was only the issue of powers that prompted consideration of a referendum.

While recommending a move to primary legislative powers on the Scottish model by 2011, the Richard Commission made no recommendation on whether or not a referendum should be required to approve such a move. This was a judgement 'for the UK Government and Parliament to make in the light of their assessment of the response to our report'.[49] An augury for the future direction of debate, however, was the letter that commission member and former Labour MP, Ted Rowlands, had appended to the published version of the report. Though not disowning the recommendations of the report – which he had apparently played a constructive role in developing – Rowlands nonetheless indicated that he saw them as no more than 'a coherent alternative model for a legislative Assembly, which, *if supported by the Welsh people in a referendum*, could form the basis for further constitutional change'.[50] But of far greater political import was that First Minister Rhodri Morgan publicly echoed this view on publication of the report. Within weeks, Welsh Labour MPs – the majority of whom remained deeply sceptical about devolution – had successfully sought assurances that any move to primary legislative powers could only occur after a referendum, and that this referendum would be post-legislative rather than pre-legislative. The latter point appeared to constitute a major victory: it seemed to ensure that any referendum would happen in circumstances more akin to 1979 than 1997.

There followed a period in which Labour's internal debate on the future of Welsh devolution seemed to polarize between distinct options. One was the Richard proposal of full legislative powers. But these powers would be conferred only after an affirmative referendum vote. The Labour leadership evinced little desire to hold such a referendum, nor much confidence that any such vote would be won. The alternative option, closely associated with Rhodri Morgan, was to construct some form of legislative empowerment short of legislative powers proper: a hybrid construct, as detailed in the following chapter, known as the '13.2 plus' option, that could be enacted without a further referendum. Yet, when the White Paper was finally published after the 2005 UK general election it became clear that the proposed legislation would contain both options, envisaged as a consecutive development. An interim legislative dispensation would be established immediately; to be replaced at some point in the future, and only after an affirmative referendum vote, by legislative powers proper. But the interim dispensation – later embodied in Part III of the resulting Act – would actually enable the National Assembly to create primary legislation. The

Rubicon of primary legislative powers would therefore be crossed immediately. Any referendum would merely be sanctioning a move to another, more expansive, form of primary law making, rather than heralding a fundamental change.

This was certainly not the result that devo-sceptic Welsh Labour MPs believed that they had secured with the agreement that a post-legislative referendum would be necessary before any move to legislative devolution. Why did the White Paper deliver so much more than they bargained for? One key point is that the '13.2 plus' plans for an interim legislative dispensation were always distinctly vague. As these plans firmed up – in apparently interminable Friday afternoon meetings in the bowels of government buildings in Cardiff's Cathays Park – the planned interim mechanism became more powerful than was originally envisaged. But it is far from clear that those involved were aware of any great principle being breached when it was agreed that Assembly measures – the product of the system installed via Part III of the 2006 Act – would have the same status in Wales as Acts of the UK Parliament.[51] Welsh devolutionists have long sought to embrace what is deliverable rather than worrying too much about constitutional dogma.

Meanwhile, Part IV was included in the legislation largely, it seems, at the behest of Peter Hain. Hain seems to have been genuinely concerned that neither parliamentary time nor a sympathetic parliamentary majority might be on hand when Labour was eventually ready to move to a less restrictive system of primary law making. The Secretary of State meant what he said: his aim was to create a piece of legislation that would last 'a generation'.[52]

Whatever the motivations of its architects, the legislation remained a source of unease amongst some Labour MPs. Several sources have suggested to us that, as a response to such concerns, Peter Hain gave verbal assurances to his own backbenchers that there was little prospect of a referendum before 2015.[53] Such a pledge was inherently impossible for any cabinet minister to redeem. The breaking of it after Labour had lost power in London may help explain Hain's obvious discomfort in the run-up to the March 2011 referendum (as discussed in chapter four). The detailed interest taken by some Welsh Labour MPs in Legislative Competence Orders (LCOs) – which saw their drafting become increasingly restrictive – may also have reflected their resentment about the 2006 Act.

With enactment of the provisions of the 2006 Government of Wales Act after the May 2007 National Assembly election, Wales became home to a legislature with primary law-making powers. The referendum envisaged within the Act would not change this. It would merely, if successful, shift the National Assembly to a less restricted system for making laws. There would be no 'fundamental constitutional issue' at stake. But as it turned out, the referendum provision would play a centrally important role in the formation of the next Welsh government.

Conclusion: the price of hubris

In summer 2007, the Labour Party in Wales was forced to pay a price for hubris; that price was the 2011 referendum. Prior to the third National Assembly election in May 2007, there were compelling reasons to believe that Labour would struggle to match their 2003 performance. There is generally an electoral cost to being in power. After a decade in office in London, and eight years in Cardiff, it was plausible to expect some of that cost to be visited upon Labour. The party had also lost a particular advantage it had enjoyed in 2003, when it had possessed – in Tony Blair and Rhodri Morgan – much the two most popular political leaders in Wales.[54] Following the Iraq debacle, the former had become a severe liability. Yet, Blair insisted on clinging on to the premiership, apparently in order to see out his tenth anniversary in power, despite the damage this would cause his party in the devolved elections. There was also clear evidence of Labour decline in Wales. The party's vote share in Wales at the 2005 UK general election was its second lowest at such an election since the mid-1920s. The April 2006 Blaenau Gwent by-elections – where, in a historic party bastion, two lavishly resourced Labour candidates were decisively beaten by two inexperienced and poorly resourced independents – further suggested particular troubles in traditional Labour heartlands.

Despite all this, Labour continued to insist until polling day that it could win an outright Assembly majority. Such a result was never remotely plausible. The party actually scored its worst share of the vote at any Westminster or devolved election in Wales since the 1918 general election.[55] Labour's vote share fell in thirty-nine of the forty constituencies and in all five electoral regions. That Labour made a net loss of only four seats was partly a reflection of the only semi-proportional nature of the Assembly electoral system; partly an indication that none of the other parties had been able to corner the non-Labour vote as effectively as the SNP managed in Scotland; and partly sheer good fortune, as several constituencies were held by Labour by tiny margins.[56]

Yet, in the aftermath of a predictably poor election performance, it rapidly became apparent that Labour had done almost nothing to prepare the ground for a post-election situation in which it had fallen well short of an overall majority. Compounding this error, Rhodri Morgan then saw fit to publicly insult potential coalition partners, declaring that the choice between Plaid Cymru and the Liberal Democrats was one between the 'inedible' and 'unpalatable'. Having made this remarkably unhelpful contribution, Labour's Welsh leader then departed on a post-election break. The possibility that a Welsh government might be formed without the Labour Party was evidently not considered a serious possibility.

It would be unfair, however, to assign exclusive blame to Rhodri Morgan. The adjectives chosen to dismiss potential partners were classic Rhodri-isms, but they spoke to a general attitude running through much of his party. Eight years after the establishment of the National Assembly, substantial sections of Welsh Labour remained resolutely 'in denial' about the implications of devolution and its semi-proportional electoral system. Only when faced with the realistic prospect of losing power did the party reluctantly accept the necessity of compromise. Even then, senior figures, including Peter Hain and Neil Kinnock, continued to resist. The result was that Labour was forced to pay a price for a coalition deal that was almost certainly higher than that it would have had to concede if the party had been willing and able to enter into serious negotiations immediately after the election.

The other three parties in the Assembly negotiated what became known as the 'Rainbow' deal. Negotiators working on behalf of Plaid Cymru, the Conservatives and the Liberal Democrats managed to find a great deal of common ground between these apparently unlikely partners. When Labour was finally ready to enter serious negotiations, Plaid Cymru was the only negotiating partner available to it. And Plaid had the alternative option of themselves leading a Rainbow coalition into government. The only prize Labour could offer to trump this was a pledge to support the enactment of the referendum provision of the 2006 Government of Wales Act. The referendum would thus take place far sooner than had been envisaged when that Act had passed through Parliament. Lured by the prospect of securing a full law-making Welsh legislature, and distrustful of the Liberal Democrats' ability to commit to the Rainbow deal, Plaid opted for the role of junior partner in a Labour-led government. The 'One Wales' agreement between Labour and Plaid was confirmed by large majorities of both parties in specially convened conferences. The agreement bound both parties 'to proceed to a successful outcome of a referendum for full law-making powers under Part IV as soon as practicable, at or before the end of the Assembly term'.[57]

Neil Kinnock, the triumphant devo-sceptic of 1979, had gone to Labour's special conference to oppose the One Wales agreement. Called to speak far earlier than he had hoped, his oratory was received very coolly by the delegates with his (normally obligatory) standing ovation restricted to a small band of hard-core followers.[58] For Labour devolutionists, their victory – and Kinnock's perceived humiliation – symbolized a shift in power in the party: from devolution sceptics to supporters of devolution, and from Welsh Labour in London to the Labour group in the National Assembly. After decades of ambivalence and often-bitter disagreements, it appeared that Wales's most important political force had finally embraced devolution. Yet, elements within the party, with Peter Hain notable among them, continued to seek to resile from the One Wales agreement, while the ever-cautious Rhodri Morgan was unwilling to publicly confront such critics. Nonetheless, the fact that the referendum commitment formed part of the coalition agreement created a logic and a momentum that, ultimately, would not be resisted.

2

The unlikely survival of the platypus: constitution building in Wales

In March 1977, Rufus Davis, an Australian scholar of federalism, gave a lecture at the London School of Economics that examined devolution in a comparative perspective. Davis's timing was opportune. Facing intransigent parliamentary opposition, the government was abandoning its Scotland and Wales Bill. Davis marked the apparent collapse of Labour's devolution plans through an arresting, Antipodean analogy:

> 'What has the platypus of my homeland, namely *ornithosynous anatinus*, in common with the nearly extinct Scotland and Wales Bill.' The answer I would like to suggest is that each is quite unique, the like of which has not been seen before, and may not be seen again.[1]

It transpired that Davis was mistaken in his immediate assessment. Separate Scotland and Wales Bills were rapidly introduced to parliament, containing essentially the same provisions as their composite predecessor. Furthermore, even after the 1979 debacle, far from becoming extinct those same proposals have enjoyed a remarkable longevity. Indeed, as we will make clear, they have survived two further devolution referendums.

Yet, though Davis's reading of the contemporary political situation proved hopelessly awry, he was nonetheless an insightful constitutional analyst. The platypus analogy, in particular, seems both inspired and highly appropriate. The platypus is a famously, even fabulously odd, beast: neither fish nor fowl, but rather an unlikely combination of features. When specimens were first scientifically examined, this semi-aquatic, egg-laying, venomous, duck-billed, beaver-tailed, otter-footed mammal was regarded as an elaborate hoax by many of the taxonomists charged with working out precisely what it was.

Davis's point was that, in comparative constitutional terms, the dispensations being proposed for Scotland and Wales in the late

1970s were an oddity. The Welsh model of so-called 'executive devolution' was a particularly weird and unlikely combination: a body with its own democratic mandate exercising executive (and related, limited legislative) authority within the context of powers granted through the actions of another legislature and executive based on a wholly separate electoral mandate; a body exercising powers that had been established and defined without any thought that they might eventually be transferred to such an entity; a body whose internal structure and organization was certainly alien to Westminster and the many political institutions in that tradition.

One potential implication of Davis's remarks is that, like the platypus, the devolved dispensations then being proposed for Scotland and Wales offered an evolutionary dead end. That may yet prove the case. But it was only through direct experience of the manifold deficiencies of the form of executive devolution operating in Wales between 1999 and 2006 that this model was finally abandoned. And its baleful legacy persisted through 2007 to 2011, when devolved government in Wales continued under a sharply attenuated and, again, oddly misshapen form of legislative devolution. Moreover – and here is the real twist in this particular tale – even after the 2011 referendum endorsed the move to a more generous form of legislative devolution, it remains true that the powers of National Assembly for Wales resemble much more closely those proposed by the 1978 Scotland Act than the very different structures finally enacted in Scotland through its 1998 replacement. Even as one version of the constitutional platypus finally became extinct, its Scottish cousin was resurrected – in Wales. This, despite the far-reaching criticisms levelled at this model both in the 1970s and then in the late 1990s, when serious consideration was again given to the most appropriate constitutional basis for a revived Scottish Parliament. Wales has followed, and largely continues to follow, a constitutional path that is as strange as it is tortuous.

In this chapter we trace the processes that have underpinned Welsh constitution building since the 1960s. First, we examine the invention of executive devolution: how this model emerged and became government policy in the mid-1970s. We then go on to explore why this model was retained when the Labour Party renewed its interest in devolution in the early 1990s. Following this, we look at the period after the 1997 referendum, when the manifest inadequacies of the original devolution dispensation provided for

Wales helped underpin a strong agenda seeking to reform that dispensation. The fourth section considers how the 2006 Government of Wales Act responded to this reform agenda, and how it provided for the referendum with which this book is concerned. Finally, we conclude by considering the broader lessons about constitution making in the context of Welsh political culture that arise from the discussion in both this and the preceding chapter.

Dyma'r ffordd: inventing executive devolution

Schemes for Welsh devolution of varying levels of seriousness and sophistication were propounded on a fairly regular basis from the 1880s onwards. But the origins of the form of devolution originally embodied in the National Assembly of Wales can be found no further back than the early 1960s, in a brief pamphlet with the unprepossessing title *A Central Welsh Council*.[2] Its author was Gwilym Prys Davies, a former Welsh republican activist but by then Labour Party member.[3] That the pamphlet was published by Undeb Cymru Fydd (a body established by the offspring of some of the leading lights of its more illustrious nineteenth-century namesake in a rather wan attempt to carry the flame) provides an interesting point of continuity with previous devolutionary schemes. More politically significant, however, was that the pamphlet's preface was provided by Jim Griffiths.

Griffiths's legacy is often appealed to by contemporary Labour devolutionists anxious to buttress their position by reference to their party's past. There is no doubt that Griffiths played a pivotal role in ensuring that Labour committed itself to establishing the Welsh Office; and as the first Secretary of State for Wales he ensured that this commitment was delivered.[4] Yet, in the early 1950s, Griffiths had sided with the party establishment when it was challenged by five Welsh Labour MPs determined to support the all-party Parliament for Wales Campaign. Indeed, Griffiths played a key role in overturning Labour's historic, if purely nominal, commitment to a Welsh home-rule parliament by ensuring that the South Wales Area of the Miners' Union supported the leadership line.[5] Rather than viewing Griffiths as a straightforward devolutionist, he is perhaps best regarded as embodying Welsh Labour's often tortu-ously complex attitudes towards the 'national question'.

Nonetheless, when this undoubted Labour giant wrote the preface to Davies's little pamphlet, it signalled that influential figures had aspirations going beyond the administrative devolution of the Welsh Office.

Prys Davies's proposals were modest. He advocated an all-Wales elected Council as the top, strategic layer of local government. Given that Myrddin-Evans's Commission on Welsh Local Government had already recommended a radical overhaul of Welsh local government, and that major changes were clearly in the offing, yoking devolution to local government reform had clear attractions to devolutionists.[6] By 1966, the Welsh Council of Labour's Annual Conference had approved a motion on 'Local government re-organisation' calling on the Secretary of State to 'examine the possibility of establishing an Elected Council for the whole of Wales to administer certain major services'.[7] In April 1967, now against a backdrop of Plaid Cymru's stunning electoral breakthrough in the 1966 Carmarthen by-election, the Welsh Office, under the direction of new Secretary of State Cledwyn Hughes, produced a draft White Paper on local government in Wales suggesting the establishment of a 'New Council for Wales'.[8] The proposed Council's powers were weak. Composed of nominated and indirectly elected members only, the council was explicitly to be denied the 'substantial executive responsibilities [that] would involve changes in the statutory responsibilities of Ministers'.[9] Rather, it was envisaged as playing an advisory, promotional and coordinating role in the fields of tourism, the arts, economic development and transport.[10]

By March 1968, however, Hughes was circulating a notably more ambitious memorandum on the *Strengthening of the Welsh Office and the Welsh Council*. As the title implies, the document had two key proposals. The first was 'further devolution of the executive work of United Kingdom Ministers by transferring some of the latter's responsibilities to the Secretary of State for Wales'.[11] The policy areas initially targeted for transfer were health, education and agriculture.[12] In addition, Hughes recommended establishment of a Welsh Council based on 'at least an element of direct election'.[13] The council's functions would be 'partly advisory and partly executive'.[14] The latter were clearly paramount in Hughes's mind. In a copy of the memorandum preserved in his papers, the words 'Dyma'r ffordd' (literally, 'This is the way') are scrawled in the margin next to a passage that suggests that the council be given 'sizeable executive functions'. These words are also underlined in the same hand. The handwriting is unmistakably Hughes's own.

The executive powers to be transferred to the council were those held by various nominated bodies. The functions of six such bodies were proposed to be transferred to the council in their entirety (the Wales Tourist Board, The Development Corporation, The Development Commission, The Countryside Commission, The Welsh Arts Council and the Sports Council for Wales), while the memorandum also envisaged the council being granted some executive functions over transport, education, water supply and health.[15]

Welsh Labour MPs' reaction to Hughes's proposal was predictably hostile. But it was not just anti-devolutionists within Wales who responded negatively.[16] The Scottish Labour leadership, under Secretary of State Willie Ross, were also implacably opposed to any all-Wales elected body, as this would create a dangerous precedent for Scotland. And while the UK party leadership was not uninterested in constitutional reform and even 'regional' government, it was very difficult to conceive any model acceptable both to Labour councillors and Labour MPs. In such circumstances, senior cabinet figures like Richard Crossman were unwilling to see themselves bounced, as they saw it, by Welsh concerns.[17] There was also a tendency within the party to view regionalism and devolution as reflecting different, even inimical, principles: the former being progressive and rational, the latter reactionary and irrational.

The rejection of Hughes's proposals for a Welsh Council was, thus, inevitable. And Hughes's devolutionist views may well have precipitated his removal from the Welsh Office by Prime Minister Harold Wilson in April 1968.[18] Under Hughes's successor, George Thomas, the Office's support for the Council proposal waned, although attempts to extend the role of the Welsh Office itself persisted.[19] A formal commitment to the council continued, but Thomas spared no effort to underline the difficulties with the proposal.[20] With other departments hostile, and the central government and Labour Party divided, the inevitable result was paralysis. By September 1968, as Duncan Tanner has noted, 'the party had no agreed strategy or policy' on devolution.[21]

But with a series of by-election victories and near-misses indicating that nationalist sentiment was continuing to grow in both Wales and Scotland, having no policy became increasingly unsustainable. The Labour government needed to be seen to be taking the issue seriously. So, in October 1968, Wilson announced the establishment of a Royal Commission to examine the constitutional relationship of the various parts of Britain.[22] It was, according to a dismissive Richard Crossman, a 'way of doing nothing'.[23] Given the extremely vague terms of references granted the commission, it was surely an attempt to draw the sting from the issue whilst waiting for the nationalist tide to ebb.[24]

If the main purpose of the Royal Commission was to give the appearance of action whilst simultaneously papering over Labour's internal divisions, this strategy contained a significant flaw. The existence of a Royal Commission examining devolution meant that the Labour Party had to define a position on the matter, so that one might be submitted to the Commission – either that, or the UK's governing party would have to decline to make any constructive proposal. George Thomas tried to persuade his party to take the latter option, but such a standpoint was clearly untenable. Yet, before Labour could submit evidence to the Commission, it had to agree a policy. The process of deciding Labour's policy has proven highly consequential for Welsh politics: the policy of executive devolution that emerged would remain Labour policy, and drive Welsh devolution, for more than three decades.

Labour's official position emerged only after a significant internal struggle in 1969 that pitched pro-devolution reformers against a party establishment that was, in contemporary parlance, decidedly devo-sceptic. The reformers were led by Emrys Jones. Organizer and secretary of the Welsh Council of Labour from 1965 to 1979, Jones remains an unsung hero of the devolutionist cause. He convened a small group to draft the Welsh Council of Labour's evidence to the Royal Commission. Jones also sought to protect that group's recommendations for a quasi-federal legislative parliament for Wales when a 'deeply concerned' George Thomas began using his power and influence to force a fundamental change of tack.[25] Given Thomas's status as Secretary of State, and with the support of most Welsh Labour MPs, he inevitably won out. But there was a price to this victory. To head off the proposals for full legislative devolution, Thomas and his supporters felt compelled to concede the scheme for 'partly advisory and partly executive' devolution contained in Cledwyn Hughes's Welsh Council proposals. Having spent his first months as Secretary of State retreating from his pre-decessor's scheme, Thomas now became their active champion.[26]

In doing so, the famously anti-devolution George Thomas achieved something no devolutionist had managed. He succeeded in giving the idea of executive devolution the imprimatur of the British Labour Party – something worth far more than any number of resolutions from the Welsh Council of Labour. Thomas's triumph was therefore highly paradoxical, even pyrrhic. Legislative devolution had been thwarted, but only by making executive devolution official party policy. This was a much weaker form of devolution than that desired by Emrys Jones and his colleagues, but it was still a form of devolution.

The scheme of executive devolution proposed to the Royal Commission in early 1970 also featured in Labour's 1970 general election manifesto, which spoke of 'an elected council for Wales with extended powers'.[27] Labour's election defeat, along with the (temporary) stalling of the nationalist surge and the predictably protracted nature of the Royal Commission's deliberations, removed some urgency from the devolution issue. But the commitment to an elected Council for Wales with limited executive powers was regularly restated: for example in *Labour's Programme for Britain* in 1972 and 1973.[28] George Thomas remained a strong advocate. In parliamentary debate on the Local Government Bill in March 1972, as shadow Welsh secretary, he moved an amendment seeking to establish an elected Council for Wales.[29] When the Kilbrandon Royal Commission finally reported in October 1973, Thomas responded by publicly restating Labour's commitment to its devolution plans. 'What we are considering', Thomas told an audience, 'is a body with powerful executive authority, but which is not a legislative assembly'.[30] A week later, a very well-attended meeting of the Welsh Parliamentary Labour Party reaffirmed support for the policy, claiming that the consensus position of the Kilbrandon report 'accorded more closely with Labour's view of an effective executive devolution than with any other proposal'.[31] Essentially, the same position was adopted in Labour's Welsh manifesto at the general election the following February:

> The Labour Party in Wales notes with some satisfaction that the Kilbrandon Report recommends all the most important points that we put forward in our evidence. Accordingly Labour will establish a directly elected council for Wales with function, power and finance to enable it to be an effective force in the life of Wales.[32]

This was, at best, a partial reading of the Commission's admittedly convoluted recommendations. Most of those who signed the Commission's 'majority' report actually recommended a scheme of legislative devolution for Wales.[33] Executive devolution was supported by only two signatories to the majority report, and the two commissioners who produced a memorandum of dissent.[34] But Thomas and his colleagues reprised their role from 1969, rubbishing legislative devolution in favour of executive devolution. The key difference, of course, was that, by 1973, and thanks in large part to Thomas's own efforts, Labour's support for executive devolution was firmly established.

Following Labour's narrow election victory in February 1974, John Morris and not George Thomas was the surprise appointment as Secretary of State for Wales. Morris used one of his first press conferences to restate Labour's commitment to an elected body for Wales with executive and administrative responsibilities. The commitment to executive rather than legislative devolution remained absolutely central to the new government's policy: as a boundary that could not be crossed, it would define the parameters of the devolution policy which the government would now seek to implement. But the new Secretary of State also raised 'the possibility of growth to legislative *functions*'.[35] While legislative powers proper were destined to remain firmly entrenched at Westminster, the proposed body – still referred to by Morris as a Council – might nonetheless be handed some legislative functions. Precisely what that might mean became clearer over following months.

Perhaps inevitably, the new government's behaviour mixed principle and pragmatic calculation. Both John Morris and Gwilym Prys Davies, by then his principal advisor and confidant on devolution-related issues, were deeply committed devolutionists. But given the political exigencies of the time, pragmatic concerns loomed large. Before that year's second general election in October the government operated without a parliamentary majority. Even after the election, its majority was narrow and destined to disappear with disconcerting rapidity. Devolution was a policy area that had already proven highly combustible and internally divisive for Labour. But the topic could not be ignored, for both Welsh and Scottish nationalism were again apparently on the rise. Ministers' room for manoeuvre was, thus, tightly constrained. As such, Morris's attempt to bolster Labour's long-standing commitment to executive devolution with some form of legislative function for the putative devolved body appears particularly astute. By remaining within the terms of Labour's Kilbrandon commitment to executive devolution, the government could reasonably hope for party unity behind its proposals. But by stressing also that the proposals could include a legislative function for the devolved body, the government also hoped to attract support from the non-Conservative opposition parties, who were committed to legislative devolution. Such support would almost certainly be required for any legislation to reach the statute book. But this wholly reasonable strategy reckoned without the strength and virulence of opposition within the governing party itself.

From the first the Labour government proceeded warily.[36] Its first step, in June 1974, was publishing a consultation Green Paper, which summarized the various proposals in the Kilbrandon report, and raised some relevant questions.[37] In reality, however, consultation is a misnomer. The broad policy for Wales was settled, and had been repeatedly affirmed in party manifestos and statements by ministers, both shadow and actual. The same was not true in Scotland: there the party entered the February 1974 election wholly opposed to devolution. The SNP surge in that election made it imperative that this policy be changed; change was eventually forced on a reluctant Scottish executive committee through the UK leadership's control of the trade union block vote. By August 1974, the party was committed to legislative devolution for Scotland (the option backed by eight signatories of the main Kilbrandon report).[38] But while dramatic change characterized policy in Scotland, continuity was the order of the day in Wales. In June, a delegate conference of the Labour Party in Wales convened in Llandrindod Wells to consider a paper, *Devolution and Democracy*, reiterating support for an elected Welsh Council. These proposals were again explicitly linked to 'the principle and points which the party made to the [Royal] Commission in 1969', which remained 'as relevant as they were then', despite the subsequent reform of local government.[39] The Kilbrandon link was restated in the conference resolution, which 'by an overwhelming majority decided to authorise the officers to submit evidence to the government based on the evidence to the Commission on the Constitution and the document "Devolution and Democracy"'.[40] Thus, the conference supported establishment of a devolved Council taking on 'powers and functions currently vested in the Welsh Office', as well as 'the various nominated and ad hoc authorities operating in Wales'.[41] The Council would 'work on a Committee System similar to local authorities'.[42]

Democracy and Devolution was the subtly different title of the government White Paper, setting out proposals for both Wales and Scotland, published in September 1974.[43] In retrospect, the paper reads as essentially a pre-election holding operation. It is remarkably thin, with nine of its twenty-one pages given over to an appendix outlining the June consultation document. Only six of thirty-eight paragraphs of the main document set out substantive plans.[44] Nonetheless, it remains an important milestone in the devolution story. Three further devolution White Papers were later published by the Callaghan government, but they were all essentially addenda to *Democracy and Devolution*, filling in the missing detail.[45] *Democracy and Devolution* set out the basic constitutional design from which the government subsequently hardly wavered. For Wales, continuity persisted. The government proposed a 'directly elected' Assembly that would 'assume some of the executive functions' of the Welsh Office and of the nominated bodies operating in Wales.[46] It also suggested that the Assembly would assume 'certain powers of the Secretary of State in respect of delegated legislation', although no detail was supplied, nor examples given, about what this might mean in practice.[47] More clear-cut was the commitment to fund the assembly through a block grant. Also made clear was that local government would not be required to concede powers to the devolved body.[48] Though the original context of local government reorganization had changed with the introduction of a new two-tier system of local authorities in April 1974, and despite the more recent stress on a legislative function, the government remained committed to the executive devolution model that had under-pinned Labour's original plans for a Welsh Council.

Labour's October 1974 manifesto for Wales pledged to 'establish a directly elected Welsh Assembly with … a wide range of decision making powers, including certain powers of the Secretary of State with respect to delegated legislation, within the broad framework of Central Government legislation'.[49] After the election, another thirteen months passed before the publication of the next White Paper, *Our Changing Democracy: Devolution to Scotland and Wales*, which would flesh out the earlier proposals.

Two features of *Our Changing Democracy* are particularly note-worthy. First, the government confirmed that the Assembly would be organized along local government lines, with powers vested 'in the Assembly as a corporate body', rather than a cabinet or execu-tive as was the case for the proposed Scottish assembly.[50] Such a system, it was argued, 'is well suited to a body which will not have to deal with primary legislation'.[51] Given that local government-style internal organization had long been integral to Labour's Welsh council proposals, and given also that such a model of internal organization was part of the two schemes for executive devolution that emerged from the Kilbrandon Commission, such an outcome was clearly over-determined, though it had been subject to internal debate within government.[52]

Secondly, the White Paper clarified the 'legislative function' to be granted the assembly. It would be an assembly with executive and not legislative powers, 'Parliament would continue to legislate for Wales', and the assembly would 'work within the limits of Westminster Acts'.[53] That said, 'in controlling the devolved services it [the assembly] will take over whatever power those Acts confer on central government, including the power to make delegated legisla-tion' – an arrangement that the White Paper conceded would produce an 'uneven' set of powers across policy areas, depending on how the relevant primary legislation had been drafted.[54]

These plans were eventually supplemented by three further White Papers, and subject to parliamentary scrutiny as part of two different pieces of legislation – the Scotland and Wales Bill, which fell in February 1977, and the subsequent Wales Bill. Nonetheless, it was this constitutional architecture that was finally passed on to the statute book as the Wales Act in July 1978.

Reading the Act against Labour's Kilbrandon proposals, two closely related developments are striking. First, while earlier plans for a Welsh Council had stressed that the proposed body would not encroach on the Secretary of State's role, by the mid-1970s it was envisaged that some (though not all) of the Welsh Office's execu-tive functions would be transferred to the assembly. This development may have been hinted at in Labour's Kilbrandon evidence, but it was not consistent with the overall spirit of that submission, which conceived of a devolved body as occupying an intermediate space between government and local authorities.[55] Five years later, the assembly was viewed as taking its place side by side with the Secretary of State, if still in a subordinate and tightly constrained role.

Secondly, the Assembly was increasingly understood as a delegated legislation-creating body. The creation of subordinate legislation was always implicit in the recurrent references to executive powers that were part of earlier schemes for a Welsh Council. But now this function became foregrounded, being presented as one of the Assembly's main functions. Indeed, pro-devolution Welsh Labour politicians trying to shore up their party's devolutionist credentials tended to elide the fundamental constitutional differences involved by equating these legislative functions with legislative powers proper. The difference between executive and legislative devolution, it was suggested, was merely words.[56] As the anti-devolution backlash within Labour gathered pace, this rhetoric was later downplayed, while official documents always differentiated the legislative powers to be vested in the Scottish Assembly and the executive powers of its Welsh counterpart.[57] Nonetheless, the role of the latter in creating delegated legislation was repeatedly stressed.[58]

In explaining these developments, both John Morris and, to a lesser extent, Gwilym Prys Davies, have in recent times attached significance to a speech that Morris made just prior to the February 1974 election.[59] It was the call in this speech to allow the assembly a legislative function, they have claimed, which led the debate and the nature of the devolution proposals to be recast.[60] The continuing relevance of Labour's Kilbrandon-evidence commitment to executive powers has been underlined repeatedly in the preceding discussion. But Kilbrandon is relevant in another way here. While the commission's final reports were widely derided, both then and subsequently, as confused and lacking in clarity – there were, after all, seven different devolutionary schemes set out in their pages – the extensive discussion of the various forms of devolution contained therein had a greater long-term impact than is often assumed.[61] In particular, the discussions of executive devolution contained within the report itself, as well as the memorandum of dissent, conceived the devolution of executive powers in more expansive terms than did Labour's 1970 Welsh Council proposals. Both schemes of executive devolution proposed by the commissioners – the weaker proposal in the majority report and the more far-reaching scheme of the memorandum of dissent

– recommended the transfer of functions from ministers to devolved assemblies, and stressed the role of the assemblies in making subordinate legislation.[62] These ideas were, at the very least, well on the way to becoming part of the generally understood meaning of executive devolution before January 1974, and in ways much more clearly articulated than in Morris's speech. It is surely also relevant in this regard that Lord Crowther-Hunt, the main driver behind the dissenting memorandum, served as a cabinet office adviser on devolution policy (between February and October 1974). We must also remember that much of the development of the 1970s devolution proposals was undertaken in Whitehall itself, not in Edinburgh or Cardiff (in contrast to the late 1990s). Thus, rather than according any great significance to Morris's January 1974 speech, it is probably appropriate to endorse the assessment made by Gwilym Prys Davies himself in 1992, when he stressed the impact of the ideas of Crowther-Hunt and, indeed, John Mackintosh, on Labour's devolution proposals for Wales.[63]

Moreover, while Labour's devolution policy certainly developed over time, continuity is much more obvious than any change. Labour's commitment to executive devolution, as established in the Kilbrandon evidence, and confirmed in the 1970 and 1974 election manifestos, was the foundation stone on which the Wales Act 1978 was built. If further confirmation of this were required, it is provided by ways in which appeals to the authority embodied in that commitment were used to try to discipline those within the party and wider Labour movement who questioned the government's policy direction. In the spring of 1974, the inaugural Wales TUC conference attempted to return legislative devolution to the Welsh Labour agenda, unanimously endorsing the idea of an elected legislative assembly.[64] This attempt was unsuccessful, with the party special delegate conference held in September endorsing plans for executive devolution as per the party's evidence to Kilbrandon (as noted above). A key argument against any attempt to adopt the legislative devolution model – following what was by then the Scottish lead – was that Labour's policy for Wales had already been settled and accepted.[65]

Internal party documents further reminded Labour MPs and activists sceptical about devolution for Wales that the central principles of the party's Kilbrandon evidence were 'precisely those at the heart of the Government's White Paper'. Specifically, the proposed

Assembly would not be granted legislative powers but would have executive, administrative and advisory powers only.[66] This line was countered by accusations that the government had gone beyond the terms of the party's agreed position.[67] Both sides were, in different senses, correct. Ministers and their supporters could rightly claim that they were respecting the letter of the Kilbrandon evidence commitment to (no more than) executive devolution. But anti-devolution MPs could point out correctly that the Assembly proposals were much farther-reaching in scope than the previous plans for a Welsh Council. To both groups, however, the Kilbrandon evidence remained a central point of reference and legitimation.

Devolutionists in the Welsh Office attempted an implicit trade-off. They would limit their ambitions by working within the constraints of executive devolution. In return, anti-devolutionists should continue to accept executive devolution as party policy. But the devolutionists' hopes were bitterly disappointed. As we have discussed in chapter one, the antis defied party policy in the most public and determined of fashions. Following several years of parliamentary trench warfare, they helped deliver the *coup de grace* in the crushing referendum result of March 1979. At the time it seemed that devolution had disappeared from the political agenda for a generation, if not permanently. In the event, however, the issue was to remain dormant for barely a decade. And as it returned, so did the model of executive devolution.

Executive devolution retained

Given the overwhelming scale of the 1979 referendum defeat, and the deep Labour divisions on the issue that had been exposed in the preceding years, it is no surprise that Labour's commitment to devolution remained effectively dormant until the end of the 1980s.[68] Moreover, initial initiatives encouraging the party to re-engage with the devolution issue came from outside Wales. In 1982, Labour's spokesman on regional policy and devolution, John Prescott, developed plans for regional bodies in England to comple-ment the established commitment to a Scottish Assembly.[69] But the Wales Labour Party remained deeply sceptical, even about devolu-tion as part of a broader, Britain-wide strategy. The idea of a Welsh Assembly was presented as being firmly embedded in plans for local government reorganization and plans for English regional assemblies.[70] There could be no suggestion that Wales would be treated separately.

So things were to remain until the early 1990s. By then, however, as was mentioned in chapter one, a wide range of factors combined to create a political opportunity for those in the Welsh Labour ranks who were determined to strengthen the 'nominal commitment' to establish 'an elected Welsh Assembly in Cardiff with powers and functions which reflect the existing administrative structure' that was contained in Labour's 1992 general election manifesto.[71]

Following the 1992 general election, and with a genuinely devolutionist party leadership now installed, an uncharacteristically bold move saw the Welsh TUC support calls for the establishment of a Welsh constitutional convention on Scottish lines. Predictably enough, the unions rapidly rowed back from this call for an all-party convention once the Labour Party made it clear that it was opposed to cross-party initiatives of this kind. But the non-event that was the Welsh constitutional convention remains significant. Since the late 1990s, the idea that Wales missed out because it experienced no Scottish-style convention has become a familiar lament, repeated on a regular basis by a number of leading politicians.[72] As if to confirm this sense of absence and loss, a recurring theme in the work of leading commentator John Osmond has been attempts to identify events or processes that might be considered the functional Welsh equivalent of Scotland's convention. Among the proposed candidates have been the Llandrindod meeting of the Parliament for Wales campaign in 1994, the first term of the National Assembly and the Richard Commission.[73]

Compared to their Scottish equivalents, the two main institutional movers behind calls for a Welsh convention – the Welsh TUC and the churches – never had the necessary autonomy, credibility or societal weight to drive such a venture forward. Even more importantly, given its dominance over the Welsh political landscape, without Labour Party support and participation any attempt to embark on such a venture would not only be doomed to failure but would likely prove counter-productive. It was precisely that dominance which meant that Labour support and participation would never be forthcoming. In dominant party systems or sub-systems, the dominant party has few if any incentives to cooperate with other actors. Little wonder then, in the words of then

Labour MEP Wayne David, that 'the Labour Party in Wales is firmly wedded to first past the post, winner takes all politics'.[74] This sentiment applied, in particular, to the dreaded 'Nats'. When the then general secretary of the Wales Labour Party, Anita Gale, was asked, in June 1992, about the prospects of entering cross-party discussions with Plaid Cymru she responded with the memorably sweeping 'There is no way we are going to sit down at the same table as the nationalists; they do not agree with anything we say or do, and we do not agree with them.'[75]

While responding to calls for a convention with a firm No, Labour's Welsh Executive established its own Constitutional Policy Commission with a remit to 're-examine policy in relation to the creation of a directly elected Welsh Assembly'. Ron Davies and his devolutionist allies sought to use this process to strengthen the party's policy beyond the now-familiar executive devolution model, but they were largely unsuccessful. Attempts to place legislative devolution on the party's agenda were stoutly and successfully resisted, both by key party officials in Wales and, it seems, elements close to Tony Blair, party leader from mid-1994 onwards.[76] Indeed, what is truly striking is the degree of continuity of Labour policy not only with the late 1970s, but with the rhetoric and arguments of the late 1960s. In the 1995 policy statement, *Shaping the Vision*, not only was the case for legislative powers firmly rejected, but devolution was yet again framed in the context of local government reform. An Assembly, it was claimed, would 'assist the process of local government reorganisation'.[77]

The only substantial policy change made by Labour from the 1978 Act concerned the electoral system for the Assembly. As was discussed in the previous chapter, the need to win a referendum on Labour's proposals generated a compelling reason for an element of proportional representation to be incorporated into Labour's plans. Yet, Ron Davies also appears to have held a principled commitment to a voting system that promised to make the proposed Assembly a more pluralist institution than the one which the 1978 proposals would likely have produced. There was also a wider concern that any new democratic chamber should not repeat Wales's dismal record on female parliamentary representation.[78] Nonetheless, it was not until the 1997 Wales Labour Party conference that resistance to a more proportional electoral system was finally overcome, and only after the intervention of Tony Blair, who had made clear his belief that 'all of Wales should ... feel repre-sented in the Welsh Assembly'.[79]

Beyond this undoubtedly significant concession, however, the rest of Labour's devolution proposals contained in the party's 1997 election manifesto, and the White Paper proposals voted upon in the subsequent referendum, followed closely the executive devolu-tion model that had been placed before the electorate in March 1979.[80] Labour's policy remained that, if Wales was to have a devolved Assembly, then it would exercise executive powers subordinate to the terms of Westminster legislation. Moreover, its internal organ-ization would be modelled on traditional local government lines. It is little wonder that a senior Welsh Office civil servant charged with making a reality of the new government's proposals reports that he and his colleagues 'went back to our beloved papers from the 1970s'.[81] As well they might. While Wales might have changed radic-ally in the intervening twenty years, Labour's proposals for devolved government in Wales remained, in almost all essentials, unaltered.

Collaborative development: 1997–2004

What is striking about the period between 1997 and 2004 in Wales – certainly compared to what had gone before, and also with what was to come later – is the extent to which the politics of devolution was characterized by inter-party cooperation in pursuit of a more workable system. This was readily visible in the parliamentary debates on the Bill that was to become the 1998 Government of Wales Act. Not only was government ministers' treatment of oppos-ition contributions unusually attentive by parliamentary standards – something that was observable from the public gallery at the time – but even more importantly, it was those interventions (including some from Conservative members of both Houses) that helped ensure that a cabinet model of government was grafted on to what had originally been envisaged as a local government model of internal organization. That this grafting was awkward, to say the least, does not diminish its subsequent importance. The work of drawing up the standing orders of the new body was also very much an all-party affair.[82]

Once the National Assembly had begun its work, it was behind-the-scenes cross-party cooperation (encompassing disenchanted Labour members, as well as those from the other parties) that precipitated the forced departure of Alun Michael from his role as the inaugural First Secretary. Following his removal, it was also cross-party cooperation that led to a de facto separation between legislature (the National Assembly for Wales) and executive (the Welsh Assembly Government), and the emergence of what Richard Rawlings termed a 'virtual parliament' instead of Michael's 'Welsh Office plus' model of devolution.[83] While First Minister Rhodri Morgan and Presiding Officer Dafydd Elis-Thomas played the leading public roles in this process, they were enthusiastically supported by many Conservatives and Liberal Democrats, as well as by members of their own parties.

But the high point of this period of 'collaborative development' was the work of the Commission into the Powers and Electoral Arrangements of the National Assembly for Wales, chaired by the independent-minded Labour peer Lord Ivor Richard.[84] The Richard Commission, as it was universally known, was one of the outcomes of the coalition agreement between Labour and the Liberal Democrats, finalized in the autumn of 2000, which brought both greater stability and some sense of policy direction to the executive that would soon become known as the Welsh Assembly Government.[85] The establishment of the Commission was one of the demands made by the junior coalition partner. The Commission's membership included not only representatives of the four main parties but also several distinguished independent experts. The Commission process was able to generate a meaningful debate on the fundamental constitutional architecture of Welsh devolution that, for the first time in many decades, was not one confined to the ranks of the Welsh Labour Party.[86] The report which the Richard Commission produced in 2004 is impressive: evidence-based, coherent and rigorous, it stands in favourable comparison even to the results of the much vaunted Scottish Constitutional Convention.[87]

The Richard Commission presented both a critique of the devolution dispensation established by the 1998 Act and an alternative model for devolved government. Their critique was devastating. A concise summary was provided by Ivor Richard at the public launch of the commission report, when he described the prevailing system as 'grotesque'.

In its place, the commissioners unanimously advocated a wholly reformed system of devolved government.[88] Their recommendations were based on a clear statement of principle:

The Assembly is the democratically representative body for the whole of Wales. The Welsh Assembly Government should be able to formulate policies within clearly defined fields, and should have the power to implement all the stages for delivery, in partnership with the UK Government and other stakeholders. The Assembly Government should be able to set its own priorities and timetables for action. It should be accountable to the people of Wales through the elected Assembly for its policies and their implementation.[89]

While this statement might appear modest and wholly unremarkable to anyone schooled in comparative government, in the context of the debates that had taken place over devolution in Wales since the early 1960s, the Richard Commission was offering something almost revolutionary in its clarity.

Based on this foundational principle, the commission made three main recommendations, relating to internal organization, powers and electoral arrangements. First, the commission recommended that full separation of the legislature and the executive should be brought about. The 'body corporate' established in the 1998 Act should be formally abolished, and both the National Assembly as the parliamentary body and the Welsh Assembly Government as the executive should be established on an appropriate legal basis. To those observers steeped in the British constitutional tradition (or indeed most other constitutional traditions), this recommendation will again appear utterly unremarkable – the reassertion of 'normality' after a period of idiosyncratic experimentation. But in the context of the historical development of Welsh devolution, the recommendation was far from anodyne. For three decades from the mid-1960s, every devolutionary scheme proposed by the Welsh Labour Party had stressed the 'local government' character of the proposed assembly. In large part this served to succour sceptics or opponents of devolution that any National Assembly would be secondary in form, as well as status, to the 'proper' parliament in Westminster. But following the de facto separation of powers that had taken place in the aftermath of Alun Michael's ouster, the commission now advocated the full, *de jure* removal of any vestiges of the local government model.

On powers, the Richard Commission went much further than most expectations. The commissioners recommended the transfer of primary legislative powers to the National Assembly in those areas where it was already exercising executive responsibilities. The model advocated was based on the Scottish model of devolution (the 1998 Scotland Act version of the Scottish model rather than the 1978 version – a distinction to which we return in the concluding chapter). The Commission further recommended that primary powers be transferred by 2011, although it made no recommendation as to whether or not such a development would require popular approval through a referendum.[90] In the intervening period before 2011, an interim dispensation was suggested that would allow the National Assembly to develop the necessary competence and experience in drafting and scrutinizing legislation. This interim dispensation – later to become known as '13.2' after a summary box in the report – would involve the development of a 'new model of framework-legislation devolution'. Specifically, this would mean 'including in future primary legislation new framework provisions designed to allow the Assembly to, for example, make any changes it wished within the field covered by the Act through secondary legislation'.[91]

Finally, on electoral arrangements, the Commission argued that the transfer of primary legislative powers to the Assembly, and the concomitant growth in its responsibilities for the proper scrutiny of legislation, would require an increase in the size of the chamber. A total of eighty members (compared with the current sixty) was advocated, with the Commission arguing that they should be elected by single transferable vote in multi-member constituencies.

These recommendations have yet to be enacted in full. To the contrary, as discussed in the next section, the Labour UK government refused even to engage with some key elements of the Richard recommendations. And yet the commissioners' labours were not in vain. They have provided a yardstick against which all subsequent proposals could be measured – and often found wanting.

Going L(o)CO: the response to Richard, the 2006 Act and the reassertion of party dominance

As we have just discussed, the period from 1997 to 2004 was characterized by a collaborative, cross-party approach to constitutional development in Wales. The years from 2004 to 2006 saw an emphatic reassertion of single party dominance. Once more it was Labour, and pretty much only Labour, that mattered. The contents of the 2006 Government of Wales Act reflected the interests of, and

45

internal compromises within, the party that remained Wales's dominant political force.

The broad thrust of Labour's initial response to the Richard
Commission recommendations was far from positive.[92] The exception was the proposed changes to the internal organization of the
National Assembly. Such was the ignominious failure of the original
arrangements that their replacement was regarded as unobjection-
able by Labour, as by the other parties. But in other respects
Labour's reaction was very different. The recommended reforms to
the electoral arrangements of the devolved chamber (eighty
members, and STV) were simply dismissed; indeed, the Labour
Party barely engaged with the substantive arguments advanced for
these proposals by the Richard report.

The response on powers was somewhat more complicated. As
mentioned in the previous chapter, Rhodri Morgan's immediate
reaction to the Richard Commission's recommendations on the
morning of the publication of its report was that a referendum
would be necessary before primary legislative powers could be
introduced. Morgan also made his own lack of enthusiasm for any
such referendum abundantly clear. At a subsequent academic
conference in Cardiff in June 2004, Morgan went on to propose the
development of a more expansive version of Richard's 13.2 proposal
– what he termed '13.2-plus' – to allow for the transfer of further
powers to the Assembly falling short of full primary powers. Details
on this mechanism were notably lacking, but the clear implication
of the First Minister's suggestion was that some such arrangement
might well be the maximum achievable for the foreseeable future.

Expectations were lowered further when the Labour Party document *Better Governance for Wales* was published in August 2004. The
contrast between the clarity and intellectual rigour of the Richard
Commission Report and that of the governing party's formal
response to it could not have been more marked. Several features
of that response appeared at the time to be particularly important.
The first was a palpable reluctance to consider the expansion of the
National Assembly's powers, with the issue posed as a choice
between primary powers on the one hand, and so-called Henry VIII
powers to amend or repeal existing legislation in areas of Assembly
responsibility on the other.[93] A second notable feature of the document was its insistence on the requirement for a post-legislative
referendum before primary powers could be transferred to

Cardiff.[94] As was discussed in chapter one, this had apparently been insisted upon by Welsh Labour MPs, and their success was regarded by many, not least the MPs themselves, as a particularly significant victory. In the summer of 2004, it appeared that the MPs had secured a re-run of 1979 rather than 1997, seemingly undermining any realistic prospect of attaining the Richard goal of primary powers for many years to come.

Another element of Labour's response to Richard that gained particular notoriety was its attack on 'dual candidacy': the practice whereby individuals could offer themselves as Assembly candidates both in a particular constituency and on the regional list. During the first Assembly, dual candidacy had not been regarded as problematic. Prominent Labour figures, including Rhodri Morgan, had been dual candidates themselves in the first Assembly election, while all four main parties had both constituency and regional list members elected to the Assembly. After the 2003 election, however, the status of regional members became subject to increasingly hostile comment from Labour AMs; it should perhaps be borne in mind that no Labour members were returned through the regional lists in 2003. In particular, the Clwyd West result was seized upon as highlighting a particularly iniquitous anomaly whereby 'failed constituency candidates' could enter the Assembly through the 'back door' of the regional list (in Clwyd West, three candidates defeated by Labour's Alun Pugh were returned through the North Wales regional list). *Better Governance for Wales* proposed a ban on dual candidacy, arguing that the present system was 'both confusing and frustrating for the electorate'.[95]

A special Welsh Labour conference in September 2004 approved a promise for further legislation to be included in Labour's 2005 general election manifesto. The vagueness of the manifesto's commitment on powers – the Assembly's legislative powers were to be 'enhanced' – contrasted sharply with the specificity of the document's uncompromising stance on dual candidacy. Labour would

> prevent candidates from standing on both the list and in a constituency in order to make all candidates genuinely accountable to the electorate, and to end Assembly Members being elected via the backdoor even when they have already been rejected by the voters.[96]

In the wake of such statements, few, if any, expectations persisted of dramatic changes to the 1998 Act. The prevailing mood is captured nicely in contributions made at the time by two close observers of Welsh politics. Writing soon after the 2005 UK general election, Alan Trench expressed surprise at the way Rhodri Morgan – 'hitherto regarded as strongly supporting devolution' – had reacted to the Richard Commission Report.[97] Morgan's reaction, he suggested, had served to ensure

> that decisions about Wales's constitutional future are not to be made in Wales, but principally in Whitehall and Westminster, by the Secretary of State. This is not a friendly setting, as interest in Wales there is limited, and there is considerable hostility toward the Assembly from a number of Welsh Labour MPs to whom Peter Hain looks for support. Securing time for new legislation and the passage of that legislation will not be straightforward, and the position taken by the First Minister ... risks further dilution in the course of the drafting of the White Paper and translating that into legislation.[98]

Meanwhile, John Osmond suggested that 'altering the political governance of Wales so as to remove the Labour Party from its dominant position may prove to be a necessary precursor for full implementation of the Richard Commission recommendations'.[99] The Richard commissioners, it appeared, had laboured mightily but to little avail.

Against such expectations, the June 2005 UK government White Paper, *Better Governance for Wales*, came as a major surprise.[100] Nothing in the internal Labour debate over the preceding year would have led observers to expect proposals so radical and far-reaching. The White Paper shared the title of Labour's initial August 2004 response to the Richard Commission, but the content of the two documents could hardly have been more different in tone or ambition.

Indeed, the scope of the White Paper's proposals was so wholly unexpected that their single most striking element – the proposal that the UK Parliament legislate immediately for the transfer of primary legislative powers to the National Assembly, those powers to be 'unlocked' after an affirmative vote in a referendum to be held at some unspecified point in the future – was missed almost entirely in initial media reactions.[101] Moreover, by legislating for primary powers immediately, while simultaneously guaranteeing that a referendum would be required before such powers come into force (albeit while stating that Wales would not be ready for such a referendum for several years), Hain effectively outflanked devolution-sceptic Welsh Labour MPs who had regarded the pledge of a post-legislative referendum as a major victory. The third devolution referendum would be no 1979 redux, and a move to legislative devolution had survived, after all. Debate on the desirability or otherwise of the primary powers model set out in Part IV of the Act was largely sidestepped during the parliamentary passage of the Government of Wales Bill on the basis that it was for the Welsh people to decide at some future point – a smaller-scale equivalent of what had occurred at the time of the 1997 general election. Greater parliamentary attention was given to the fact that the wording of the referendum question was to be set out in the Order in Council for the referendum, and was not set out in the Bill. There were also some denunciations of the various 'locks' insisted upon in the White Paper before a referendum could be held (there would need to be a two-thirds majority in the Assembly in favour, as well as the agreement of a Secretary of State and the UK Parliament as a whole). But much of this criticism had a ritualistic air. There was no doubting the fact that, on legislative powers, the White Paper was a significant victory for devolutionists.[102]

Indeed, in one important respect, the White Paper went further than the Richard Commission. A form of Rhodri Morgan's 13.2-plus mechanism also found its way into the UK government's proposals. But while Morgan had implied that this mechanism might be a substitute for the Richard goal of primary powers, in the White Paper it became the interim dispensation. Moreover, the mechanism allowed for greater powers to be conferred on the Assembly than Morgan had suggested. By permitting the Assembly to create Measures, Part III of the legislation would in reality be conferring primary legislative powers on the National Assembly even without a referendum being held. Even if those legislative powers were tightly constrained, nonetheless the Rubicon of principle would be crossed. Wales would have a national legislature with the power to create its own primary legislation.

This modified 13.2-plus mechanism ('13.2 plus plus' according to one prominent civil servant[103]), was underspecified at the time of the White Paper's publication and remained so even after the legislation came into force. In particular, the pledge to allow MPs to undertake 'pre-legislative scrutiny' of Assembly requests for legislative competence remained vague and an obvious potential point of friction. But optimists chose to emphasize the potential of this new system, assuming that Legislative Competence Orders (LCOs) would be widely drawn and lead to a relatively rapid empowerment of the Assembly.[104] As will be discussed in chapter four, these hopes were to be disappointed. Nonetheless, they were real enough at the time.

Other aspects of the White Paper were much less surprising. The legislation would abolish the body corporate and separate executive and legislature. More controversial was confirmation of the UK government's standpoint on the electoral arrangements for the National Assembly. The White Paper made no attempt to engage seriously with the possibility of increasing the numbers of Assembly Members, nor with adopting the single transferable vote.[105] It did, however, confirm the government's determination to legislate a ban on dual candidacy in Assembly elections. The White Paper's claim was that dual candidacy 'both devalues the integrity of the electoral system in the eyes of the public and acts as a disincentive to vote'.[106] Unsurprisingly, the other parties took a different view, attacking the change as deeply partisan. Indeed, much of the subsequent debate on the White Paper focused not on the issue of powers, but rather on the proposed dual candidacy ban.

As the Bill proceeded through Parliament, successive attempts by the government to construct an intellectual underpinning for banning dual candidacy collapsed. Having initially claimed that the ban reflected deep public disquiet at the 'Clwyd West' issue, Hain subsequently admitted that there was no evidence from Wales to support this claim.[107] Evidence collected by the Scottish Arbuthnott Commission was cited in support, even though that commission's report explicitly rejected a ban on dual candidacy.[108] Comments by Lord David Steel and even the Electoral Reform Society were then invoked to justify the ban – much to their surprise and even indignation.[109] Attempts to justify the ban descended into the farcical by January 2006, when research produced by the Bevan Foundation on behalf of a Labour MP was hailed as evidence in support of the government's case, a claim that was rapidly discredited.[110] Hain also came under almost unprecedented criticism from the Electoral Commission who, along with the current authors, pointed out the rare and highly inauspicious international precedents for the government's proposal (notably the banning of dual candidacy in pre-Orange revolution Ukraine).[111] Unsurprisingly, given both the second chamber's political composition and Labour's failure to establish any plausible case for the dual candidacy ban beyond crude partisan advantage, the House of Lords voted to overturn the ban in April 2006. Ultimately, however, the fact that the ban was specifically trailed in the 2005 manifesto – as well as a notably helpful intervention from Assembly Presiding Officer Lord Elis-Thomas – saw the Lords drop their objection.[112]

However dubious the reasoning behind the ban on dual candidacy, the major question about the 2006 Government of Wales Act is surely how it was, following Labour's initially very cool reaction to the Richard Commission, that Labour actually delivered so much of the Richard agenda? Indeed, in the Measure-making interim dispensation of Part III, it had gone significantly further than envisaged by the Commission, and without the referendum that Rhodri Morgan had claimed would be necessary. The full story of this turnaround remains to be told, and will likely remain elusive. But a number of points are surely pertinent. First, as was mentioned in chapter one, to overcome resistance from many of those Welsh Labour MPs who remained deeply distrustful of devolution, Peter Hain seems to have given private assurances that there would be no referendum on a move to the Part IV provisions before 2015 at the earliest. Or this is what the recipients of these assurances seem to have believed, at any rate.

Secondly, the controversy about dual candidacy helped, in that it distracted much attention (both inside and outside parliament) away from the provisions of the government Bill concerning powers and towards this proposed reform of the electoral arrangements. Moreover, the dual candidacy ban united virtually everyone in the Labour Party – from the strongest devolution enthusiasts to the most devo-sceptic – in a way that a focus on powers never could.

Nonetheless, the passage of the Bill required fighting internal battles successfully within the Labour Party. Peter Hain has spoken publicly of his own role in overcoming opposition at cabinet level to at least some of the provisions of the 2006 Act:

> [s]ome arm twisting was required but that's in the nature of government. There's nothing particularly conspiratorial about this, but there were one or two very senior members of the government – one particular senior member of the government – with whom I had to have some serious engagements; and a bit of a kind of stand-off at one

point; and a bit of a kind of power struggle. But that person was persuaded in the end and all to the good.[113]

The key interlocutor referred to here is Geoff Hoon, who was at that stage Lord Privy Seal and Leader of the House of Commons – and thus, as the government's senior Commons business manager, potentially in a position to be highly obstructive to Hain and his Bill.[114] It was not only Hain who had to lobby senior government figures. Rhodri Morgan made a direct intervention to Prime Minister Blair to ensure that space was found in the legislative calendar for the Bill that would eventually become the 2006 Act. Indeed, it appears that Morgan made clear to the Prime Minister that he could not survive as First Minister should parliamentary time not be found.[115]

Beyond the various personalities involved, the making of the 2006 Government of Wales Act also highlights a wider analytical point: that despite having been weakened by devolution, 'one-partyism' retained a considerable grip on Welsh politics. The Richard Commission, in the processes it followed and the final report it produced, had appeared to embody a new, more pluralistic Welsh politics. Subsequent events – from the publication of that report to the final passage of the Government of Wales Act – demonstrated the resilience of a different and far less inclusive politics. The 2006 Act was undoubtedly a major piece of constitutional legislation; according to Peter Hain it was intended to provide the basic building blocks for Welsh political life for a generation. And yet – notwithstanding all the sound and fury surrounding dual candidacy – the only debates that really mattered with regard to the final content of the Act were those conducted within the Labour Party. To the extent that they were relevant at all, prominent devolutionists in Wales's other political parties mattered for how they related to the divisions within Labour (Lord Elis-Thomas's previously mentioned intervention being merely one example). Such behaviour is characteristic of what political scientists term one-party dominant political systems (or sub-systems): systems where the most important divisions occur within the dominant party, rather than between parties, and where other political actors are required to provide implicit recognition of this state of affairs by orienting their behaviour around the battles occurring within the dominant political force.[116] The 2006 Government of Wales Act showed that there clearly remained some distance still to be travelled before a mature, pluralistic democracy could be said to exist in Wales.

Conclusion: party dominance and the failure of Welsh constitution building

This chapter has sought to trace and analyse the key political proc-esses that have underpinned Welsh devolved constitution building. From the welter of detail about particular debates, individuals and institutions, two general points stand out.

The first point is that the record of Welsh constitution building is a record of failure. To say so is not meant to disparage either the efforts or the ingenuity of many of those involved. But the reality should be faced squarely: the successive edifices constructed have been characterized by almost continual instability. And – as we will discuss further in the concluding chapter – it is unlikely that the latest version will prove much more durable.

Lest this verdict appear too damning, we should remind ourselves of key milestones since 1997. First we might recall that the White Paper proposals placed before the Welsh electorate in September 1997 were subject to substantial changes before the passage of the 1998 Government of Wales Act: most notably the decision to replace the local government-style committee system envisaged in the White Paper with a model of cabinet government, creating what we might euphemistically term a highly original hybrid of local govern-ment and parliamentary-type structures and practices.

We should then remember that, following Alun Michael's enforced resignation in early 2000, the body corporate model estab-lished by the 1998 Act (that is, the local government elements of the hybrid) was effectively effaced by the introduction of a more orthodox parliamentary division of powers between executive and legislature. Strikingly, while this move was clearly contrary to the spirit (if not quite the letter) of the 1998 Act, it was supported by every actor involved in devolved Welsh politics: eloquent testimony to the fundamental problems with the 1998 Act.

We might now also remind ourselves that by 2004 the Richard Commission had unanimously recommended that the de facto executive–legislative split be rendered *de jure*, and had also recom-mended fundamental changes to the powers of the National Assembly, amidst a general characterization by Lord Richard of the devolutionary dispensation provided for Wales by the 1998 Act as 'grotesque'. At least partly in consequence, a new Government of Wales Act reached the statute book in 2006.

At this point we should probably pause to reflect on this simple fact: Wales's first devolved constitution lasted scarcely eight years. The only genuinely memorably line from the No campaign in the 1997 referendum was Tim Williams's quip that a devolved Wales would be 'a banana republic without the bananas'.[117] Having to rewrite a constitution after eight years – indeed, only seven years of actual operation – does indeed leave us squarely in banana-republic territory. Furthermore, the successor dispensation lasted scarcely four further years before it too was replaced, this time by an alternative already encoded in the 2006 Act – a rare, if not unique, example of the principle of built-in obsolescence being extended from the design of household appliances to that of national constitutions.

Some of those schooled in the British constitutional tradition – or, more precisely, the justificatory panegyrics that often surround it – may well object to our criticism on the basis that flexibility and evolutionary adaptability are precisely the defining qualities of what, in more confident times, used to be regarded as Britain's 'unique constitutional genius'.[118] It might thus be argued that the almost constant change to the foundations of devolved government just outlined is an example of effective constitutional adjustment: a source of vindication rather than cause for condemnation. It is true that constitutional and political *immobilisme* is a pathological state of affairs. But the choice should not be between absolute stasis and wholesale flux. A certain level of durability is a feature of all reasonably successful constitutional regimes. Moreover, in the Welsh case it has less often been a positive choice for a coherent alternative than the manifest inadequacies of the status quo that has driven change. From Assembly regional committees to Legislative Competence Orders, huge amounts of time and scarce resources have been diverted from dealing effectively with the problems facing Welsh society to keeping flawed structures and processes functioning.

A more serious defence of Welsh constitution builders and their efforts would be that, given the realities of Welsh society and politics, nothing better was realistically possible with the material and in the circumstances at hand. This is an argument with real substance. Perhaps there was no other way for Wales to approach legislative

devolution than in a piecemeal and crab-like fashion. Welsh devolutionists may well have been wise in never allowing the genuinely
viable to be the enemy of the achievable. But even if this point is
conceded, a high price has been paid for proceeding in this manner.
A highly flawed process of constitution building has resulted in
governmental structures and processes that have repeatedly proven
inadequate to the task at hand.

Mention of political realities leads to our second main point. This
is that, as we have shown, constitution making in Wales has been a
process determined almost exclusively within one party. The story
of Welsh constitution making is not only a story of failure; it is also
a story of party dominance. Indeed, devolution arguably provides
the paradigmatic example of party dominance in action. To focus
on the role of the Labour Party in the constitutional design of Welsh
devolution is therefore not only essential to understanding the
various designs adopted; it also opens up a unique window on the
nature of Welsh politics more generally.

Labour's decades-long domination of Welsh electoral politics is,
by international standards, highly unusual. But it is not totally
without precedent. Other democratic societies have also witnessed
extended periods in which one party has enjoyed a hegemonic position. At the state level, the Japanese Liberal Democrats, the Swedish
Social Democrats and Ireland's Fianna Fáil all offer examples. At
the sub-state level, the Ulster Unionist Party controlled the Stormont
Parliament throughout its existence; the Christian Social Union has
now enjoyed more than six decades of almost unbroken domination in Bavaria, and the Democrats dominated the former
Confederate South for almost a century after the end of the
American civil war.

Labour's domination in Wales is not exactly analogous, of course.
Before 1999 there was no directly elected layer of government at the
Welsh level. This meant that in the post-Second World War period,
with the exception of the 1964 and 1974 general elections, it was the
electoral behaviour of the English electorate that determined how
Wales would be governed. The absence of a Welsh legislature and
government may have served to mitigate some of the pathologies
widely associated with long-term periods of one-party domination.
For example, the absence of the spoils of government obviated the
dangers of the serious, systemic corruption often associated with
single-party domination. But by the same token, the absence of the

disciplining realities of government arguably gave other negative traits even freer rein. So, for example, it would be hard to argue that Welsh Labour's long electoral dominance was accompanied by any substantial intellectual vibrancy or creativity. Comforting shibboleths could be maintained with little danger that they might need to be tested in the crucible of practice.

As the evidence adduced in this chapter has underlined, all of the key debates about the government of Wales – and, in particular, on the form that devolution might take – have taken place within the Labour Party. The most politically consequential cleavages on the devolution issue have been those within Labour ranks, rather than between Labour and some of its opponents. Moreover, as is also typical of dominant party systems, other political actors in Wales have sought to position themselves around the Labour Party's internal cleavages, actively assisting those forces within the party most closely associated with their preferred position on the issue. In the 1997 referendum, for instance, this meant Plaid Cymru and the Liberal Democrats supporting Labour pro-devolutionists like Ron Davies, while their Conservative opponents provided practical help to Labour dissidents like Betty Bowen and Carys Pugh. For all concerned, this appeared the most likely means to promote their own favoured position.

But with the most important divisions lying within Labour ranks, the party's devolution plans have often been aimed at least as much at trying to bridge those divides as they have towards providing a basis for effective devolved government. Compromises that would avoid damaging internal arguments have been placed at a higher premium than adherence to basic constitutional principles; backroom fixes preferred to potentially rancorous public debate. It is at this point that the two wider points underlined by this discussion connect.

The failure of devolved constitution building in Wales has not occurred because the parliamentary drafters of the 1978 Wales Act or the 1998 and 2006 Government of Wales Acts were peculiarly inept. Nor is it the case that those politicians who gave them their instructions suffered from a particularly stubborn form of constitutional illiteracy. It is not to the conjunctural or the contingent that we need to look for an explanation, but to the deeper structures of Wales's political culture. The deeply flawed process of Welsh constitution building is itself a consequence of single-party dominance.

3
The evolution of public attitudes

The previous two chapters in this book have set out much of the political context for the 2011 Welsh referendum. In chapter one, we examined the road to the referendum and placed the vote in historical perspective. We did this by reviewing both the longer-term processes that led to the establishment of democratic devolution in Wales, and also the particular and peculiar political path that culminated in the holding of a referendum on extending devolution in March 2011. In chapter two we explored the constitutional politics of Welsh devolution in more detail. By examining the complex model for devolution that was introduced in the late 1990s, how that model had evolved and changed in subsequent years, and the provisions of the 2006 Government of Wales Act, we were able to establish what was at stake in the referendum and make clearer what differences would follow for the government of Wales if the people voted Yes or voted No.

However, one very important dimension of the context for the 2011 referendum has not yet been considered at any length. Thus far we have barely talked about the views of those who would ultimately decide the matter – the people of Wales. The task for the present chapter will be to explain what we know about those views and how they had evolved over the months and years preceding the referendum.

Considering public opinion requires us to address a rather substantial puzzle. One necessary condition for the referendum occurring was that a substantial proportion of Wales's political elite had become persuaded that a vote on extending devolution could be won. As was discussed in the previous chapters, the process by which this came to pass was far from straightforward, and doubts certainly lingered in many minds. Nonetheless, enough of the major political leaders had come to regard the referendum as winnable. But how could this be so – in the land that had over-whelmingly rejected self-government in March 1979 and then, in just about the most favourable circumstances possible for devolutionists, only very narrowly supported the idea in September 1997? Was it really credible to believe that people could now confidently be expected to endorse a strengthening of devolution? And if so, what changes in the landscape of public attitudes had made this possible?

To answer these questions, this chapter pulls together the available evidence on public attitudes to self-government in Wales. We first assess the 'long history' of public attitudes to devolution in Wales, from the mid-1960s to the mid-1990s. Here we consider the limited available evidence from the period prior to the 1979 referendum before outlining the overwhelming victory of the No campaign in that vote. We then explore the extent to which public attitudes began to change during the 1980s and 1990s. The second section of the chapter assesses the 1997 referendum. In doing so, we consider what the result of this ballot said about attitudes towards devolution in Wales – both the extent of change since 1979 and the substantial divisions that still persisted. The third section will be devoted to exploring the years after 1997, about which we have much more detailed evidence than for earlier years. We draw on much of this evidence to document the evolution of public attitudes after the referendum: showing how opposition to devolution declined surprisingly rapidly and substantially, while an enhanced level of devolution began to attract significant support. We also discuss the factors that best explain these changes. Were they down to the practical achievements of devolution? Did changes in public attitudes reflect the people of Wales becoming significantly more 'Welsh' in their identities after the creation of the National Assembly? Or were other factors at play – and if so, what were they? Finally, we conclude the chapter by assessing what the evidence in the period immediately prior to the 2011 referendum campaign suggested about the state of public attitudes. With what degree of justifiable optimism could the respective forces march on to the campaign battlefield?

The 'long history': public attitudes from the 1960s to the 1990s

Any attempt to trace the evolution over recent decades of public attitudes towards how Wales is governed almost immediately runs into a significant problem: the fragmentary nature of the available evidence. In this section of the chapter, we draw the pieces together as best we can, while also acknowledging that considerable gaps remain.

Systematic attempts to gauge public attitudes in Wales can first be witnessed in the mid-1960s. By this time, representative sample surveys had become widely recognized as a legitimate method for gauging public opinion. And the emergence of Plaid Cymru and the Scottish National Party as potentially serious political forces created a practical urgency among much of the British political class to use this tool to discover more about the apparently changing landscape of Scottish and Welsh attitudes.

The earliest survey on public support for self-government for Wales seems to have been one commissioned by the Conservative Party in 1966, in which ORC found 42 per cent of respondents supporting a 'Parliament for Wales'. The following autumn, a survey for the *Western Mail* by the same company found 61 per cent of Welsh respondents agreeing that 'Wales should have its own parliament to deal with Welsh affairs'. And in 1968, ORC (in another survey for the Conservatives) found 59 per cent endorsing a Welsh Parliament, and 54 per cent favouring 'more power to make government decisions being given to authorities in Wales'.[1] By the summer of 1970, NOP was observing virtually half of Welsh respondents favouring home rule for 'Welsh affairs'. In short, a number of different surveys in this period seemed to suggest quite substantial public support for some Welsh self-government. But other surveys pointed to rather different conclusions. In November 1967, NOP found only 24 per cent support for 'self-government for Wales'. A survey for the BBC in May 1968 found majority support in Wales for at most only limited constitutional change.[2] And a Gallup poll in September 1968 found 51 per cent of respondents opposed to a Welsh Parliament. These early surveys also tended to show the low salience of the issue: few of those surveyed considered Wales's constitutional status a major priority.[3]

This early survey evidence is far from unproblematic. In some polls, only a fairly small number of Welsh respondents were included within a wider British sample; such small samples greatly increase the survey 'margin of error'. Even where full samples were conducted in Wales, the absence of previous experience in conducting political surveys in Wales possibly increased the likelihood that samples unrepresentative of the wider population might be drawn. But most problematic of all was that surveys were asking about matters of low public salience, where the terms of public debate were far from settled. It was not clear what options should be put to survey respondents, nor how respondents would interpret them: the apparently contradictory evidence we have just seen can probably most readily be explained by many respondents, lacking deeply thought-through views on the matter, being very sensitive to the exact wording of the question asked.

The problem of presenting sensible alternatives to survey respondents was well illustrated by research into public attitudes conducted by the Crowther/Kilbrandon Royal Commission. The Royal Commission carried out a survey with substantial samples in all major regions and nations of Britain in the summer of 1970; included in this survey was a question on constitutional preferences. Findings for Wales, alongside those for Scotland, are reported in table 3.1.

Table 3.1 Constitutional preferences (%) in Wales and Scotland, 1970: Crowther/Kilbrandon Royal Commission Survey*

Q. For running the region as a whole, which of these five alternatives would you prefer?

Response	Wales	Scotland
Leave things as they are at present	15	6
Keep things much the same as they are now but make sure that the needs of the region are better understood by the government	27	19
Keep the present system but allow more decisions to be made in the region	21	26
Have a new system of governing the region so that as many decisions as possible are made in the area	23	24
Let the region take over complete responsibility for running things in the region	12	23
Number of respondents	726	892

* Survey conducted by Social and Community Planning Research in the summer of 1970; findings reported in 'Devolution and other aspects of governance: an attitudes survey', *Royal Commission on the Constitution Research Paper 7* (London: HMSO, 1973).

The most striking feature of the table is not the results, but the distinctly nebulous alternatives given to survey respondents. A golden rule of closed-ended survey questions (where respondents are required to choose between predefined answers) is that the options presented should be clearly differentiated and as unambiguous as possible. But what unambiguous meaning can be given to 'Keep things much the same as they are now but make sure that the needs of the region are better understood by the government'? And how does this clearly differ from 'Keep the present system but allow more decisions to be made in the region'?[4]

But to the extent that the Royal Commission's survey evidence can be meaningfully interpreted, it is also striking that support in Wales for substantial self-government was only half that found in Scotland, and was the joint lowest of any region in Britain (along with the south-west of England). A very similar question in the February 1974 British Election Study again showed limited enthusiasm in Wales for significant change.[5]

During the extended parliamentary debates on devolution in the 1974–9 parliament, and prior to the March 1979 referendum, occasional opinion polls were conducted to gauge the public mood. The results of these surveys (reported in table 3.2) show a continued lack of enthusiasm for self-government for Wales, and substantial endorsement of the status quo. Not once did even a plurality of

Table 3.2 Opinion polls on Welsh devolution in the 1970s*

Survey	% Yes	% No	% Don't know
December 1975[a]	30	39	31
March 1976[b]	30	39	31
December 1976[a]	27	40	33
March 1977[a]	27	53	21
May 1978[c]	34	39	27
September 1978[c]	27	41	31
1 February 1 1979[c]	33	46	21
21–2 February 1979[c]	22	65	13

* Adapted from D. Balsom, 'Public opinion and Welsh devolution'. Numbers of respondents for surveys not given.
Sources: [a] Research and Marketing Ltd poll for Western Mail/HTV Wales; [b] Research and Marketing Ltd poll for Y Cymro; [c] Abacus poll for BBC Wales

survey respondents support devolution. And the final poll prior to the referendum suggested opposition to be hardening.

In retrospect, the outcome of the 1979 referendum appears inevitable. But few at the time were prepared for quite the scale of the defeat for devolution. The final result (set out in detail in table 3.3) was overwhelming. Not a single area of Wales voted Yes; even the most 'Welsh' by language and identity rejected self-government for Wales by around two to one. Nor can this result be attributed simply to faults with the particular scheme of devolution put before the Welsh people. The 1979 Welsh Election Study (WES) found that even when offered a range of choices, the people of Wales overwhelmingly rejected self-government. WES also showed that the referendum campaign had turned certain defeat for devolution into an abject humiliation. Table 3.4 gives results from three surveys (the final two pre-referendum BBC polls and the WES conducted after the referendum) where respondents were asked to choose between four constitutional options for Wales. The substantial shift in public opinion, even in the short period covered by these polls, is unmistakeable.

The emphatic defeat of devolution in the March 1979 referendum was swiftly followed by the May general election victory of Margaret Thatcher's Conservatives, who had no desire to revive devolution. As was briefly discussed in the previous chapters, the subject thus disappeared for many years from the Welsh political agenda. Largely in consequence, few surveys of any kind examined

Table 3.3 The 1979 Welsh devolution referendum

Area	Yes (%)	No (%)
Clwyd	31,384 (22.0%)	114,119 (78.0%)
Dyfed	44,849 (28.0%)	114,947 (72.0%)
Glamorgan – Mid	46,747 (20.2%)	184,196 (79.8%)
Glamorgan – South	21,830 (13.1%)	144,186 (86.9%)
Glamorgan – West	29,663 (18.7%)	128,834 (81.3%)
Gwent	21,369 (12.0%)	155,389 (88.0%)
Gwynedd	37,363 (34.4%)	71,157 (65.6%)
Powys	9,843 (18.5%)	43,502 (81.5%)
Wales	**243,048 (20.3%)**	**956,330 (79.7%)**

Turnout = 58.3%

Table 3.4 Constitutional preferences (%) in Wales, 1979

Response	Early Feb[a]	Late Feb[a]	May[b]
Complete self-government	16	9	5
Stronger assembly	19	12	12
Proposed assembly	10	9	8
No change	56	70	75
Number of respondents	805	1,589	817

Sources: [a] = Abacus polls for BBC Wales (as reported in table 3.2); [b] = Welsh Election Study, 1979

public attitudes to devolution for many years. This is very unfortunate, because it leaves us with only fragmentary evidence about when opinions in Wales started to change. That evidence which does exist suggests that public attitudes in Wales began to shift during the mid- to late 1980s, and that this process continued into the 1990s. A question on constitutional preferences was included in the 1983, 1987 and 1992 British Election Studies; the results, presented in table 3.5, indicate a steady erosion of support for the status quo and growing endorsement of some Welsh self-government.[6]

As was discussed in chapter one, devolution had assumed a renewed salience by the mid-1990s. This prompted further polling, which indicated that self-government for Wales was now much more popular than a decade earlier. In October 1994, a poll for the BBC found a bare majority (51 per cent of respondents) supporting an 'elected assembly' for Wales. Two years later, a slightly higher proportion of the Welsh public (55 per cent) appeared to favour the idea.[7]

Table 3.5 Constitutional preferences (%) in Wales, 1983–96

Response	1983	1987	1992	1994/6
Independence	6	6	14	16
Assembly	12	23	40	50
No major change	82	71	46	34
Number of respondents	202	206	141	131

Sources: British Election Studies, 1983, 1987, 1992; British Social Attitudes Survey 1994 and 1996. Entries in the final column represent merged 1994 and 1996 BSA findings.

To review the evidence on public attitudes towards devolution before 1997 is to rely on an evidential base that is, for the most part, both limited and fragmentary in nature. Nonetheless, it seems reasonable to conclude that the rather inchoate picture in the late 1960s had, by the beginning of the 1970s, developed into clear public opposition to devolution. While the particular political circumstances of the 1979 referendum may have exaggerated the scale of the result, it is very probable that at no point in the 1970s would the result of a devolution referendum in Wales have been any different. Only during the latter part of the 1980s did the land-scape of opinion begin to shift significantly. By the mid-1990s, much greater support for devolution seemed to exist. What remained to be seen was whether this increased support would be enough to tip the balance in a future poll.

The 1997 referendum

The political agenda in the months prior to the September 1997 referendum was largely dominated by the lead-up to May's UK general election, and then by the extraordinary political honey-moon that Tony Blair's New Labour government initially enjoyed. (We should also recall that for most of the three weeks immediately prior to the referendum the news agenda concentrated heavily on coverage of the death of Princess Diana.) Nonetheless, a number of polls were commissioned in the weeks and months prior to the referendum: results are reported in table 3.6. It is interesting, in view of the closeness of the eventual referendum result, that most of these polls showed the Yes camp in a fairly clear lead.

When the final referendum result was declared, in the early hours of 19 September, there were two remarkable things about it. Its first, and most obvious, remarkable feature was the closeness of the result (detailed in table 3.7). A mere 6,721 votes separated Yes from No. Half of all registered voters had failed to vote, and of the half that did, the split was right down the middle. Wales was clearly divided about devolution, and closer examination of the results and of a survey conducted among voters immediately after the vote rein-forced this point. All of the areas that Denis Balsom had classified as British Wales in his famous Three-Wales Model voted No; all those which he had termed Welsh Wales or Y Fro Gymraeg voted Yes.[8] Yet, in not a single area did either the Yes or No camp win as

Table 3.6 Opinion polls on the 1997 referendum

Date	%Yes	%No	% Don't know
March 1997	41	33	27
April 1997	34	37	30
July 1997	39	27	34
July 1997	43	29	28
August 1997	42	22	36
September 1997	37	36	26
September 1997	37	29	34

Source: David McCrone and Bethan Lewis, 'The Scottish and Welsh referendum campaigns', in B.Taylor and K. Thomson (eds), *Scotland and Wales: Nations Again?* (Cardiff: University of Wales Press, 1999), p. 36.

much as 70 per cent of the vote: every part of Wales was divided, though the balance of opinion varied from place to place. Data from an academic survey conducted immediately after the vote suggested that a clear majority of Welsh speakers had supported devolution, but most of those speaking only English had opposed it. Similarly with national identity, those identifying themselves primarily as Welsh had tended to back devolution, but most who identified as British had not done so.[9] The referendum held in Scotland a week prior to that in Wales had indicated a clear consensus behind devolution – that it was, in the late John Smith's oft-quoted phrase, the 'settled will of the Scottish people'. No remotely similar claim could possibly have been sustained for Wales at this time.

But the very closeness of the final result, and the clear divisions in Wales, tended to distract attention away from the second respect in which the 1997 referendum result was remarkable. This was the extent of the change since 1979. The swing in favour of devolution between the 1979 and 1997 referendums in Scotland was a very substantial 22.7 per cent. Yet, in Wales – where, as discussed in previous chapters, the issue had engaged civil society and the wider public in the years prior to 1997 to a far lesser degree than it did in Scotland – the pro-devolution swing was even greater, at exactly 30.0 per cent. Some observers pointed out that, in sharp contrast to 1979, in 1997 devolution was being advocated by a highly popular new UK prime minister. Holding the Welsh referendum a week after that in Scotland had also been expected to favour the Yes

Table 3.7 The 1997 Welsh devolution referendum

Area	Yes (%)	No (%)
Blaenau Gwent	15,237 (56.1%)	11,928 (43.9%)
Bridgend	27,632 (54.4%)	23,172 (46.6%)
Caerphilly	34,830 (54.7%)	28,841 (45.3%)
Cardiff	47,527 (44.4%)	59,589 (55.6%)
Carmarthen	49,115 (65.3%)	26,119 (34.7%)
Ceredigion	18,304 (59.1%)	12,614 (40.9%)
Conwy	18,369 (41.0%)	26,521 (59.0%)
Denbighshire	14,271 (40.8%)	20,732 (59.2%)
Flintshire	17,746 (38.1%)	28,707 (61.9%)
Gwynedd	35,425 (64.1%)	19,859 (35.9%)
Merthyr Tydfil	12,707 (58.2%)	9,121 (41.8%)
Monmouth	10,592 (32.1%)	22,403 (67.9%)
Neath/Port Talbot	36,730 (66.6%)	18,463 (33.4%)
Newport	16,172 (37.4%)	27,017 (62.6%)
Pembrokeshire	19,979 (42.8%)	26,712 (57.2%)
Powys	23,038 (42.7%)	30,966 (57.3%)
Rhondda Cynon Taff	51,201 (58.5%)	36,362 (41.5%)
Torfaen	15,756 (49.9%)	15,854 (50.1%)
Swansea	42,789 (52.0%)	39,561 (48.0%)
Vale of Glamorgan	17,776 (36.7%)	30,613 (63.3%)
Wrexham	18,574 (45.3%)	22,449 (54.7%)
Ynys Môn	15,649 (50.9%)	15,095 (49.1%)
Wales	*559,419 (50.3%)*	*552,698 (49.7%)*

Turnout = 50.1%

campaign, by creating a sense of momentum behind devolution. In short, the political circumstances were favourable to a Yes vote. In only a slightly different political context the vote might very well have tipped the other way. But the contrast with 1979 was still stark. Then, the rejection of self-government had appeared to be the clear 'settled will'. Even to reach the point in 1997 where Wales was split down the middle on the issue indicated a huge shift in the public mood.

Public attitudes after 1997

Although public opinion in Wales moved considerably in a pro-devolution direction between the two referendums, the outcome in September 1997 demonstrated the country to be very much divided on the issue of self-government. Considerable scepticism about the merits of devolution remained. Indeed, if one allows for non-voters (and thus takes into account the fact that turnout in the referendum was only 50.1 per cent of registered voters) merely a quarter of the Welsh electorate actually supported the establishment of the National Assembly.

In the years since the 1997 referendum, an extensive body of evidence has been gathered on public opinion in Wales. Major academic surveys were carried out after the referendum, as well as after the 1999, 2003 and 2007 National Assembly elections, and the 2001 and 2010 UK general elections. Additional evidence on public opinion can be drawn from polls and surveys conducted for the BBC, ITV Wales, the Electoral Commission, the All-Wales Convention and the National Assembly Commission. The Electoral Commission also conducted extensive focus group research in both 2002 and 2006, as did the All-Wales Convention in 2009. Taken together, this accumulated body of research means that we know far more about public attitudes in the decade and more since the referendum than we do for any previous period.

The picture that emerges from this wealth of evidence is surprisingly dramatic. There has been no noticeable growth in support for Wales to seek political independence from the United Kingdom. But opposition to devolution declined very substantially in the years after the second devolution referendum. Devolution began increasingly to look like the settled will of the Welsh people. And there was a significant growth in support for the National Assembly to become a rather more important institution.

Some of these changes can be seen in table 3.8, which reports results from a question on constitutional preferences that was asked in several academic surveys in the decade after the 1997 referendum and in a 2006 Electoral Commission study. The question asks respondents to indicate their preferred option from four broad possible models of government for Wales:

- independence
- a Parliament with substantial law-making and some tax powers

Table 3.8 Constitutional preferences (%) Wales, 1997–2007

Constitutional preference	1997	1999	2001	2003	2006	2007	2009
Independence	13	10	12	13	11	12	15
Parliament	18	28	37	36	40	42	34
Assembly	25	33	25	25	24	26	27
No elected body	37	24	23	20	20	16	17
Don't know/refused	7	5	4	5	5	5	6
Number of respondents	686	1,256	1,085	988	1,000	884	1,078

Sources: 1997 Welsh Referendum Study; 1999 Welsh Assembly Election Study; 2001 Wales Life and Times Survey; 2003 Wales Life and Times Survey; 2006 Survey by NOP for the Electoral Commission; 2007 Welsh Election Study; 2009 YouGov poll for Aberystwyth University and Cardiff University.

- an Assembly with only limited law-making powers, and
- no devolution.

The table confirms the striking decline in opposition to devolution, and the growth of support for taking devolution further. Immediately after the 1997 referendum, 'No devolution' was favoured by a clear plurality of respondents. A decade on, the proportion choosing the 'No devolution' option had more than halved. And the 'Parliament' option had become the plurality choice, often favoured by more than two in five, in all major surveys from 2001 onwards.

Lest these trends be thought to be in some way an artefact of a particular question wording, we can look at the evidence from other surveys which framed the choices somewhat differently. For instance, table 3.9 reports results from a survey conducted immediately after the 2010 UK general election, in which the constitutional options were presented in a rather different way. But the results are very similar. The 'More Powers' option was the plurality choice, and those believing that devolution should be abolished were fewer than one in five. Indeed, between 2006 and 2010 some thirteen separate publicly reported surveys were conducted which asked some form of multiple-option constitutional preference question. The exact question wordings differed considerably; the surveys differed in other respects as well.[10] Yet, every single one of these

Table 3.9 Constitutional preferences Wales, 2010

Option	%
Wales should be independent	8
NAW should have more powers	37
Leave things as they are now	26
NAW should have fewer powers	5
No devolved government	17
Don't know/refused	8
Number of respondents	1,475

Source: 2010 Welsh Election Study.

surveys found that support for 'Independence' for Wales was always below 20 per cent, and support for a 'No devolution' option was always at 20 per cent or lower. And the proportion of those supporting either the constitutional status quo or more powers for the devolved institutions in Wales was always at 60 per cent or more. In short, the survey evidence was by now remarkably consistent.

Other survey questions (as well as the evidence from focus group research conducted by the Electoral Commission and the All-Wales Convention[11]) tended to reinforce this picture. A number of surveys used a pair of twinned questions: these asked respondents first to indicate which level of government they believed 'has the most influence over the way Wales is run' (the options given being local councils, the National Assembly, the UK government and the European Union), and then to indicate which of those levels of government they thought 'ought to have most influence over the way Wales is run'. As the figures in table 3.10 demonstrate, while there was some fluctuation from survey to survey, all showed the UK government to remain the most important level in the perceptions of most voters. But every survey indicated that a majority of voters desired the National Assembly to be the most important institution in running Wales.

The survey evidence also indicated that the decline in opposition to devolution had been most rapid in those parts of Wales, and among those identity groups (particularly those with a predom-inantly 'British' national identity), that had been most opposed to the idea in 1997. There were also interesting gender differences: while women had been significantly more likely than men to oppose

Table 3.10 Most influence over 'the way Wales is run' (%), 2001–10

A. *Does* influence				
Response	2001	2003	2007	2010
NAW	17	22	36	28
UK government	64	58	53	60
Councils	16	15	5	6
EU	3	5	6	7
Number of respondents	1,033	917	827	1,329
B. *Ought to* influence				
Response	2001	2003	2007	2010
NAW	56	56	74	59
UK government	26	29	18	31
Councils	17	14	8	9
EU	1	1	0	1
Number of respondents	1,033	917	857	1,368

Sources: 2001 Wales Life and Times Survey; 2003 Wales Life and Times Survey; 2007 Welsh Election Study; 2010 Welsh Election Study

devolution in 1997, a decade on surveys tended to show them being more enthusiastic about devolution.[12]

The survey data also allowed analysts to explore a number of potential explanations as to why attitudes had changed. A first plausible candidate is that public opinion had responded to the concrete, practical achievements of devolution and the devolved bodies. Such a process has been observed in many other political systems. In post-war West Germany, for example, the specific success of the Federal Republic in rebuilding the economy and establishing social and political stability appears to have been integral to the gradual development of a more diffuse sense of public support for the institutions and democratic principles of that republic.[13] However, the evidence that something similar had occurred in Wales was very limited. Evaluations of the policy record of the NAW and WAG in key areas such as health, education and the economy were distinctly moderate. Devolution was not linked in the public mind to great advances in any of these areas – although few people, at least, seemed to think that devolution had directly contributed to making things much worse. The most positive thing that could be said for the policy record of the devolved bodies was that the public appeared far more willing to attribute any improvements to them than to the actions of the UK authorities: both in devolved areas like health and education, and non-devolved ones such as the economy and law and order, perceived positive changes were disproportionately linked to the actions of government in Cardiff rather than that in London; perceived negative changes, on the other hand, were overwhelmingly blamed on London.[14] But, overall, there was only a limited sense of devolution having had substantial and positive practical consequences for Wales.

A second potential explanation for the changing landscape of attitudes to devolution in Wales was one based on identities rather than practical consequences. The idea here, put simply, is that creating distinctly 'Welsh' political institutions, and giving more of a Welsh focus to the political life of the nation, might have led to a significant change in the political identities of many people in Wales. Put even more simply, devolution could have made the people of Wales feel more Welsh. Once again, the plausibility of this potential explanation is strengthened by the fact that such processes have been observed in other political contexts: the development of widespread national identities have often followed, rather than led to, the creation of national political institutions.[15] But in Wales – thus far at least – the evidence here is distinctly negative. It is true that, at any single time for which we have relevant data, there is a positive correlation between individuals' strength of identification with Wales and their support for greater self-government for Wales. It is not true, however, that as support for further devolution has grown and opposition to devolution declined since 1997, there has been an increase in the proportion of strong Welsh identifiers in the population. To the contrary, the national identity profile of the Welsh population has remained remarkably consistent since the 1970s.[16] While the people of Wales did become more Welsh in their desired centre of government in the first decade of devolution, in their basic sense of national identity they became no more Welsh at all.[17]

If the rise in support for, and decline in opposition to, devolution can only partially be explained through its policy consequences and not at all through its impact on the identities of the people of Wales, what can explain the changes in public attitudes that were observed in the first decade of devolution? It is not clear that a wholly comprehensive and satisfactory answer has yet been arrived at. But the most detailed analysis of the available evidence suggested that, as in Scotland, in Wales too there had come to be a widespread belief in the appropriateness of the country having substantial self-government. Public attitudes, the evidence indicated, were 'most strongly associated with perceptions of how devolution has altered the process of government ... increasingly [to] the people of Wales, self-government has come to be viewed as the appropriate political expression of how they wish to be governed'.[18]

Given the closeness of the referendum result, it might have been expected that devolution would continue to divide the people of Wales down the middle. In fact, that was not what occurred. Opposition to devolution began to decline significantly after the referendum, and continued to do so more or less throughout the first decade of the NAW's existence. At the same time, support for enhancing the powers of the Assembly also began to grow somewhat. This does not appear to have happened primarily because devolution was associated with great policy achievements, nor because it had in some way made the people of Wales feel more Welsh. Rather, a growing sense of the appropriateness of a Welsh institution making major political decisions for Wales appears to have become established among many of the people of Wales. The final part of this chapter will consider what such attitudes appeared to promise for the referendum of 2011 as it began to loom larger on the political horizon.

The approaching referendum

As was discussed in some detail in chapters one and two, the passage of the 2006 Government of Wales Act established a framework in which a referendum might be held on granting the NAW more extensive legislative powers. The likelihood of that referendum occurring increased substantially in summer 2007, with the 'One Wales' coalition agreement between Labour and Plaid Cymru. In response to these successive developments, polls conducted by media organizations and some other surveys began to investigate how voters intended to behave if and when the referendum finally happened.

The first publicly reported poll on the subject was conducted in the summer of 2007. At that stage, polls were addressing a matter that was both of low public salience and considerable uncertainty. It was rather unclear at this stage quite when the referendum might occur (if, indeed, it happened at all), what the actual referendum question would be, or the manner in which public debate about the referendum would be cast. Thus, the polls were at first infrequent, and were conducted using a number of varying question wordings. Over time, polling became more frequent. The vast majority of polls also converged on the same, simple wording: a question which asked, 'If there were a referendum held tomorrow on increasing the law-making powers of the National Assembly for Wales how would you vote?' (An Appendix at the end of this book includes details on all the publicly reported polls conducted, including the precise question wordings used.)

In addition to the appropriate question wording for polls to ask, it was not at all clear how the public attitudes revealed in the research on public opinion discussed above might translate into referendum voting intentions. For instance, it might seem to make sense that all those reported in table 3.9 as favouring 'More powers' for the Assembly would also intend to vote Yes in a referendum on greater powers for that body. It might also seem logical that all those supporting independence would wish to vote Yes, as such a result would enhance Wales's degree of self-government and thus move the country closer towards the ideal of those supporting independence. Similarly, it would seem to make sense for all those believing that 'we should leave things as they are now' should intend to vote No in the referendum. And those favouring 'Fewer powers' for the NAW, or even 'No devolution' at all, might be thought to be heavily inclined towards voting No, as a No vote would at least inhibit Wales moving further away from their most-preferred position. Were all voters to take such apparently logical positions, the overall implication would be that prospective No voters would slightly outnumber those intending to vote Yes.

In fact, as table 3.11 reveals, while many survey respondents take such apparently logical positions, it is certainly not the case that all of them do so. The table compares referendum voting intention with constitutional preferences among respondents to a survey conducted immediately after the 2010 UK general election. As is readily apparent, the relationships are far from perfect: a significant minority of voters, particularly those who chose the 'leave things as they are now' constitutional preference, took apparently

Table 3.11 Referendum voting intention by constitutional preference (%), May 2010

Option	% Yes	% No	% Wouldn't vote/DK
Wales should be independent	94	1	5
NAW should have more powers	91	2	7
Leave things as they are now	24	47	30
NAW should have fewer powers	3	94	3
No devolved government	4	90	6
Don't know/refused	24	3	73

Number of respondents = 1,476
Source: 2010 Welsh Election Study

'illogical' positions. This is a salutary reminder to avoid the overinterpretation of survey data. All surveys involve some degree of measurement error; when they are asking about matters that are not of great salience to many of those responding to the surveys (and certainly of lesser salience to them than they are to the people writing the surveys) there can be substantial 'noise' introduced. These results also remind us – as will be explored in much greater detail in chapter six – that referendum voting behaviour can be shaped by things other than simply people's views on the matter ostensibly at stake.

Nonetheless, notwithstanding the inevitable fluctuations introduced by measurement and sampling error, as well as more systematic effects that can follow from different question wordings or survey techniques, a clear pattern did emerge in the polls conducted on referendum voting intention, which are reported in table 3.12. Not a single poll ever showed prospective No voters outnumbering those indicating that they intended to vote Yes. And, gradually, the Yes camp began to extend its lead. The average Yes lead in the four polls published in 2007 and 2008 was 8.8 percentage points. In the five polls conducted in 2009 that average lead had grown to 11.4 per cent. And in the fourteen polls reported in 2010, the average Yes lead was no less than 21.2 per cent. Moreover, as some of the polls began to investigate the potential effect of low levels of public participation in the referendum, turnout effects seemed likely to increase the Yes advantage still further. The ICM poll conducted for the BBC in November 2010 found that a Yes lead

Table 3.12 Opinion polls on the 2011 referendum

Date	% Yes	% No	% Don't know
June 2007	47	44	9
February 2008	49	42	9
June–July 2008	46	32	22
Nov–Dec 2008	49	35	16
February 2009	52	39	9
July 2009	44	36	21
July 2009	47	37	16
October 2009	42	37	21
November 2009	51	30	20
January 2010	49	32	20
February 2010	56	35	10
March 2010	53	31	16
March 2010	50	34	17
May 2010	51	32	18
June 2010	55	28	17
July 2010	48	34	19
August 2010	48	32	21
September 2010	49	30	20
October 2010	52	29	20
November 2010	48	30	22
November 2010	57	24	18
November 2010	60	28	13
December 2010	46	25	29

Sources: See Appendix

of 33 per cent increased to one of 54 per cent (77 per cent to 23 per cent) once the company took into account likelihood to vote. Similarly, the YouGov poll for ITV Wales the following month found that a Yes lead of 21 per cent in voting intention increased to one of 29 per cent when one considered only those respondents who stated their likelihood to vote in the referendum to be at least 7 on a 0–10 scale.

As 2010 drew to a (snow-covered) close, and the beginning of the formal campaign period drew in sight, the Yes camp appeared to be in a very strong, though not invulnerable, position with those whose votes would ultimately decide the matter. There was a clear, and generally growing, Yes lead in all the opinion polls. And there seemed to be an even greater advantage for the Yes camp when one looked closely at those who were the most likely to participate in the referendum.[19] The following chapter will now go on to tell the story of the period leading up to the referendum campaign, and the campaign itself.

4

From coalition agreement to polling day

On 6 July 2007, a Wales Labour Party special conference met to decide whether or not to ratify the One Wales coalition agreement with Plaid Cymru. The vote in favour was substantial – 78.4 per cent supporting the agreement.[1] The following day Plaid Cymru endorsed the deal even more strongly.[2] With Labour and Plaid Cymru between them holding forty-one of the sixty seats in the Assembly, their coalition government had little to fear from the opposition benches. But serious questions remained about the ability of the two parties to work together following many years of competition and enmity. Particular doubts concerned the willingness of the defeated minorities in both parties to accept the deal: perhaps most notably many Welsh Labour MPs, who continued to harbour deep reservations about the coalition agreement.

An obvious potential source of problems was the referendum commitment that formed the centrepiece of the coalition agreement. For Plaid Cymru that commitment was the critical difference between One Wales and the 'Rainbow' deal they had negotiated with the Conservatives and Liberal Democrats.[3] The latter would have seen Ieuan Wyn Jones installed as First Minister. The prospect that a deal with Labour could deliver the referendum, and ultimately an Assembly with full legislative powers, was the only substantial incentive for Plaid to choose the One Wales deal. For Plaid, therefore, this element of the agreement simply had to be delivered upon.

But for many Welsh Labour MPs the referendum commitment was a bitter pill to swallow. They had supported the 2006 Government of Wales Act in Parliament on the understanding that there was no prospect of a move to substantial greater legislative powers for the National Assembly in the foreseeable future. They were now on a conveyor belt leading to a referendum on those powers within four years. They were also aware, following recent Scottish precedent, that an affirmative vote in that referendum would likely mean an end to Welsh over-representation in the House of Commons. That several Welsh Labour MPs were now deeply resentful is very understandable.

What exactly had the two parties committed themselves to? The relevant passage in the coalition agreement stated:

> There will be a joint commitment to use the Government of Wales Act 2006 provisions to the full under Part III and to proceed to a successful outcome of a referendum for full law-making powers under Part IV as soon as practicable, at or before the end of the Assembly term.
>
> Both parties agree in good faith to campaign for a successful outcome to such a referendum. The preparations for securing such a successful outcome will begin immediately. We will set up an All-Wales Convention within six months and a group of MPs and AMs from both parties will be commissioned to set the terms of reference and membership of the Convention based on wide representation from civic society. Both parties will then take account of the success of the bedding down of the use of the new legislative powers already available and, by monitoring the state of public opinion, will need to assess the levels of support for full law-making powers necessary to trigger the referendum.[4]

Two key elements here were major concessions to Plaid Cymru. The first was the timetable: a 'successful outcome of a referendum … at or before the end of the Assembly term'. The second was that both parties 'agree in good faith to campaign for a successful outcome'. Thus, not only was a clear time frame for the referendum established, but Labour was formally committed to campaigning for a Yes vote. Remembering 1979, Plaid negotiators realized that a formal commitment would not necessarily translate into a wholly united Labour campaign. But this was as firm a commitment as they could realistically have hoped for.

The role envisaged for the All-Wales Convention was notably vague. But it was an aspect of the agreement to which both sides were equally committed – to the extent that both subsequently believed that it was their own idea![5] Part of the explanation for this pervasive commitment is a sense amongst Welsh devolutionists of all stripes that Wales somehow 'missed out' by not having a constitutional convention on Scottish lines. As we shall see, to equate the

All-Wales Convention to the Scottish Convention is to miss the real significance of both bodies. But Wales's convention was a key stage towards the eventual referendum.

The final element of the One Wales agreement that requires comment is the clear commitment to a successful outcome. Neither party wanted to hold a referendum that they might well lose. A No vote would be the worst possible outcome for devolutionists. But who would determine whether or not victory was likely? A careful reading – in particular of the final sentence quoted above – indicates that this potentially vital question was not resolved by the One Wales agreement. A potential fault-line existed if the parties disagreed in their assessment.

The One Wales agreement was the key political reference point in the process leading to the referendum. But there was also a new legal context, provided by the 2000 Political Parties, Elections and Referendums Act (PPERA). Regulation of the 1979 and 1997 referendums had been very much ad hoc; in 2011, everyone would have to work within the statutory framework created by PPERA. The referendum-related parts of this legislation had been prompted not only by a belief that referendums were likely to become a more regular feature of the UK's political life, but also by a concern that the previous make-it-up-as-we-go-along arrangements had been inadequate. Some of this concern had focused on the 1997 referendum in Wales, which critics regarded as too one-sided.[6] PPERA allowed for the possibility of state funding for officially designated 'lead' campaigns on both sides, but with tight constraints on how such funding could be used. PPERA also regulated, and imposed spending caps on, other 'permitted participants' in a referendum campaign. This regulatory framework was to be administered by the Electoral Commission, who would be responsible for designating the various categories of participants and policing their behaviour. But prior to 2011, this new framework remained largely untested. The 2004 vote on establishing a regional assembly in north-east England had been the only significant referendum to have been held under its auspices. As will become clear, when tested in Welsh circumstances, PPERA was found wanting.

This, then, was the political and legal context for the 2011 referendum. In what follows we will first examine the All-Wales Convention. We then consider the period between publication of the convention report and the vote in the National Assembly that triggered the formal request that the referendum be held. After this, we explore the processes by which the main Yes and No campaigns were constructed, before we present an account of the period between the official campaign launches and polling day itself. We conclude by summarizing the relative strengths and weaknesses of the two campaigns.

The All-Wales Convention

A joint statement from First Minister Rhodri Morgan and Deputy First Minister Ieuan Wyn Jones on 23 October 2007 announced the appointment of Sir Emyr Jones Parry to chair the convention promised in the One Wales agreement. Recently retired from diplomatic service after a distinguished career that culminated as the United Kingdom's Permanent Representative to the United Nations, Sir Emyr was undoubtedly a heavyweight figure. His long experience as a diplomat was also likely to be of value in a potentially delicate role.

Before Sir Emyr could begin work, however, the precise role of the Convention had to be defined. The One Wales agreement had indicated who would establish its remit – 'a group of MPs and AMs from both parties' – and stated that that the Convention's membership should be based 'on wide representation from civic society'. But the coalition document had said nothing at all about what, precisely, the Convention might seek to achieve. It soon became clear that political realities would ensure that its room for manoeuvre was tightly constrained. Comparisons with the Scottish Constitutional Convention that was its inspiration are instructive. Beyond ruling out independence, that had been afforded a largely blank piece of paper on which to draw up plans for a Scottish Parliament. The Welsh version would be restricted to consideration of a move to a model of devolution already established by Part IV of the 2006 Government of Wales Act. There was no question of altering the possible destination; the All-Wales Convention was to play some, as yet undetermined, role in helping determine the timing of the journey.

In the event, the elected members charged with drawing up the convention's remit, a group jointly chaired by Plaid AM Helen Mary Jones and the Labour MP Nick Ainger, agreed the following terms of reference:

- Raise awareness and improve understanding of the current arrangements for devolved government in Wales and of the provisions of Part 4 of the Government of Wales Act 2006, and their future implications for the governance of Wales.
- Facilitate and stimulate a widespread, thorough and participative consultation at all levels of Welsh society on the issue of primary law-making powers.
- Prepare an analysis of the views expressed and the evidence presented through this process.
- Assess the level of public support for giving the National Assembly for Wales primary law-making powers.
- Report to the One Wales Government on its findings, with recommendations relevant to the holding of a referendum.[7]

These suggestions were accepted by the First Minister and his Deputy in March 2008; by July, sixteen members had been appointed to serve on the convention.[8]

The Convention's main tasks, thus, were to educate – improving understanding of the current and proposed models of devolved government – and to collect and assess information on attitudes towards a move to Part IV. Given the lack of clarity in the One Wales document about who should ultimately decide whether or not a referendum was winnable, it was the final element of the remit – 'recommendations relevant to the holding of a referendum' – that was always likely to prove most important. It would be difficult for either coalition partner to avoid charges of bad faith if they sought to ignore or override the Convention's conclusions in this regard.

When the Convention's report was published in November 2009, most interest focused on two statements. The first was the unanimous verdict of the commissioners that 'a "yes" vote in a referendum is obtainable'.[9] This declaration was sensibly qualified to the effect that this did not mean that an affirmative vote was certain. There were no such caveats, however, to the second statement:

> We are convinced that Part 4 offers substantial advantage over the present arrangements in Part 3. It would offer greater efficiency, permit a strategic approach to the drafting of the legislation, provide greater clarity, be more consistent with the rule of law and democratic tradition, and reflect the growing maturity of the National Assembly for Wales.[10]

There was none of the fence-sitting of diplomatic cliché here. The judgement of Sir Emyr and his colleagues was clear and emphatic: not only could Wales move to Part IV, but it should. The latter half of this verdict, we should at least note, was not something that the Convention was actually asked to deliver. But by creatively over-interpreting their mandate in this way, the Convention gave a clear direction to a report that might otherwise have struggled to have an impact. After all, in concluding that a referendum was winnable the Convention was doing little more than endorsing the findings that researchers had been pointing to for some years (as discussed in chapter three). The same was true of the Convention's wholly predictable finding that the Welsh electorate 'has scant knowledge' of the system of government established by the 2006 Act.[11] Such was hardly news. Indeed, one might ask (and some did ask) what point there was in spending the £1.3 million that the Convention cost to tell people what most observers of the Welsh political scene already knew.[12]

It would be a mistake, however, to conclude that the Convention was an irrelevance. It was important in several respects. That an authoritative, external voice had concluded that a referendum was winnable mattered. A feature of Welsh politics since 1997 had been a widespread reluctance to accept the consistent research evidence pointing to declining opposition to devolution and growing support for further devolution. Such reluctance had been observable not only among opponents of more powers (with consequences we return to below); it was also very evident among supporters of devolution, many of whom remained scarred by the 1979 debacle.[13] That the conclusions of other analysts were confirmed by the Convention served to give them greater political credibility.

The Convention was also important because it created space and time for other processes to take their course. That the most potentially contentious issue between Labour and Plaid Cymru was, in essence, 'parked' while the Convention went about its business, allowed the two parties to become more used to working together in government, and permitted at least a modest reservoir of mutual trust and understanding to be developed between the partners, which could then be called upon when the issue re-emerged from the Convention process. Equally importantly, the Convention period gave time for any illusions about the Part III model of legislative powers to be thoroughly disabused. Many in 2007 – including

First Minister Rhodri Morgan and Presiding Officer Lord Dafydd Elis-Thomas – had expected the Measure-making system to work in a relatively straightforward manner.[14] They hoped that requests for transfers of legislative competence to the National Assembly would encounter few obstacles in Whitehall or Westminster. More specifically, they envisaged a system that would transfer parts of the wording from Schedule 7 of the Act (outlining the powers that the Assembly would enjoy if Part IV were enacted) directly to Schedule 5 (outlining the powers under Part III). In this way, the Welsh legislature would rapidly develop a fairly generous – and generously drawn – legislative competence. Indeed, this expectation underpinned the All-Wales Convention's own attempts to frame and explain the difference between Part III and Part IV. It contrasted:

- Firstly, the current arrangements, where the National Assembly for Wales acquires powers to make laws step by step, with the permission of the UK parliament (Part III);
- Or for the National Assembly for Wales to get powers to make laws in all 20 areas all at once after an affirmative vote in referendum (Part IV).[15]

The juxtaposition of 'step by step' with 'all at once' here clearly implies that Part III and Part IV were tending towards the same destination, even if on somewhat different timelines. But by late 2009, with LCOs being drafted in increasingly restrictive fashion on the insistence of Whitehall and Westminster, it was clear that Schedule 5 would bear no relationship to Schedule 7. Indeed, there were real concerns that Schedule 5 was becoming so complex and burdened with so many exceptions that it was in danger of becoming wholly unworkable.[16] Moreover, the seemingly interminable delays associated with the whole process had become obvious to all. In 2007 at least some Labour AMs were inclined to defend the new system – or at least give it a chance to prove itself. Two years later, a general sense of frustration with the whole system was pervasive across the Welsh political class. By the time the All-Wales Convention had reported, most Welsh politicians – certainly at the devolved level – had already drawn their own conclusions.

A final question to consider is whether the Convention actually played any role in shifting public attitudes. When it was established, some critics of enhanced legislative powers were deeply suspicious that the Convention would prove to be some kind of state-funded propaganda exercise.[17] After the fact, most seemed to accept that the Convention went out of its way to behave in an even-handed fashion, even if some of its early efforts at raising awareness and stimulating debate were subject to caustic criticism.[18]

Under Sir Emyr's energetic leadership, the Convention held twenty-three public events across Wales, attended by some 1,700 people, as well another thirteen formal evidence-gathering sessions. It received 608 written submissions from various organizations and individuals as well hearing oral evidence from another seventy-six. Furthermore, the Convention used the connections of its members – and other organizational links that it nurtured – to disseminate information through various community groups. In absolute terms, the numbers involved were not large in the context of a Welsh population of some three million. But it is in the nature of such things that those attracted to take part in such events tend to be above average in their levels of political engagement and social connectedness. In the context of a referendum debate that remained rather low key throughout, engaging with these social elites probably had a rather greater influence than might otherwise have been the case. The Convention at the very least ensured that Wales did not enter the referendum completely 'cold'. And although we lack sufficient data to trace such matters with any degree of causal certainty, we can observe that it was from about the time of the launch of the Convention report that the Yes camp moved into a clearer opinion poll lead.

Pulling the trigger

The immediate aftermath of the publication of the All-Wales Convention report was always likely to be a potentially hazardous time for the Labour–Plaid Cymru coalition. And so it proved. Within a week of the report's launch on 18 November 2009, the One Wales government was plunged into its only bona fide crisis. The crisis was short-lived – lasting no more than a few, intense hours. And its outcome – a public capitulation by one partner – ensured that a referendum would indeed be held within the time frame envisaged in the original coalition agreement.

Two factors must be borne in mind in trying to understand the 24 November crisis that briefly threatened the collapse of the Welsh Assembly Government. The first is that internal tensions within the Welsh Labour Party on the referendum issue were, at that specific moment in time, being refracted through the process occurring to elect a new leader to replace Rhodri Morgan. The winner was due to be announced on 1 December. The electoral system used by the Labour Party rendered Welsh Labour MPs as important figures: they formed a significant proportion of one of the three elements of the electoral college, and were seen as potentially influential in the other two parts as well.[19] These MPs therefore found themselves being courted assiduously by the three leadership contenders: Edwina Hart, Carwyn Jones and Huw Lewis. Given many MPs' sensitivities about the prospect of a referendum, the respective leadership campaigns all tended to downplay the likelihood of such a poll during the campaign period. This in turn had generated increasing unease within Plaid Cymru about whether Labour would fulfil this key coalition commitment.

The additional complicating factor was the process specified by the 2006 Act for triggering the referendum. For the vote to occur, several hurdles would have to be cleared. First, the National Assembly would need to vote in favour of a formal request that a referendum be held, with the support of two-thirds of the total membership (that it, forty Assembly Members). This request would then pass to the Secretary of State, who would have 120 days to consider whether or not it should be forwarded to the UK Parliament. If (and only if) the Secretary of State was willing, an order permitting the holding of the referendum would then go before both Houses of Parliament, requiring the support of a simple majority in both. This was not only a convoluted process with several potential veto points; it was also a potentially time-consuming one. The All-Wales Convention itself had estimated that the Assembly 'trigger vote' would need to be held by June 2010 at the very latest if there was to be any prospect of the referendum occurring by the end of the One Wales government's term. Given the imminence of the next UK general election, with the upheavals and delays that might inevitably follow from any change of government, even this estimate may have been optimistic.

It was in this political and legal context that ministers and officials began to discuss the formal government response to the

Convention report. This would be given in a statement to the National Assembly on 24 November. Plaid Cymru's understanding – even after an hour-long bilateral meeting between the First and Deputy First Ministers on the morning of 24 November specifically to discuss the issue – was that this statement would promise an Assembly debate on the Convention report and a subsequent trigger vote early in the new year, with the referendum to take place by the end of the Assembly's term.[20] Later that same morning, however, a joint statement was issued by Rhodri Morgan, Secretary of State Peter Hain and Welsh Labour Chair, Gary Owen. This indicated clearly that 'wider Party consultation with AMs and MPs, councillors, trade unionists and members', on the convention's recommendations and the timing of any referendum, would not begin until after the forthcoming UK general election.[21]

Being charitable, a case could possibly be made that the three signatories were merely seeking to exercise the right of the Labour Party, as enshrined in the coalition agreement, to assess for itself the state of public support for a move to Part IV. Yet, the statement made no attempt to couch its stance in terms of the One Wales agreement. And it was a clear breach of the 'No Surprises' clause that had also been part of the One Wales agreement: Morgan having failed to mention the forthcoming statement to Ieuan Wyn Jones when they had met earlier that same morning.[22] But most serious of all for Plaid Cymru, with the UK election expected to take place in May or June 2010, the clear implication of the Labour Party statement was that there would be no realistic prospect of holding a referendum 'at or before the end of the Assembly term'.

Unsurprisingly, Plaid's leadership were livid, interpreting Labour's statement as a direct attack on the coalition agreement. Their suspicions about Labour's intentions were hardly assuaged when, in response to Ieuan Wyn Jones's urgent request for an immediate meeting to clarify matters, Morgan's officials responded that the First Minister was resting and would then have to prepare for First Minister's Questions and a subsequent statement on the convention report. He would not, therefore, be able to meet with his Deputy until later that afternoon. With their coalition partners apparently acting in bad faith, Plaid raised the stakes dramatically. Ieuan Wyn Jones authorized his special advisors Simon Thomas and Rhuanedd Richards to brief journalists that the coalition would collapse unless Rhodri Morgan backtracked immediately and made a public commitment to the holding of a referendum during the current Assembly term. Plaid also made clear that they possessed a mechanism for bringing down the government: they would not vote to allow Morgan's successor to take office as First Minister unless Labour retracted its statement.[23]

Almost immediately an excited press corps began to report Plaid 'senior sources' as stating, 'There is no way the party would allow its ministers to sit around the table with Labour if this is allowed to stand.'[24] As these reports began to emerge, several Labour AMs who themselves seem to have been in the dark about the joint statement also began briefing the BBC that they too were 'shocked and angry'; 'this cannot be allowed to stand' was again the message from one Labour backbencher.[25]

The First Minister's statement to the Assembly adopted a more emollient tone than his joint statement with Hain and Owen. The key passage made it clear that

> The Assembly Government intends in the new year to bring forward a motion for a full debate on the Convention's Report. I am reassured that the Convention believes that our One Wales agreement to hold a referendum during this Assembly is both practical and achievable, but I must leave the details to my successor as First Minister.[26]

But there was no mention of a trigger vote, and by this stage Plaid were in no mood for equivocation. A difficult meeting ensued between Morgan and Jones: this resulted in a further joint statement, where the two party leaders both reaffirmed their commitment to the One Wales referendum pledge, and explicitly held open the possibility of a referendum in autumn 2010.[27] The latter would require a trigger vote early in the new year. This rendered the Labour statement's commitment to only begin consideration of the timing of a referendum after the 2010 general election null and void. The coalition agreement and its dynamics had trumped the Secretary of State and the internal party process that he and Labour's Welsh Chair had attempted to establish.

Any remaining doubts about Labour's commitment to a referendum, and the survival of the coalition, were put to rest in the aftermath of Carwyn Jones's decisive victory in the race to succeed Rhodri Morgan as Labour leader in the National Assembly. Jones adopted a far more positive approach to the prospect of – and prospects for – a referendum than had characterized the public utterances of his predecessor. He certainly appeared less worried about the sensitivities of his Westminster colleagues.[28] The trigger vote in the Assembly was now imminent; it was held on 9 February 2010, and passed unanimously. Such unequivocal support from all parties in the Assembly rendered the various other potential 'veto points' irrelevant: it was now politically impossible to prevent a referendum on a move to Part IV.

In retrospect, the events of 24 November 2009 brought to a head tensions within the Welsh Labour Party that had existed at least since the 2007 special conference that approved the One Wales coalition with Plaid, and which arguably reflected much longer-standing ambivalences within the party. The internal culture of Welsh Labour, nurtured by generations of party dominance, clashed with the more pluralistic culture and practices that had been generated by the semi-proportional system used to elect members of the National Assembly. Many Labour MPs (including Peter Hain) had seemed unable to reconcile themselves to the coalition agreement; Rhodri Morgan had been equally unwilling to face them down. On 24 November, force of circumstances, if nothing else, meant that Morgan had to make a choice.[29]

For Plaid Cymru, the episode might be offered as an example of the surprising ease with which the party in general adapted to the demands of being in government for the first time. Having given their coalition partners considerable time and space with which to deal with the referendum issue, Ieuan Wyn Jones and his team nonetheless held the line with great firmness when faced with a direct attack on the terms of the coalition agreement. This was subtle and mature coalition politics. By seeking to undermine the terms of the One Wales agreement in such a crude manner, the signatories of Labour's joint statement overplayed their hand. Once Plaid Cymru responded, as was inevitable and entirely predictable, by threatening to bring down the government, Labour had little option but to cave in.[30] The referendum then moved from probability to certainty.

Building the campaigns

In the next and subsequent sections we trace the development and then the operation of the opposing Yes and No campaigns in the referendum. The two sections are divided chronologically. First, we explore developments until approximately the end of 2010. We then focus on the official campaign period from early January 2011 to the vote on 3 March.

Yes: waiting for Labour

Perhaps the most striking thing about the Yes campaign is quite how slow it was to take shape. Not until the final weeks of 2010 was anything resembling a functional national organization established. And to the end it remained a relatively small, if highly dedicated, group. While the Yes campaign ultimately managed to achieve a great deal in a compressed timescale, clearly outperforming their No rivals in every area, to trace its emergence and then perform-ance is to be struck by a sense that those involved were always 'playing catch-up'.

One forerunner of the Yes campaign, the constitutional ginger group Cymru Yfory-Tomorrow's Wales, had been in existence since July 2004, when it was created to support implementation of the Richard Commission's recommendations. Given that it contained representatives from various civil society organizations, and indi-viduals associated prominently with all four main parties in Wales, it might have been expected that Cymru Yfory would transform itself into the Yes campaign proper. In political contexts other than Wales this might have been the case. But the more politically experienced members of the organization, at least, never regarded this as a remotely realistic prospect. They consciously attempted to prepare the way for the Yes campaign – by attempting to establish a network of local groups and seeking to develop a consensus on core campaign messages. But they always recognized that for it to success-fully corral the potential affirmative vote, the Yes campaign would have to be created and 'owned' by the political parties.[31]

Plaid Cymru in turn realized that this meant, in essence, waiting for the Labour Party to be ready to participate. Having been scarred by the experience of 1979 (and to a lesser extent 1997), when Plaid believed that they had been left holding Labour's devolution baby, the nationalists were determined to ensure full Labour participa-tion in 2011.[32] This required patience from Plaid Cymru: a long, and at times nervous, waiting game. Even after the February 2010 trigger vote, Plaid knew that Labour would not be willing to engage seriously in any cross-party campaign until after the UK general election. Yet, even after that election, Labour's involvement for some time remained stumbling and hesitant.

A complicating factor here is the meaning of 'Labour' in the Welsh context. What limited machinery the party has in Wales, centred in Cardiff's Transport House, works for and is ultimately loyal to the party leadership in London, rather than Carwyn Jones and the Labour National Assembly group.[33] As if reflecting this, the attitudes of salaried Labour officials in Wales towards the cross-party referendum Yes campaign remained ambiguous, at best, throughout. Initially, Labour officials did not play any direct part in the Yes for Wales organization. Even when they began to do so, the party machine was not represented at the same level of seniority as either Plaid Cymru or the Liberal Democrats. Moreover, some party officials continued to treat those Labour activists centrally involved in the cross-party campaign with suspicion. Thus, while the Morgan–Owen–Hain statement did not succeed in undermining the prospects for a referendum, the sentiments that led to its commissioning did not disappear.

But even among those in the Labour Party in Wales who were eventually to prove wholehearted in their support, there seems to have been little foresight as to what a successful Yes campaign would ultimately entail. Prior to the trigger vote, to the extent that there was any willingness at all to consider the issue of what such a campaign might look like, the stock answer was that it would somehow emerge from civil society. The parties would take a back seat. Given that Cymru Yfory was an almost textbook example of a civil society-based organization, the neuralgic reaction its activities engendered among key Labour activists suggests that this was always a highly fanciful notion. In Wales, at least, one person's social entrepreneur appears to be another's *crachach*.[34] Moreover, even when, after the UK general election, Carwyn Jones and his colleagues belatedly began to engage more seriously in the task of constructing a cross-party campaign, they managed to compound the problems caused by this slow start.

When a steering committee finally began, in the summer of 2010, to plan a Yes campaign, Carwyn Jones asked Rhodri Morgan to represent Labour on the committee.[35] This was undoubtedly a well-intentioned request. The former First Minister is a genuine political heavyweight, and was at the time by far the most popular political figure in Wales. Inviting him to be involved in the campaign was a token of seriousness and good faith. But the move backfired. Treated with understandable deference by his interlocutors, and doubtless used to playing such a role in cabinet, Rhodri Morgan gravitated to the chair of the steering committee. Yet, he was singularly ill-suited to this role. Notwithstanding his considerable strengths as a doorstep campaigner and media communicator – which were amply demonstrated in the final weeks of the campaign – the practicalities of campaign organization, fund-raising and the rest were not Morgan's forte. Other steering committee members soon found his long, discursive interventions frustrating. Even more frustrating was a lack of progress from one meeting to the next. Matters were not helped by the nature of Labour's representation. Plaid Cymru and the Welsh Liberal Democrats both deputed representatives from the lay and professional sides of their parties to participate in the steering committee: Leanne Wood AM and chief executive Gwenllian Lansdown for Plaid, former party chair Rob Humphreys and chief executive Joanne Foster for the Lib-Dems.[36] This not only ensured that both parties were contributing a broad range of expertise; it also meant that each had two sources of information about how the preparations were proceeding. In the initial stages, the Labour leadership in Cardiff Bay was limited to one source: precisely the person whose role was proving problematic! Moreover, even when a Labour staff representative did eventually begin to attend, it is doubtful whether he was in a position to start calling into question the role being played by one of his party's most senior and respected figures. There was thus no obvious intra-party route by which this serious situation could become known, let alone be addressed. Meanwhile, Labour's partners found themselves in a delicate situation: on the one hand they were aware that time was now desperately short if a proper campaign was to be established; on the other, they were also wary of creating inter-party tensions in a situation where cross-party unity was vital.

By late summer 2010, a series of increasingly concerned messages about lack of progress were being circulated both within and between the parties. The combined efforts of Lansdown and Foster had ensured that at least some basic preparatory work had been undertaken; efforts were also underway to draw Daran Hill (national organizer of the 1997 Yes campaign) into the core team. But the level of activity was in no way commensurate with the urgency demanded. Things simply could not continue in this vein. On 5

October, the four party leaders in the Assembly acted together to reorganize the putative Yes campaign; or perhaps, more accurately, to allow Labour to reorganize its input into the campaign. Rhodri Morgan continued as a steering committee member, but Education Minister Leighton Andrews was installed as campaign convenor and Lee Waters introduced as Labour's official representative on the committee. Andrews in turn brought in Labour activist Cathy Owens to play a key organizational role in the campaign.[37] Andrews, Owens and Waters had all been active in Carwyn Jones's successful Labour leadership campaign (with Andrews acting as campaign manager and Owens as organizer); their involvement signalled a step change in the level and intensity of Welsh Labour's engagement, and thus in the seriousness of the campaign itself.[38]

Substantial challenges faced the revamped team. Scarcely five months before polling day, Yes for Wales had almost no funds – indeed, it did not even have a bank account until late October. Some preparatory work had been undertaken in terms of establishing a national organization, but it remained a ramshackle affair. At the local level, while the campaign inherited twelve local groups established by Cymru Yfory, these varied greatly in terms of their capabilities. Some were rapidly able to develop an impressive momentum of their own and become largely self-sustaining; others would require much more support. Moreover, much of the country remained, as yet, 'uncovered' by any local group.

Some work had been done on key campaign messages. Carwyn Jones himself had alighted on the slogan that 'Laws that apply only in Wales should be made in Wales' in the wake of the publication of the Richard Commission report. This was to become one of Yes for Wales's most frequently used campaign lines. In January 2010, key Cymru Yfory activist and former Plaid MP and AM, Cynog Dafis, had chaired a productive, if occasionally tense, unofficial cross-party meeting which had forged consensus around a few key themes; these themes were later further refined in a *Western Mail* article by Lee Waters.[39] But even here, much remained to be done. In particular, work on branding, which is crucial to contemporary political campaigning, had hardly begun. Nor was there yet a formal campaign chair in place.

Yet, notwithstanding these problems, Yes for Wales also had considerable strengths on which it could draw. It now had in place a core team who were expert and highly dedicated campaigners;

who were very closely linked to the Labour Party in general, and the First Minister in particular, and who were also respected by the other parties and stakeholders in the Yes coalition. Moreover, given the centrality of the referendum to Plaid Cymru's core mission, and despite the proximity of the Assembly election, Plaid were willing to commit resources for the campaign. Two members of staff were deputed to provide assistance to the core national campaign team, while Plaid supporters provided most of the financial support – with Dafydd Wigley and party treasurer Dafydd Trystan Davies playing key fund-raising roles. Meanwhile, although patterns varied greatly from area to area, with considerable effort made everywhere to construct and maintain a genuinely cross-party campaign, there is little doubt that Plaid members and sympathizers formed the largest group of Yes for Wales activists on the ground.

From their more limited resources, the Welsh Liberal Democrats also made a significant contribution. In addition to participating positively in the steering committee, Liberal Democrats made important contributions to the local campaign in a number of areas. Cymru Yfory also played an important role, not only because of the local networks it had established but also in mobilizing resources for the campaign. These included not only tasking a member of staff to work with the core campaign team but also a vital initial contribution towards fund-raising, something at which its prominent activist Hywel Ceri Jones excelled. Several Conservatives (such as Nick Ramsay in Monmouth) made impressive individual contributions to local campaigns. But perhaps their most important contribution was the 'cover' provided by their presence. A cause supported by a number of prominent Tories was difficult to portray as one that was ultimately about Welsh independence.

The Yes campaign had one further, and very considerable, strength. This was, quite simply, the weakness of their opponents.

No: a grass-roots campaign?

True Wales was by far the most significant element in the No campaign. Founded in response to the establishment of the All-Wales Convention, True Wales constitutes an interesting case of a self-proclaimed grass-roots movement that largely failed to establish any substantial roots. It remained throughout a tiny organization: quite unable to attract either significant funds (it spent less than £5,000 during the referendum campaign) or, despite its best efforts, the support of substantial political figures. Apart from Labour activists Diane and (daughter) Rachel Banner, the organization's core group was made up of individuals with some experience of local government politics and several political neophytes. True Wales's main concentration of relative strength was in the eastern valleys of south Wales; beyond this it had no more than a very patchy presence in the rest of the country. A token of its failure to develop a genuinely national presence was True Wales's inability to find even one plausible Welsh speaker to make their case.[40] Given that its supporters were so limited in number and lacking in political experience, it is unsurprising that the national campaign developed by True Wales was, at best, rudimentary. Furthermore, under the pressure of the campaign, the group began to splinter.

Notwithstanding its anti-establishment self-image, it was only the official 'rules of the game' that gave True Wales a substantial presence and importance during the referendum campaign. Rules requiring impartiality and equal coverage in television and radio coverage meant that the BBC and other broadcast companies needed spokespeople from the No side in discussions of the referendum.[41] This gave True Wales a public platform, making a minor political celebrity out of Rachel Banner. She, along with Len Gibbs, provided the main public faces and voices of the No campaign and Banner – who despite her limited experience emerged as a plausible and articulate media performer – became True Wales's main, perhaps only, asset. In addition, as we explore below, the PPERA rules gave True Wales the power to stymie the Yes campaign, especially its ability to raise and spend money. By any reasonable definition, True Wales failed to approximate a successful grass-roots campaign. That it succeeded in having an impact on the campaign out of all proportion to its own strength was because of the rules under which the referendum was organized.

Why did the No side fail to mobilize a more effective campaign? After all, in 1979 the No side was able to completely outperform its rivals in campaign effectiveness. Even in 1997, the No side was able to attract support from a number of established political figures, and to raise more than £100,000 to fund its activities. In 2011, no major established political figures were willing to identify with the No camp, and True Wales could raise barely one-twentieth of the money raised fourteen years previously. A number of factors appear relevant to explaining this failure.

First, the extensive polling conducted over several years, and the increasingly lop-sided findings of those polls (as discussed in the previous chapter), may well have persuaded potential opponents not to expend political capital on what increasingly looked like a lost cause. If so, the polls became something of a self-fulfilling prophecy.

Secondly, the decision of the Conservative–Liberal Democrat UK government to decouple the size of Welsh representation at Westminster from the powers of the National Assembly may have served to stay the hand of MPs who would otherwise have been more willing to join the No camp. Fears that the numbers of Welsh MPs would be cut if the National Assembly were given full legislative powers had long underpinned opposition to such a development. Now the London coalition planned to reduce the number of Welsh MPs anyway. A major plank of opposition to legislative powers for Cardiff had been kicked away.

Labour's defeat in the 2010 UK general election also strengthened the hand of Labour devolutionists. With the UK government in the hands of the Conservatives and Liberal Democrats (and the SNP in power in Edinburgh), Carwyn Jones was now the most senior Labour figure in government anywhere. Could opposing the transfer of greater powers to an institution where Labour was likely to remain the strongest party for the foreseeable future, and inflicting a humiliating referendum defeat on Labour's First Minister, really be in the party's best interests?

Another factor explaining the weakness of the No campaign is simply the obvious deficiencies of the status quo that No campaigners were, in effect, campaigning to maintain. By late 2010, the system of LCOs and the rest had few defenders. Indeed, retaining this system was not what most No campaigners really wanted: most undoubtedly wished to see the devolved Assembly and Government completely abolished. Indeed, a referendum offering the prospect of abolition may well have produced a more motivated and well-organized No campaign – even if the shifts in public attitudes witnessed since 1997 suggest that such a campaign would have had no greater prospect of ultimate success.

Two other points are worth considering. In 1997, devolution was an unknown, hypothetical prospect about which apparently believable apocalyptic scenarios could be woven. In the parliamentary debates preceding the referendums in Scotland and Wales, the Conservative spokesman Michael Ancram warned of the 'dark, cold night' that would follow Yes votes.[42] By 2011, devolution was now a familiar and – to most people – rather unthreatening reality. Although many remained fairly unimpressed by what it had delivered, few believed that they had been living through the dark, cold night. Arguments about its dangers, such as the contention that devolution was a 'slippery slope' leading inevitably to independence, seemed to have lost much of their traction.

Such changing perspectives on devolution might be seen as part of broader changes in attitudes, and society, in Wales. Explaining her initial involvement in the moves that led to the establishment of True Wales, Rachel Banner cites her experiences on her return to post-devolution Wales after a period working as a teacher in Italy. She relates her sense that something had changed while she had been away. This was a change of which she did not approve and subsequently sought to counter.[43] We would suggest that it is not entirely fanciful to widen the point. To attend the launch of True Wales's No campaign on 19 January 2011 was to encounter a group of, in the main, rather angry elderly men raging, if not exactly at the dying of the light, then at the changing face of Wales and Britain. There was a palpable sense of resentment at the way a familiar order had been overturned. But as it transpired, the majority of people in Wales were either entirely unconcerned about or even supportive of this development.

From the campaign launches to polling day

The Yes for Wales campaign was formally launched in Cardiff on 4 January 2011. A morning press conference was followed by an evening launch event at the Atrium Building, the University of Glamorgan's shining new outpost in the heart of Wales's capital. Both events demonstrated the image that Yes campaigners sought to project throughout the campaign: multi-ethnic, bilingual, committed yet non-partisan, youthful, forward-looking and, crucially, Wales-wide in perspective and support.[44] Particularly striking was the extent to which politicians were relegated to a supporting role in proceedings. Yes for Wales would seek to speak though 'ordinary people'. This strategy represented a change from that adopted in 1979, where the primary focus was on celebrity endorsement, and 1997 where endorsements had been sought from various sectional groups, but its adoption was surely over-determined. Given the low esteem in which all elected politicians were held, in particular following the 2009 Westminster expenses scandal, to place them front and centre of the campaign would simply have played to True Wales's argument that the latter represented ordinary people campaigning against a self-serving elite. While politicians could not be kept out of the picture entirely, focusing on ordinary people and their concerns was a way of deflecting charges that the powers of the National Assembly were a concern only of the political elite. Throughout the campaign, Yes for Wales sought to present the proposed move to enhanced legislative powers in terms of a natural, common-sense development that was directly relevant to delivering solutions to the problems faced by ordinary people.

These themes all featured in the speech of campaign chair Roger Lewis at the Atrium. Characterizing the Part III system as a 'cumbersome, time-consuming and costly bureaucratic procedure which can and has led to misunderstandings and unnecessary tension between Cardiff and London', Lewis went on to argue that:

> A Yes for Wales vote ensures that primary law making powers, laws for Wales, are passed in Wales in a timely fashion, following full and proper Welsh Assembly debate.
> A Yes for Wales vote will enable our Welsh Assembly to get on and do the job for which it was intended.[45]

It was all a matter, therefore, of evolution rather than dramatic revolution: this would be the heart of the campaign's core message over the coming two months.

Roger Lewis had been announced as the Yes campaign chair in mid-December and proved an inspired choice for the role. Honed during senior executive roles in broadcasting and the music business, as well as in his current role as chief executive of the Welsh Rugby Union, his 'relentlessly positive' management style helped build bridges between the various stakeholders of Yes for Wales.[46] He also proved adept at smoothing occasional ruffled feathers. That he himself had no party axe to grind, and was not by nature a large 'p' political person, was also helpful: Lewis cheerfully admits to have been drawn to Plaid, Labour and the Conservatives at different points in his life.[47] What was most impressive, however, for those who worked closely with him during the campaign was the way in which Lewis proved a willing and adept learner. During his first media appearances, and in particular when debating with Rachel Banner on the BBC's *Dragon's Eye* programme on 21 January, his tone struck many as somewhat hectoring.[48] By the close of the campaign, however, he was a much more fluent political communicator, refusing to be distracted from hammering home his own points. This was no coincidence: Lewis actively sought and accepted advice on how to improve. The result was that, as even Len Gibbs ruefully admits, Roger Lewis bested Banner in their final BBC television debate broadcast from the former Miner's Institute in Blackwood.[49]

Yes for Wales operated as a series of concentric circles. Surrounding Lewis was a small inner circle consisting of Lee Waters, Daran Hill and Cathy Owens, who each dedicated an enormous amount of time and effort to the campaign from October onwards. This core group had operational control. While responsibilities were shared between them, unsurprisingly each gravitated towards their own areas of expertise: Waters on messaging, Hill on operational management and Owens bringing to bear her expertise on branding and political campaigning. Assisting this core group were several members of staff, including one part-time press officer employed directly by Yes for Wales, two Plaid Cymru staffers, a part-timer employed by Cymru Yfory, as well as various volunteers.

Removed slightly from the day-to-day activity was the steering committee, which continued to meet on a weekly basis. Leighton Andrews retained his role as chair, although he retreated from detailed involvement having injected the campaign with momentum in the autumn. These meetings were important in providing direction, ensuring coordination, and in heading off – or ameliorating – inter-party tensions. With regards the latter, there was also a very conscious effort by those involved to pre-empt problems, either by checking potentially contentious issues or by self-censorship. Cathy Owens recalls asking herself regularly 'what would [then Conservative leader] Nick Bourne say?'[50] One result of this was that, however professionally produced, the Yes campaign's literature had a 'lowest common denominator' feel to it. With so many different constituencies to satisfy, blandness was hard to avoid. Nonetheless, it was a price that had to be paid in order to ensure a harmonious campaign. And it was remarkably harmonious, especially considering that the Assembly election was only a few weeks away. Labour–Plaid tensions proved notable only by their absence. Those spats that did occur seem rather to have been a spillover of tensions from Westminster, where the decision of the Liberal Democrats to enter a coalition with the Conservatives was bitterly condemned by Labour. But even if the relationship between the central campaign team and the Welsh Liberal Democrats was on occasion somewhat strained, there remained a healthy appreciation on both sides of the contribution that each was making. More fundamentally, as Rob Humphreys makes clear, there was a determination on the part of those Liberal Democrats most centrally involved to ensure that short-term pressures arising from developments at the UK level should not deflect the party from its 'historic role as part of Wales's national movement'.[51]

Outside the central organization, some twenty-five local campaigning groups were eventually established. As already noted, these varied significantly in terms of their composition, organization and levels of activity. One that we were able to observe particularly closely was in Ceredigion. Like the national campaign, this only coalesced into an effective, functioning organization relatively late in 2010. Also like the national campaign, it functioned in 'concentric circles'. At the core was a group of four, led by chair, Lisa Francis – a former AM who, as a Conservative, was able to navigate the tensions caused by the fierce local rivalry between Plaid Cymru and the Liberal Democrats. Outside this core group were others who made more or less regular contributions to the main activities of fund-raising, leafleting, media work and the holding of regular street stalls in the market towns of this rural area. And, with the active support of both the local MP (Liberal Democrat Mark Williams) and AM (Plaid Cymru's Elin Jones), the machinery of the two main local parties was drawn upon. The Ceredigion campaign liaised regularly with the national campaign, but in the main, it functioned autonomously, raising its own resources and planning its own activities.[52]

Ceredigion held one of the first 'regional launch' events of Yes for Wales, in Aberystwyth on the night of 5 January. Local organizers had hoped that fifty people might attend: they were taken aback, ten minutes before the event was due to start, to find people queuing out of the door for admission, and the fifty seats set out already full. In the end, over 200 people heard speeches from Elin

Jones and Mark Williams, as well as contributions from former (Labour) MP Lord Elystan Morgan and Lisa Francis, as well as many contributions from the floor. On the evening of 10 January (at a time when True Wales had barely exceeded thirty supporters on Facebook), twenty-nine people attended the first organizational meeting of Yes for Wales in Ceredigion. Participants packed into a room that would hardly have been spacious for half that many. In addition to representatives from the main parties, other participants included representatives of the Aberystwyth University Students Union and local business. There was considerable awareness of the limited resources available, and the makeshift nature of the campaign. But with an apparent determination not to fall into partisan squabbles, participants set to work allocating duties across the rural county and planning the programme of activities.

The contrast between the strength and organization of the respective Yes and No campaigns in this part of mid-Wales was highlighted when the BBC broadcast the first of three referendum debates from Aberystwyth University on Monday, 14 February. The only spokesperson that the No side could supply for the panel was a local small businessman, Nick Martin, who freely acknowledged his lack of previous experience in such matters. Despite his best efforts, this inexperience was telling once the cameras began to roll.[53] The BBC's efforts to ensure a balanced audience were hampered by the fact that the No campaign was only able to supply two people (in addition to Mr Martin's wife) to attend. By contrast, Yes for Wales in Ceredigion could with little difficulty have filled the entire hall.

By referendum day, the Yes campaign in Ceredigion had leafleted most households three times, and had also persuaded many people to display their posters or stake-posts. The latter meant, as one member of the core team observed, that Ceredigion was one of the few parts of Wales where it was visibly obvious that a referendum was occurring. While it is hard to be definitive, it is very likely that by the time the referendum was held the Yes campaign in Ceredigion had actually undertaken more activity in the county than True Wales and its supporters had managed across the country as a whole. It was undoubtedly the case that they succeeded in raising and spending more money in Ceredigion than True Wales managed nationally.[54] Moreover, while the Ceredigion group was certainly active, other local Yes campaigns were equally so. The Swansea group, for example, was particularly active. Given the 1997 result, when the capital city rejected devolution, the Cardiff group was another success story of the Yes campaign. Across rural and urban areas alike, and in only a few short weeks, the Yes campaign managed to establish a presence in most (though not all) communities in Wales.

The national No campaign, organized by True Wales, was formally launched at Newbridge Rugby Club on 19 January to an audience of around seventy people. Two particular things stood out. The first was the message that the organizers attempted to communicate to the electorate. On a stage emblazoned with the slogan 'Vote NO for Better Devolution', the speakers eschewed an abolitionist line while maintaining what can only be regarded as a deliberately ambiguous position about the likely fate of the devolved Assembly and Government in a Wales where 'Better Devolution' operated. Instead of demanding abolition, the three speakers, Rachel Banner, Nigel Bull and Paul Matthews, offered withering attacks on the record of devolved government in Wales since 1999, in particular in economic development and education policy. The logic of their position was encapsulated in Banner's (rhetorical) question:

> If you cannot get the economic and educational basics right for the future of Wales in the first devolution decade – which were years of plenty – how can you ask the people of Wales in this referendum for more 'tools' after a botched job?[55]

This statement was hardly likely to endear Banner (an approved party candidate) to her fellow Labour members. Nonetheless, it was astute political positioning. As was discussed in chapter three, while fundamental opposition to devolution diminished considerably after 1997, public attitudes towards the achievements of the devolved government were far more ambiguous. In what was clearly a tightly controlled event, Rachel Banner was determined to focus on the Yes side's most vulnerable point. There were nonetheless clear indications from the floor of the meeting that abolition was what actually excited many, if not most, of those present in support. In retrospect, it is also significant that Len Gibbs was not present on the platform.

This general message of standing up for the 'ordinary people' of Wales against an incompetent and overweening political class in Cardiff was reinforced by an announcement that was to attract most attention in press coverage of the launch. True Wales stated that it

would not seek official designation as a 'lead campaign' organization for the No side, a decision that was presented in the following
terms:

> We say that far too much public money has already been spent on Bay
> politicians' efforts to amass more power for themselves. After the £1.3
> million All Wales Convention ... and the amount run up by politicians
> who will spend their days canvassing for more power, rather than
> sorting out the economic fundamentals and the state of the hospitals
> and schools, we in True Wales say 'Enough is enough'. Enough of the
> hard earned money from the hardworking people of Wales has been
> spent on getting more power for politicians.[56]

Under the terms of PPERA, this decision by True Wales meant that
Yes for Wales would also be denied lead campaign status. There
clearly would be cost savings following from this decision. There
would not now be a publicly funded mail-shot to each household in
Wales from the opposing campaigns. Nor would the Electoral
Commission provide any financial support for the campaigns
themselves. It is difficult to quantify how much money this might
amount to, given that we cannot know precisely what spending the
Commission would have been prepared to support. Nonetheless,
we can estimate the total amount to be around £200,000.[57] In the
context of a referendum that was to cost some £5.89 million to
organize, this was not a huge saving; moreover, the spending
forgone was specifically designed to inform the electorate of the
opposing positions on the issue at stake.[58]

Given True Wales's organizational weakness, the decision to
eschew lead campaign status is best understood as an attempt to
level (down) the playing field. Indeed, it appears to have reflected
a fundamental pessimism, even defeatism, at the heart of the No
campaign. True Wales did not at that point have the financial means
to print the leaflets required for the mail-shot (funds from the
Electoral Commission being specifically debarred from this
purpose). Apparently overwhelmed by what they regarded as the
combined might of the 'establishment led Yes campaign, which
formed an umbrella over the leaders of the main political parties,
unions, third sector groups as well as the Church hierarchy', neither
did they believe that they would be able to raise the money
required.[59] They were therefore 'deeply concerned at the idea of
Yes material reaching every household while we would have had no

choice but to forfeit the not-so-free postal delivery'.[60] Furthermore, given the conditions attached to public funding, True Wales also seem to have been pessimistic about their prospects of using any financial support that might be forthcoming to develop the infra-structure required for a genuinely national campaign.[61] But by refusing to apply for designated lead status, the ability of the Yes side to campaign effectively would, of course, be hampered. Greater emphasis in the campaign would thus be placed on the broadcast media, an arena in which, as True Wales were fully aware, the regu-lations would ensure equal coverage.

True Wales's decision to deny both itself and Yes for Wales desig-nated lead campaign status had a big initial impact on their opponents. Indeed, for a short period, Yes for Wales appear to have been thrown completely off-balance. They had certainly enter-tained the possibility of True Wales using the PPERA rules to their advantage, but this was not the particular scenario that had been envisaged. Rather, they had suspected that True Wales would accept official designation while refusing to accept any public funding, and then challenge Yes for Wales to do the same. The announce-ment that they would not even apply for official designation was a shock. Yes for Wales were already well aware that Electoral Commission funding would be so tightly constrained that relatively little of it might be usable. But the absence of the national mail-shot was a considerable blow. Even more serious was the dawning realiza-tion that as a 'permitted participant' the Yes campaign would now not be allowed to raise and spend more than £100,000. Simply the cost of printing and posting a single leaflet to every household in Wales would have consumed the lion's share of their allowable expenditure! The spending cap was also less than the sum that had been spent by either the Yes or No sides in 1997 – a referendum in which both sides had also benefitted from a publicly funded mail-shot.

After the initial shock had dissipated, the Yes campaign decided nonetheless to print a million leaflets and distribute them through its local groups. (Eventually it was to print one and a half million pieces of campaign literature.) Quite how effective a single leaflet stuffed through the letterbox is as a campaigning tool is doubtful. As we show in chapter six, the evidence suggests that for most people such communications join the piles of leaflets advertising takeaway food and double-glazing that are immediately transferred from doorstep to (recycling) bin. But the initial decision to print and distribute the million leaflets had a galvanizing effect on the Yes campaign, giving their activities a very clear focus. Moreover, it also supplied what those involved in the central organization universally regard as a key, cathartic moment of the campaign.

The leaflet initially produced – in reality a colourful, four-page, bilingual newspaper-style publication – featured a large photograph of, and supporting statement from, Welsh rugby hero Shane Williams. Distribution was to begin on Monday, 14 February, after a weekend when the Welsh rugby team would play Scotland at Murrayfield. As it happened, this match produced not only a Welsh victory, but one secured by two Shane Williams tries. Following a difficult period, there was a feeling among the core Yes for Wales group that this was the point at which 'our luck changed'.[62] Whilst the survey evidence presented in chapter six indicates that voting intentions actually changed very little, these few days were a genuinely significant moment in terms of the psychology of the campaign. After it, the Yes for Wales organization was more composed and increasingly confident.

The confidence of Yes for Wales was further boosted as the inadequacy of True Wales became ever clearer. Beyond promenading its inflatable pig mascot down the occasional high street and sporadic leafleting in a few areas, True Wales failed to establish an effective local campaigning presence. Worse than that, True Wales was not able even to deliver the minimal national campaign that had been promised at the Newbridge launch. The promised daily updates of its website ceased in early February. The 'message discipline' of the True Wales campaign also broke down. By mid-February, Len Gibbs had launched his own blog, which he proceeded to update regularly with material that adopted a very different tone from that presented at the Newbridge launch. Rejecting the deliberate ambiguity of 'Better Devolution', Gibbs's new line was, in effect, a pox on the Assembly and all its work: or, in short, abolition.

This development reflected personal differences and tensions within the No campaign. While Gibbs viewed Rachel Banner's abilities as a communicator as constituting the No campaign's main asset, he also believed that the dominant role played by the Banners (mother and daughter) within True Wales as virtually guaranteeing its defeat. Regarding the campaign as 'chaotic to the nth degree' and as being organized in an 'authoritarian' manner, Gibbs baulked at the tight message discipline that had been so obvious at the Newbridge launch. But in addition, Gibbs seems to have genuinely believed that there was a 'silent majority' in Wales who took an anti-devolution view. He therefore regarded giving voice to – and mobilizing – this apparent majority as the key to victory.[63] Like several other inhabitants of the blogosphere, and others involved in the No campaign, Gibbs simply did not accept the overwhelming survey evidence that opposition to devolution had fallen off considerably after 1997. Such figures apparently believed that this evidence had been contaminated by the supposed pro-devolution bias of the researchers involved. In Gibbs's case, he preferred to believe the 'polls' conducted on a limited number of Welsh high streets, under the auspices of True Wales, that purported to show that perhaps 40 per cent of the Welsh electorate favoured complete abolition.[64] Banner's strategy of maintaining deliberate ambiguity about the meaning of 'Better Devolution' whilst attacking the record of Welsh politicians and the devolved institutions was far more likely to succeed than Gibbs's groundless faith in the popularity of an abolitionist stance. But in the end, these differences between Banner and Gibbs were almost certainly of little consequence. Neither True Wales nor anyone else was able to construct an effective No campaign at national or local level.

Their understanding of the potential campaigning impact of communications via the 'new media' illustrates nicely how inexperience and even naivety characterized and bedevilled the efforts of the No campaign. The Yes for Wales team understood that although such methods might allow them to get their message across to some undecided voters, Facebook, Twitter and their campaign website were primarily a means of communicating with and inspiring their own core supporters as well as influencing journalists. Such an understanding is very much in line with what research evidence on the use of such media in elections has hitherto suggested.[65] Prominent campaigners on the No side, by contrast, seem to have regarded these media as a means of communicating with the mass of the Welsh electorate itself. Their various efforts in this regard were certainly studied in detail by their opponents. But as the evidence presented in chapter six indicates, few among the wider electorate were taking any notice.

Conclusion

By the end of February, with referendum day looming and the polls continuing to show a large and stable Yes lead, the No campaign was clearly subsiding. Journalists report having had to make multiple calls to secure information from No activists about their campaigning plans for a particular day.[66] In stark contrast, Yes for Wales felt confident enough to effectively cease their money-raising efforts to ensure that they did not breach the £100,000 limit. Had the referendum been a boxing match, a humane referee would have called a halt to proceedings well before 3 March 2011. The campaign had proved a complete mismatch. Only the rules under which the referendum and its media coverage were conducted acted to keep the No side in the ring at all. The deficiencies of the No campaign were displayed all-too-publicly in the Senedd in Cardiff on the afternoon of 4 March. After the final result of the referendum had been announced by the Electoral Commission, a number of participants were allowed to make a speech. In the event, three different figures from the No side elected to do so. First, Rachel Banner gave a dignified speech on behalf of True Wales in which she accepted the verdict of the electorate while pointedly warning her audience of the challenges that Wales's devolved institutions had yet to overcome. She was followed by Len Gibbs who, although still associated with True Wales, was by then director (and apparently sole member) of Vote No Day. He concluded his somewhat hectoring address by advocating a vote for UKIP in the forthcoming Assembly election. Finally, Mark Beech, a former candidate for the Monster Raving Loony Party who had also run a one-person campaign, took to the podium. Beech elected to begin his remarks by speaking in Klingon.

By substantial contrast, and even after a delayed start and a definite, if short-lived, wobble in late January 2011, the Yes campaign proceeded to an ultimately assured and comfortable victory. Campaigning on a question that, to say the least, did not lend itself to generating public interest, for a referendum that was largely ignored by the London news media, Yes for Wales nonetheless managed to generate sufficient enthusiasm in local networks to deliver substantial material over a large part of the country. They also managed the delicate task of crafting a campaign image and campaign messages that did not offend the campaign's widely differing stakeholders. Moreover, the materials that they produced in order to propagate those messages were professional and well designed.

Indeed, by the end there was a sufficient sense of inevitability about the final outcome that the result itself had ceased to be the main preoccupation of the various party staff present for the final announcement in the Senedd. They were rather more concerned about the composition of the final 'victory' photograph. Labour Party staff who were already thinking about the forthcoming National Assembly election had no desire to recreate the iconic image from 1997 when Ron Davies and his Labour Welsh Office ministers joined hands in celebration with Plaid Cymru's Dafydd Wigley and Richard Livsey of the Liberal Democrats. In the event, arrangements were made to photograph the four leaders standing adjacent to each other among the audience in the Senedd. Meanwhile, two prominent members of the Yes campaign were deputed to form a 'human shield' ensuring that Secretary of State Cheryl Gillan did not encroach on the scene. The very banality of these exchanges showed how far devolutionists had come from the utter humiliation of 1979 and the raw relief of 1997.

Lee Waters used a striking simile to encapsulate the position in which he and his fellow Yes campaigners found themselves in the run-up to the 2011 referendum. Their position, he mused, was akin to a skater navigating an ice rink holding an expensive vase. Only if the vase was dropped would anyone take notice.[67] Given the support that they enjoyed from Labour, Plaid Cymru, the Liberal Democrats, the Conservative Assembly group and almost every civil society organization in Wales, a Yes victory in the referendum was, for many, taken for granted. Yes for Wales had little to gain and much to lose: their efforts would only really be noticed if they messed up. In the end, however, Waters and his colleagues managed to negotiate their journey with some aplomb. It was rather their opponents who ended up in an untidy heap.

5
The referendum result

The previous chapter of this book examined in considerable detail the campaign for the Welsh referendum of 3 March 2011, and the campaigning efforts during this period of the two sides. We sought to explain how the main Yes and No campaigns were established, how they functioned at national and local level, and how their work (at least in the case of the Yes campaign) linked with any related efforts from the political parties and others. This chapter moves on from that to explore the degree of ultimate success with which the campaigners' efforts met. That is, we devote this chapter to examining in detail the result of the Welsh devolution referendum. The following chapter will then go on to assess why the people of Wales made the choices that they did.

The chapter proceeds as follows. We begin by presenting the result itself, giving the final figures for turnout, and for the number and percentage of Yes and No votes cast for each local authority area, and the aggregate outcome for Wales as a whole. We then devote the remainder of the chapter to analysing these results and placing them in some perspective. We examine a number of issues. First, we consider participation levels in the referendum, and to what degree an official turnout of 35.6 per cent should be regarded as disappointing. We also explore why turnout in the referendum varied by as much as 17.4 per cent across the different areas of Wales. Next, we assess the performance of the opinion polls. In the period prior to the referendum, political polling became far more frequent in Wales than it had ever been before. But to what extent did this relative proliferation of polls actually supply useful information? Thirdly, we examine in detail the geography of the referendum result. How far had the patterns of voting behaviour in 2011 changed from those observed in the previous devolution referendum in 1997? To what degree did the result show a Wales that continues to be politically divided along geographic lines? Finally, we offer some concluding observations.

The overall result

The polling stations closed in the Welsh devolution referendum at 10 p.m. on 3 March 2011. As was mentioned in chapter four, the final opinion polls reported before the vote had already indicated that the most likely outcome was a clear Yes victory. But whether the result was to be a landslide as in 1979, achingly close as in 1997 or somewhere in between, one thing was already certain: the formal counting of the votes was not going to begin until the following morning. There was to be no early-hours-of-the-morning drama as had happened last time. Everyone involved – except those guarding the sealed ballot boxes – could get some, generally much-needed, sleep.

Work at each of the twenty-two Welsh local authority counting centres began at 9 a.m. the following morning. Before very long, it became apparent that the polls were going to be broadly vindicated: that the final outcome of the referendum would be a victory for the Yes campaign. At 11.53 a.m., the first local authority to announce a result was Blaenau Gwent. This area is part of the south-east Wales valleys, where True Wales had their only remotely significant concentration of support. But the outcome here, in an area that had voted Yes to devolution by a fairly comfortable margin in 1997, was a very clear Yes, with nearly 69 per cent of those voting supporting the proposed increase in the National Assembly's law-making powers.

The second area to declare was Denbighshire. This county, in the north-east of Wales, had voted heavily against devolution in 1997. Moreover, it was located in a part of the country where there had long been grumblings, often given voice in the *Daily Post* newspaper, about the Assembly being too heavily focused on Cardiff and the south of Wales. Yes campaigners had been far from confident that they would win here. But Denbighshire also voted Yes, and by the very clear margin of 61.8 per cent to 38.2 per cent. This was to be the second highest 'swing' to Yes from 1997 of any local authority in Wales.[1] After this result had been announced, there was no longer room for any serious doubt as to what the final outcome of the referendum was going to be.

Results continued to be announced from the other twenty counts over the following hours, until the final declaration was made by Cardiff at 3.18 p.m. In 1997, everything had still been in the balance until the very final announcement from Carmarthen had tipped the result from the No that had seemed the inevitable outcome into a narrow victory for Yes. This time around it was all much less dramatic. This final result simply filled in the last details of an outcome that had long been clear in its outline. Wales had voted Yes. And to many in the victorious camp, it seemed fitting that Wales's capital city – which had voted against devolution in 1997 – now put the seal on the victory.

The precise details of the result in each local authority, as well as for Wales as a whole, are laid out in table 5.1. This lists the total number of votes cast for both Yes and No, as well as the percentage of the vote gained by each side, and the official percentage turnout. We can observe immediately that there was significant variation

Table 5.1 The 2011 Welsh devolution referendum

Area	Yes (%)	No (%)	% Turnout
Blaenau Gwent	11,869 (68.9)	5,366 (31.1)	32.4
Bridgend	25,063 (68.1)	11,736 (31.9)	35.6
Caerphilly	28,431 (64.3)	15,751 (35.7)	34.6
Cardiff	53,427 (61.4)	33,606 (38.6)	35.2
Carmarthen	42,979 (70.8)	17,712 (29.2)	44.4
Ceredigion	16,505 (66.2)	8,412 (33.8)	44.1
Conwy	18,368 (59.7)	12,390 (40.3)	33.8
Denbighshire	15,793 (61.8)	9,742 (38.2)	34.5
Flintshire	21,119 (62.1)	12,913 (37.9)	29.4
Gwynedd	28,200 (76.0)	8,891 (24.0)	43.4
Merthyr Tydfil	9,136 (68.9)	4,132 (31.1)	30.1
Monmouth	12,381 (49.4)	12,701 (50.6)	35.8
Neath/Port Talbot	29,957 (73.0)	11,079 (27.0)	38.0
Newport	15,983 (54.8)	13,204 (45.2)	27.9
Pembrokeshire	19,600 (55.0)	16,050 (45.0)	38.7
Powys	21,072 (51.6)	19,730 (48.4)	39.7
Rhondda Cynon Taff	43,051 (70.7)	17,834 (29.3)	34.6
Swansea	38,496 (63.2)	22,409 (36.8)	32.9
Torfaen	14,655 (62.8)	8,688 (37.2)	33.8
Vale of Glamorgan	19,430 (52.5)	17,551 (47.5)	40.1
Wrexham	17,606 (64.1)	9,863 (35.9)	27.0
Ynys Môn	14,011 (64.8)	7,620 (35.2)	43.8
Wales	**517,132 (63.5)**	**297,380 (36.5)**	**35.6**

both in the proportions of people voting Yes and No across the different areas, and in the numbers of those who chose to participate. Rhondda Cynon Taff could claim the honour of the highest absolute Yes majority, although the highest percentage margin was in Gwynedd. The highest turnout figure had been in Carmarthenshire, and the lowest in Wrexham. In the remainder of this chapter, we will explore and analyse these results in greater detail. We begin with an analysis of one of the most striking features of the result – turnout.

The results in perspective

Turnout

In the immediate aftermath of the announcement of the final result, the one thing that virtually all participants in the referendum campaign could agree upon was that the final turnout figure was disappointingly low. Although 35.6 per cent was not as bad as some gloom-mongers had been suggesting, nonetheless it could hardly be viewed as a triumph for democratic participation. Wales had held a referendum – but few of its people had bothered to come and take part.

Just how disappointing was this turnout figure? Some historical perspective can be given by comparing the participation rate in the 2011 Welsh referendum with those in the previous major referendums that have been held in the UK. Table 5.2 lists official turnout figures for all of these votes. We can see immediately that 35.6 per cent is well towards the lower end of the spectrum. Higher turnouts occurred in all four previous devolution referendums held in Scotland and Wales. A greater proportion of voters also took part in the 1975 UK referendum on EC membership, as they did in the two major referendums held in Northern Ireland. Indeed, the 1973 'border' referendum in Northern Ireland attained a turnout level more than 20 per cent higher than that in Wales in 2011, despite it being hit by a campaign of mass non-participation from a large proportion of Ulster's Catholic population. The only previous major referendum in the UK that had produced a lower turnout than 35.6 per cent was that held in 1998 on the issue of whether London should establish the office of a directly elected mayor alongside a Greater London Assembly, which produced a turnout

Table 5.2 Turnout in major UK referendums

Referendum	% Turnout
'Border' vote, Northern Ireland, 1973	58.7
EC membership, UK, 1975	64.5
Devolution, Scotland, 1979	63.8
Devolution, Wales, 1979	58.8
Devolution, Scotland, 1997	60.4
Devolution, Wales, 1997	50.1
Good Friday Agreement, Northern Ireland, 1998	81.0
Elected mayor & GLA, London, 1998	34.1
Devolution, north-east England, 2004	47.7
Devolution, Wales, 2011	35.6
AV electoral reform, UK, 2011	42.0

of only 34.1 per cent. Only nine weeks after the devolution referendum, the UK-wide vote on reform of the electoral system for House of Commons elections produced a turnout figure of 42.0 per cent across the UK as a whole, and 41.7 per cent in Wales. Compared with almost all other experience in the UK, therefore, the 2011 Welsh referendum turnout does look rather pitiful.

Why was turnout this low? The following chapter will examine detailed, individual-level evidence on why some people participated in the vote while others chose not to. But even before we explore this evidence, there are a number of factors that can help account for the level of participation experienced in Wales in 2011. A first point is that, as much evidence both from the UK and elsewhere indicates, participation rates in referendums tend to be lower than in equivalent national elections (at least when those referendums are not held simultaneously to elections).[2] The UK's referendum on EC membership in June 1975 saw 64.5 per cent turnout, compared to 72.8 per cent in the previous October's general election. Turnout in the four previous devolution referendums in Scotland and Wales was lower than at the nearest UK general election.[3] Looking outside the UK, the June 2006 Catalan referendum on a new statute of autonomy – one of very few across the globe that might be seen as broadly similar in nature to the 2011 Welsh referendum, concerning as it did the possible enhancement of the status of already-existing sub-state regional political institutions – saw only

48.9 per cent of voters take part, whereas the election held to the parliament of the Catalan Autonomous Community the following November had a 56.0 per cent turnout.[4] Given also that only 42.2 per cent of people took part in the May 2011 National Assembly for Wales election, 35.6 per cent turnout in the preceding referendum looks a bit less surprising.

Nonetheless, differences between prevailing turnout levels in referendums and legislative elections cannot obviously account for why participation in the 2011 Welsh devolution referendum was so much lower than for those in either 1979 or 1997. Other reasons must be found for this. One of them is surely the general decline in voting participation that has occurred in the UK, and in much of the democratic world, in recent times.[5] A vivid illustration of this can be given simply by comparing average turnout in the three UK general elections prior to the 2011 referendum (those in 2001, 2005 and 2010) with the average in the three previous such elections (1987, 1992 and 1997). The figure for the more recent trio is 62.0 per cent; for the earlier elections it is 74.8 per cent. Falling levels of voter participation are not something specific to Wales in 2011; but nor can we reasonably expect that Wales will be exempt.

Four other factors, all of which we have touched upon in previous chapters, also appear to be obvious contributors to low turnout in the 2011 referendum. The first is the nature of the question that was put to the voters. With no clearly explicable issue of principle at stake in the referendum, it was difficult for those campaigning, as we have seen, to communicate to voters why they should care about the issue that was on the ballot. Secondly, the absence of official campaigns, along with the paucity of grass-roots campaigners in all but a very few places on the No side of the argument, did nothing to raise the public profile of the referendum. Thirdly, the lack of interest from the UK-wide media, and lack of active participation by major UK-level politicians in the referendum, also contributed to lowering public awareness and interest. Most Welsh voters consume London-based media as their main sources of information about politics. And these media had little interest in a referendum that was apparently relevant only to Wales. Fourthly and finally, the timing of the vote was less than ideal in a couple of respects. There are good reasons why elections are very rarely held in winter in the UK: campaigning in the dark and the cold is not much fun. Although February 2011 in Wales was actually a little drier and

warmer than typical, daylight hours for campaigning were inevitably limited. Moreover, while many politicians and grass-roots party
members gave very generously of their time on behalf of the Yes
campaign (and a tiny number were very active on the No side), the
parties themselves were, quite understandably, seeking to husband
their limited resources for the May Assembly elections. These
factors further limited the ability of the campaign period to inform
or inspire the potential voters.

The contrast between the two major 2011 referendums on the
last three of these points is striking. The referendum on the alternative vote had officially recognized campaigns, and a fairly equal
balance between the forces on the two sides of the argument. The
AV referendum saw active participation from all the major UK party
leaders and many other very well-known political figures, and
received a significant amount of coverage from the main UK-wide
newspapers and other media outlets. Finally, the AV referendum
was held in May – not merely a more congenial time for campaigning
and voting, but also one long established in the public mind as a
time when elections are held; in addition, the same time at which
elections were being held for the Scottish Parliament, National
Assembly for Wales, many English local authorities and both the
Assembly and local government in Northern Ireland. While this
proliferation of other events may have drawn some attention away
from the AV vote, it also gave people throughout the UK other
reasons to be going to the polls on 5 May 2011. In this context, it is
hardly surprising that turnout in Wales for the AV referendum was
higher than for the March devolution referendum. Indeed, the
surprise perhaps is that the gap between participation levels in the
two votes was not greater than 6.1 percentage points.

The other aspect of turnout in the 2011 devolution referendum
that is readily apparent from table 5.1, and worthy of some
detailed attention, is how much participation rates varied across
the twenty-two Welsh local authorities. Nowhere could turnout be
described as high, but there was more than a 17 per cent difference between the areas with the highest and lowest levels of
public participation. At first glance there seems an obvious pattern
to these variations. The two highest Yes vote shares were recorded
in Gwynedd and Carmarthenshire, which were also among the
four highest turnout levels – suggesting that participation was
highest where there was the greatest degree of enthusiasm for the

Table 5.3 Correlations with local authority 2011 referendum turnout

% Yes vote	.16
1997 referendum turnout	.91*
2010 UK election turnout[†]	.57
NAW 2011 turnout[†]	.92*
% Welsh identity	−.07
% Welsh-speaking	.68*
People per sq km	−.35
% rural population	.75*
% professional/managers in workforce	.18
% in employment	.13
% economically inactive	.03

* Statistically significant (p < .05)
†These variables were measured at the level of the eight 'preserved counties' of Wales, and correlated with the 2011 referendum turnout at this level (see n. 3).

Yes cause. But a closer examination of the data shows that among other relatively high turnouts were Powys and the Vale of Glamorgan, two local authorities which recorded among the lowest levels of Yes support. And overall, there was no more than a very weak correlation between levels of Yes voting and turnout (see table 5.3).

There was, however, a very strong relationship between local authority turnout in the 2011 devolution referendum and that in the previous such vote in Wales some thirteen and a half years previously. Indeed, the correlation (r = 0.91) is very strong. There was also a very high correlation between levels of turnout in the 1979 and 2011 referendums, and between the 2011 referendum and the NAW election, and a weaker but still substantial relationship between the turnout levels in an area in the 2011 referendum and that in the 2010 UK general election.[6] This suggests that local differences in turnout in the referendum were largely shaped by the same factors that shape the differences between different areas' voter turnout levels in general, but also that there are some factors which have a particular influence on turnout in devolution referendums.[7]

Some of these factors are explored in table 5.3. One factor strongly related to turnout in Scotland in 1997 was the 'rural-ness' of an area; such was also the case in Wales in 2011. While a direct measure of population density per local authority was negatively correlated with turnout (although insufficiently strongly to reach statistical significance), the proportion of the population actually living in a 'rural area' was strongly and positively associated with higher turnout levels across the twenty-two local authorities. Socio-economic prosperity is also generally associated with higher turnout, and two measures of this – the proportion of the employed workforce employed in professional or managerial occupations and the proportion of the working-age population actually in employment – show a positive, though fairly modest, correlation with higher turnout in Wales in 2011. However, a measure of deprivation – the proportion of the working-age population in a local authority who are economically inactive – was not substantially related to turnout.[8]

These broad socio-economic factors tend to shape turnout across most voting contexts. Any factors shaping localities' turnout levels specifically for referendums on Welsh devolution might plausibly be expected to be related to the 'Welshness' of an area. Again, the evidence is at least partially supportive of this idea. While the levels of Welsh identity in a local authority area were not substantially related to referendum participation rates, there was a very strong positive correlation between local authority turnout and the proportion of Welsh-language speakers in an area.

Combining the various factors examined in table 5.3 into a multivariate regression analysis of turnout (reported in table 5.4) we find that these socio-demographic variables alone enable us to account statistically for most of the variation in the 2011 referendum turnout in Wales. Once other factors are controlled for, there is a strong and positive association between levels of both Welsh identity and Welsh-language competence in an area and participation rates in the 2011 referendum. Turnout was also notably higher in more rural areas, and in those with greater levels of the working population in professional or managerial roles. When the percentage Yes vote in the region and 1997 referendum turnout are also included in the model, the inter-correlations between several of these variables means that few of them are now statistically significant, although the overall model fit increases.

In sum, turnout at the 2011 Welsh referendum was distinctly poor, by most historic UK and international standards. But it was poor for reasons that are readily explicable. Indeed, one might

Table 5.4 Multivariate analyses of local authority 2011 referendum turnout

Variable	Model 1		Model 2	
% Welsh identity	.20	(.06)**	.11	(.08)
% Welsh-speaking	.12	(.04)*	.06	(.06)
People per km²	.00	(.00)	.00	(.00)
% living in rural area	.21	(.04)**	.14	(.05)*
% working in professional/ managerial role	.59	(.14)**	.34	(.19)
% 16–64 in employment	.08	(.36)	.26	(.35)
% economically inactive	.69	(.41)	.60	(.39)
% Yes vote			.04	(.11)
% 1997 referendum turnout			.46	(.23)
(Constant)	−22.86	(34.51)	−42.45	(33.70)
Adjusted R²	.84		.86	

Number of observations = 22
(Cell entries are unstandardized OLS regression coefficients, with standard errors in brackets)
* $p < .05$; ** $p < .01$

suggest that if ever a referendum had been designed to elicit a low turnout, it was the 2011 Welsh referendum. Participation in the referendum also varied across the different areas of Wales. For the most part, this variation is also explicable. Turnout was lower in those parts of Wales that mostly have lower election turnouts. But it also reflected factors specific to the politics of devolution referendums: it was lower in the more anglicized areas of Wales, and where participation had been lower in the previous devolution referendums of 1979 and 1997. In chapter six, we will examine survey data to explore the extent to which the factors we have just examined help explain directly the decisions of individuals as to whether or not to participate in the referendum.

The opinion polls

Compared both with previous devolution referendums in Wales and previous National Assembly elections, the 2011 referendum saw a far greater number of opinion polls conducted beforehand. Those in the years, months and weeks prior to the referendum itself were discussed in chapter three. Here we analyse the performance of the final polls conducted immediately prior to the vote.

Four polls were carried out and/or reported in the final few days of the campaign. On the Monday of referendum week, the S4C programme *Y Byd ar Bedwar* (which is produced by ITV Wales) reported results from a YouGov internet survey. Fieldwork for this poll was actually conducted over the previous week – some eight to ten days prior to the referendum. As shown in table 5.5, once the undecided and likely non-voters were excluded, this poll placed the Yes camp ahead by a two-to-one margin. On the day prior to the vote, two further polls were published. Media Wales, publishers of the *Western Mail* and *Daily Post*, reported a telephone poll conducted by RMG across the previous weekend. Later that same day, ITV Wales presented findings of a further YouGov internet poll conducted during the week prior to the vote. Among those giving a clear voting preference the two polls reported exactly the same result: both placed Yes voting intention on 69 per cent, No on 31 per cent. The final poll reported was one conducted by telephone for BBC Cymru-Wales by ICM. Fieldwork for this survey was carried out on the final two days before the referendum; results were released by the BBC only on the morning after the polls had closed. Remarkably, this poll gave exactly the same result as the two previous ones: Yes voting intentions were at 69 per cent, No at 31 per cent.[9]

The final polls were unanimous, then, in suggesting that the referendum outcome would be a clear Yes victory. And a clear Yes victory was indeed the result. Nonetheless, the polls did not perform flawlessly. As table 5.5 also shows, all the final pre-referendum polls overstated Yes support compared to the final result. The two telephone polls and YouGov's final poll were inaccurate by approximately 5.5 percentage points; YouGov's slightly earlier effort was actually a

Table 5.5 The final polls compared

Poll	% Yes	% No	% Error
YouGov/ITV Wales, 21–3 February	67	33	3.5
RMG/Media Wales, 25–8 February	69	31	5.5
YouGov/ITV Wales, 24 Feb–1 March	69	31	5.5
ICM/BBC Wales, 1–2 March	69	31	5.5
Final result	63.5%	36.5%	

bit closer, with an error of 3.5 percentage points. These differences are not huge but are substantial enough to be significant – given that, with sample sizes of around one thousand, the 'margin of error' for these surveys is approximately three per cent. Given also that the surveys were all wrong in the same direction, it suggests a moderately serious degree of systematic bias, rather than merely random error.[10] Indeed, comparing 2011 to 1997, one finds that the performance of the final polls in 2011 was marginally worse. The two final polls conducted in September 1997 gave (once the undecided and intended non-voters are excluded) an average of 53.5 per cent support for Yes and 46.5 per cent for No – an error in relation to the final results of just over three per cent.[11] Although lower turnout in 2011 probably made the pollsters' job more diffi-cult, the marginal decline in their performance between the two votes is undoubtedly disappointing.

The period between the 1997 and 2011 referendums in Wales saw some important developments in political polling, most notably the development of internet polling. The very low costs associated with this method helped underpin the conduct of regular surveys in the years, months and weeks leading up to the March 2011 referendum. The regularity of these surveys undoubtedly adds to our under-standing of the dynamics of the campaign, as we saw in chapter three and will see in chapter six. Unlike for much of contemporary Welsh political history, there are no 'black holes' here – no lengthy or important periods for which we have no measures of public atti-tudes. By providing us evidence on the evolution of public attitudes over key time periods, polling adds much to our understanding of the 2011 Welsh referendum. But we must also note that polling remains a less-than-perfect science: the final polls prior to the refer-endum were all incorrect by more than the standard margin of error, something that actually constitutes a slightly worse perform-ance than that produced by the equivalent polls in 1997.

Comparing 2011 with 1997: the geography of referendum voting

Comparing the results of the 2011 Welsh referendum with those of previous devolution referendums is problematic in some respects. They were not votes on the same issue. Those of 1979 and 1997 can be more easily compared. Although the broader political context was strikingly different, the 1979 and 1997 referendums were both about creating an Assembly for Wales. Indeed (as discussed in chapter two), they were votes on strikingly similar schemes for devolution. The vote in 2011 was different. The Assembly was now in place; at issue was whether (and how) it acquired greater legislative powers. In this context, it is somewhat dubious to invoke the psephological concept of swing when describing differences in voting patterns between the 1997 and 2011 referendums. Swing refers to the net proportion of the electorate that has moved towards or away from one side between two votes. Its use to describe changes between the 1979 and 1997 referendums is pretty unproblematic: the Yes side in 1997 was essentially arguing for the same thing as the Yes side had been in 1979. But there is no such equivalence between 1997 and 2011.

However, while the referendums of 1997 and 2011 were clearly different in nature, and while much of the broader political landscape was also very different, some continuities remained. Much of the impetus behind the No campaign and much of its support on the ground came from those who were still essentially opposed to devolution. It was also true that, prior to the vote, campaigners on both sides expected that the hardest areas for the Yes side to win would be those that had rejected devolution in 1997. And when all the votes had been counted, these expectations were shown to have a substantial basis in reality: there was a very strong correlation (r = .90) between the share of the vote won by the two sides in each local authority in 1997 and in 2011. Reflecting the different nature of the two votes, we will place any references to changes in voting patterns between 1997 and 2011 in inverted commas. But it is still of considerable interest to examine such 'swings'.

In 1997, 50.3 per cent of those taking part in the referendum had voted Yes. In 2011, Yes votes were 63.5 per cent of the total. This meant a 'swing' to Yes across Wales of 13.2 percentage points. These figures are displayed in table 5.6, which also includes the equivalent figures for each of the twenty-two local authorities in which results were declared, with authorities listed in order of 'swing' from highest to lowest. None of the twenty-two saw a 'swing' to No between the two votes.

Notwithstanding the substantial continuities in voting patterns with 1997, there were also some interesting and important differences. Examining the table, a few things are immediately obvious. One is that the greatest 'swings' to Yes from 1997 were in those areas

Table 5.6 1997–2011 'swing' by area

Area	1997 % Yes	2011 % Yes	% 'Swing'
Flintshire	38.1	62.1	24.0
Denbighshire	40.8	61.8	21.0
Wrexham	45.3	64.1	18.8
Conwy	41.0	59.7	18.7
Newport	37.4	54.8	17.4
Monmouth	32.1	49.4	17.3
Cardiff	44.4	61.4	17.0
Vale of Glamorgan	36.7	52.5	15.8
Ynys Môn	50.9	64.8	13.9
Bridgend	54.4	68.1	13.7
Blaenau Gwent	56.1	68.9	12.8
Torfaen	50.1	62.8	12.7
Pembrokeshire	42.8	55.0	12.2
Rhondda Cynon Taff	58.5	70.7	12.2
Gwynedd	64.1	76.0	11.9
Swansea	52.0	63.2	11.2
Merthyr Tydfil	58.2	68.9	10.7
Caerphilly	54.7	64.3	9.6
Powys	42.7	51.6	8.9
Ceredigion	59.1	66.2	7.1
Neath/Port Talbot	66.6	73.0	6.4
Carmarthen	65.3	70.8	5.5
Wales	**50.3**	**63.5**	**13.2**

Note: areas that had voted No in 1997 in italics

that had voted No in 1997. To be precise, the eight highest increases in the Yes vote share were all in areas that had rejected devolution thirteen and a half years previous. The average 'swing' in the eleven local authorities that had voted against devolution in 1997 was 16.7 percentage points; the average among those that had supported the establishment of the National Assembly was a notably more modest 10.5 percentage points. This is very much consistent with the findings of the body of work on public attitudes to devolution that was conducted in the years prior to the referendum. This had found a distinct homogenization of attitudes across Wales. Far from devolution becoming a more divisive issue in Wales in the wake of the narrow 1997 referendum outcome, in subsequent years attitudes had actually come a little closer together; the greatest falls in opposition to devolution were seen in those areas, and amongst those groups in the population, that had harboured the highest levels of opposition in 1997.[12] The referendum result confirmed that, across the twenty-two local authorities, such homogenization had occurred. In 1997, the gap between the highest percentage Yes vote in any local authority (66.6 per cent in Neath-Port Talbot) and the lowest (32.1 per cent in Monmouthshire) was huge, at 34.5 percentage points. In 2011, the gap between the highest Yes (76.0 per cent in Gwynedd) and the lowest (49.4 per cent, again in Monmouthshire) was 26.6 percentage points: still a significant gap but also significantly smaller.

The second thing that is most immediately noticeable from table 5.6 is that the four greatest 'swings' to Yes were all in north Wales. This was distinctly counter-intuitive. A significant undercurrent to public debate and discussion of devolution across the previous decade had been complaints from many in north and mid Wales in particular that the Assembly and its associated political class had become too enclosed within their own 'Cardiff Bay bubble', and too concerned with the problems of Cardiff and its immediate south Wales hinterland. There had also been concern from some in the Yes campaign that the people of north-east Wales were, in the main, culturally disengaged from much of the life of Wales, and insufficiently aware of devolved politics in general or the referendum campaign in particular. Yet, despite these problems, it was in north Wales that the biggest 'swings' to Yes occurred.

Despite the degree of homogenization in voting patterns noted above, there were still significant differences across local authorities in the overall levels of voting support for the Yes and No camps. As with our analysis of turnout earlier, we can examine various factors that might be expected to be associated with voting patterns across the twenty-two areas. First, we compare the broad geographical regions of Wales. One way of dividing the country is by a simple tripartite split between south Wales, north Wales, and mid and west Wales.[13] Comparing these three areas we see that average levels of Yes support across the twelve local authorities in south Wales was

63.2 per cent; in the six local authorities in north Wales the Yes vote share averaged 64.8 per cent; across the four in mid and west Wales the Yes vote share averaged 60.9 per cent. Interestingly, the three regions actually reversed places from 1997: then, mid and west Wales had been the most enthusiastic for devolution (an average of 52.5 per cent support across the four local authorities), and north Wales the least (with an average Yes vote per local authority of only 46.7 per cent.) As now, south Wales occupied the middle position (with 50.1 per cent having voted Yes). Overall, this comparison reinforces the point that, notwithstanding grumbles about the Cardiff Bay bubble, the people of north Wales had not become alienated from devolution: if anything, the opposite was the case.

Another approach to examining referendum voting is to invoke the most well-known of all geographic analyses of Welsh politics, Denis Balsom's much-cited Three-Wales Model.[14] This posited an alternative tripartite division of the country to that considered immediately above: one, based on historic lines of language and identity, between British Wales, Welsh Wales and Y Fro Gymraeg. Dividing the map of Wales along these lines we see that:

- the average Yes vote in the four local authorities that clearly fit within Balsom's Y Fro Gymraeg was 69.5 per cent (compared with 59.9 per cent in 1997)
- among the seven local authorities within Welsh Wales the average Yes vote was 67.4 per cent (having been 56.6 per cent in 1997)
- and in the eleven local authorities in British Wales, the average Yes vote of 58.2 per cent compared with an average of 41.4 per cent in the previous referendum.

Here we see some difference, but also significant evidence of homogenization. While enthusiasm for the Yes cause remained at lower levels in British Wales, and was the highest in Y Fro Gymraeg, the differences between the areas were of a notably lower order than in 1997. Wales had not become wholly unified on devolution, but it was clearly less divided than before.

As with our earlier analysis of turnout, we can also examine whether the level of Yes voting in different local authority areas correlates with aspects of the social or political profile of the area. We do so in table 5.7. We find that the extent of Welsh identity and

123

Welsh language speaking in an area is associated positively with greater levels of Yes voting. While there is no relationship between the rural-ness of an area and its proclivity to vote Yes, there are strong relationships between measures of socio-economic prosperity and referendum vote. More middle-class areas were significantly less likely to vote Yes; those more economically deprived were more inclined to support strengthening devolution. Such socio-economic associations with referendum voting may reflect in part the political colouration of different localities. For example, those with higher levels of Conservative support at the 2010 UK general election also tended to vote No in greater numbers; those that produced higher levels of support for Plaid Cymru at the 2011 National Assembly elections were also notably more inclined to vote Yes.

Combining most of the factors included in table 5.7 into a multiple regression analysis of referendum voting (presented in table 5.8), we find that socio-demographic variables are less able to account for variation in Yes voting across local authorities than they could account for turnout levels. Once other factors are controlled for there is a strong and positive relationship between the proportion of a local authority's population that is Welsh-speaking and the level of Yes votes in that area in the 2011 referendum. No other variables are significantly related to referendum voting. When we also include the level of Yes votes in each local authority in 1997 in the equation, the overall model fit increases substantially. Levels of

Table 5.7 Correlations with % Yes in local authorities, 2011

% Welsh identity	.55*
% Welsh-speaking	.38
People per sq km	.02
% rural population	−.12
% professional/managers in workforce	−.61*
% in employment	−.44*
% economically inactive	.47*
% Conservative vote in 2010[†]	−.55
% Plaid Cymru vote in 2011[†]	.70

* Statistically significant (p < .05)
†These variables were measured at the level of the eight 'preserved counties' of Wales, and correlated with the 2011 referendum turnout at this level (see n. 3).

Table 5.8 Multivariate analyses of % Yes in local authorities, 2011

Variable	Model 1		Model 2	
% Welsh identity	.18	(.13)	−.14	(.04)
% Welsh-speaking	.34	(.09)**	.12	(.05)**
People per km^2	.00	(.00)	.00	(.00)
% living in rural area	−.14	(.09)	−.20	(.04)**
% working in professional/ managerial role	−.34	(.31)	−.24	(.14)
% 16–64 in employment	.10	(.82)	.46	(.37)
% economically inactive	.54	(.92)	.15	(.41)
% Yes vote 1997			.70	(.09)**
(Constant)	32.93	(77.53)	9.99	(34.47)
Adjusted R^2	.58		.92	

Number of observations = 22
(Cell entries are unstandardized OLS regression coefficients, with standard errors in brackets)
* $p < .05$; ** $p < .01$

Welsh-speaking remain positively associated with Yes voting levels, while the proportion of an authority's population living in rural areas now has a significant negative coefficient – indicating that, holding other factors constant, more rural areas were less supportive of enhancing Welsh devolution.

To summarize, voting patterns in the 2011 Welsh devolution referendum were in many respects quite predictable. Areas of Wales that had voted Yes to devolution in 1997 tended to be those which most strongly supported extending devolution in 2011. Similarly, areas that have recently supported the party most closely associated with that agenda – Plaid Cymru – also voted Yes in greater proportions, while those more supportive of the party historically most cautious about devolution – the Conservatives – were less likely to vote Yes in 2011. But the results were not just a mirror of the past. By 2011, Wales was notably less divided on the issue of devolution and how it wanted to be governed than it had been in 1997. What substantial research on public attitudes had indicated for several years was now confirmed by the referendum vote. Wales remained far from totally united, but divisions between the different parts of Wales were significantly reduced in scale from what they had once been.

Conclusions

The purpose of this chapter was to present and analyse the result of the 2011 Welsh referendum. We have seen that the outcome of the referendum was a clear Yes vote, with an almost two-to-one margin across Wales, and victory for the Yes camp in twenty-one of the twenty-two Welsh local authorities. We have also analysed some major features of the result: the low turnout, the relationship of the final outcome to that predicted by the opinion polls and the geography of referendum voting across Wales. Turnout, as we have seen, was low but explicably so. The polls, we suggested, provided valuable information but remained a somewhat imperfect guide to public voting intentions. And the geographic divisions across Wales were shown to be still significant, but to have diminished in scale as the country has become more unified on the issue of devolution.

The analysis in this chapter has been conducted using aggregate data – information gathered at the level of the twenty-two Welsh local authorities, the eight 'preserved counties' of Wales, or Wales as a whole. While this has been able to tell us many valuable and important things, there are also limits to the insights it can offer. To understand more fully why people did or did not vote, and why many of them voted the way that they did, we need information directly on individuals. Thanks to the 2011 Welsh Referendum Survey, plenty of such information is available. This will be presented, and analysed, in chapter six.

6

The people's choice: explaining voting in the referendum

The previous chapter of the book set out the result of the 2011 Welsh referendum and examined it in some detail. We saw that while turnout in the referendum was low, it was so for reasons that are largely explicable. We also observed that while the 2011 referendum on enhancing the powers of the NAW produced a much more comfortable Yes vote than that on its creation in 1997, there were still considerable continuities in local voting patterns between the two votes. But where the two differed – other than in the general level of Yes support being higher everywhere – they did so in the direction of homogenization. Differences in referendum voting patterns between local authority areas in Wales in 2011 were notably smaller in scale than they had been in 1997.

Analysis of the referendum results can tell us a lot. But there are also some limits to what such analysis can contribute to our understanding. Most obviously, the results can only supply information on the twenty-two local authority areas where the referendum vote was counted. They can offer us no other direct information about the voters of Wales. They do give us some strong hints. For instance, the previous chapter found a strong correlation between the proportion of Welsh-speakers in an area and its level of support for the Yes side in the referendum. This would seem to suggest that Welsh speakers were strongly supportive of enhancing the powers of the National Assembly for Wales. But such 'ecological inferences' – drawing conclusions about the behaviour of individuals from aggregate information – are notoriously unreliable.[1] To understand properly the behaviour and decisions of individuals, we need detailed information about those individuals.

This chapter is devoted to the analysis of such information. We draw on the 2011 Welsh Referendum Study (WRS), which gathered substantial survey data from large, representative samples of voters in Wales both before and after the referendum.[2] Moreover, in most cases the same people were included in both pre- and post-referendum surveys. These 'panel data' enable us to see whether particular individuals changed their attitudes or intended voting behaviour.

We use WRS data to investigate three main issues. First, we explore turnout. As discussed in the previous chapter, participation levels in the 2011 Welsh referendum were low. The discussion in the previous chapter also considered some factors shaping differences in turnout across the different areas of Wales. Here, we draw on WRS data to investigate who voted and who did not, and to explore why some people chose not to participate in the referendum. We also consider whether the low turnout may have made any significant difference to the final outcome of the referendum.

Secondly, we assess the impact of the campaign period. We examine not only whether it influenced people's decisions about participating in the referendum, and which side to vote for, but also the extent to which the campaigns shaped voters' wider perceptions of the issues at stake. Did the campaign matter for the referendum outcome? And might it have left any lasting legacy on public attitudes? In addition, we explore the role of parties in the referendum. How did voters perceive the positions of the different political parties?

In the final main section of the chapter, we use WRS data to examine the voting choices of those who did participate in the referendum. What were the major factors shaping how they voted? We examine several issues here. We assess the extent to which social factors – such as language, class and national identity – divided Yes from No voters. We also consider the extent to which voters may have been swayed by their attitudes to devolution and the perceived performance of the National Assembly. We also explore how supporters of different parties voted, and whether voting in the Welsh referendum was influenced substantially by attitudes to the UK government.

The concluding section of the chapter addresses two questions. First, why did Wales vote Yes in 2011? What major conclusions does the evidence suggest about why the referendum produced a decisive victory for this side? Secondly, how uniquely Welsh was the 2011 referendum? How idiosyncratic were the factors shaping voting behaviour and the referendum outcome in Wales in 2011?

To what extent does Wales fit within wider international experiences of referendums as a form of political decision-making?

Turnout in the referendum

This section of the chapter will first seek to identify which types of people did and did not vote in the 2011 Welsh referendum, before exploring further why some participated and others did not. Finally, we will consider the consequences of turnout: what, if any, difference did it make to the referendum outcome that only 35.6 per cent of registered voters took part?

Who voted?

The previous chapter demonstrated that turnout in the 2011 Welsh referendum was low by almost any standard. It also showed that turnout levels across the different local authorities were quite predictable: they correlated highly with turnout rates in previous referendums and elections, and to some degree with key social markers such as levels of Welsh-speaking and the economic prosperity of an area. This, along with broader understandings of voting turnout, gives us much to explore here.

First, we examine social characteristics. In the past such factors have probably been over-emphasized as determinants of political attitudes and behaviour in Wales. But it remains true that voter turnout is often strongly linked to social location.[3] We consider several such potential influences. Some are factors associated with turnout across many democratic contexts. *Age* is a prominent example. Both for life-cycle reasons (people's likelihood to vote increases as they move into middle-age and become more socially rooted) and generational ones (growing evidence that more recent generations do not possess to the same degree as their elders the belief that voting is a social duty), a common finding is that propensity to vote increases with age. *Education* is also commonly pointed to. The more highly educated tend to vote more: whether because education is related to higher social status (and those further up the social scale vote in greater numbers) or because it facilitates understanding and engaging with politics. Similarly with *housing status*: homeowners, typically more deeply-rooted in their communities than those who rent, are more likely to vote.[4] Finally, *social class* and *income* levels have also been associated with likelihood to vote, with the more affluent generally expected to turn out in greater numbers.

Other factors potentially salient to understanding participation in the 2011 referendum are more specific to Wales. Evidence from the previous chapter, and from previous devolution referendums, suggests that those with a strong attachment to Wales may be particularly motivated to take part.[5] We gauge attachment to Wales in two ways: first, via a measure of *national identity* (using the Moreno scale that allows for gradations of adherence to British and Welsh identities) and secondly through ability to speak the *Welsh language*.

We examine first individual relationships of these variables with referendum turnout. Table 6.1 presents reported turnout levels in the 2011 Welsh referendum among different groups for the variables outlined above.[6] There is a strong association between reported turnout and age, in the expected direction: turnout rates increase steadily with age. Little relationship is seen for household income: those from poorer households were not much less likely to vote in the referendum. And though middle-class voters were more likely to participate, the relationship is modest. Similarly, there is no consistent relationship between education

Table 6.1 Reported referendum participation by social characteristics

Variable	% Reported turnout
Age	
18–24	39
25–34	54
35–44	67
45–54	72
55–64	80
65+	87
Education	
No formal qualifications	75
GCSE/O level/equivalent	70
A level/equivalent	54
University or equivalent	74
Other qualifications	68
Don't know/refused	50

Variable	% Reported turnout
Housing status	
Owner occupiers	74
Council/hous. assoc. renters	72
Private renters	47
Don't know/refused	39
Household income	
< £10,000	69
£10,000–£14,999	74
£15,000–£19,999	70
£20,000–£29,999	70
£30,000–£39,999	66
£40,000–£59,999	71
£60,000+	73
Don't know/refused	64
Social class	
Middle class (ABC1)	73
Working class (C2DE)	65
National identity	
Welsh not British	69
More Welsh than British	66
Equally Welsh and British	76
More British than Welsh	69
British not Welsh	60
None of these/don't know	52
Welsh language	
Fluent	76
Non-fluent	70
Non-Welsh speaker	66

Number of respondents = 2,569
Source: 2011 Welsh Referendum Study

levels and referendum turnout. But there is more of a link between referendum participation and housing status: owner occupiers, as well as those renting from councils and housing associations, voted in significantly greater numbers than those renting privately. But overall, most of these standard social predictors of voting turnout seem only modestly related to participation in the 2011 Welsh referendum.

The WRS data also suggest that the referendum did not attract participation only from the more 'Welsh' within society. There are few observable turnout differences across national identity groups, except for those with an exclusively British identity who were less inclined to vote. In line with the aggregate analysis reported in the previous chapter we find that Welsh speakers were somewhat more likely to vote, but even this relationship is modest in scale.

The results in table 6.1 illustrate well that while social location significantly influences how people experience and relate to politics, it does not determine attitudes or behaviour. On the whole, this is a positive thing. While overall turnout in the referendum was low, it is healthy that it does not appear to have been heavily skewed in favour of the more educated, more wealthy or the more 'Welsh'. This means that the referendum outcome did not result from certain sectors of society systematically excluding themselves from the vote.

If we wish to comprehend how and why people behave politically, we need to examine more than just their social background. We must also consider the political foreground – their attitudes to political processes, institutions and actors. In doing so, we will again explore both generic factors found to be important in other political contexts and things more specific to Wales and the referendum.

Among factors previously found to be relevant to voter participation is an individual's level of interest in politics: unsurprisingly, those more interested in politics tend to vote in greater numbers. Another important variable, according to many studies, is one's attitude to the act of voting: those who regard voting as a social responsibility participate in much greater numbers than those lacking such a belief.[7] Among factors more specific to the referendum were perceptions of its importance. Even some people with substantial interest in politics may have taken the view that the referendum itself was of little consequence. Finally, we look at individuals' attitudes towards devolution in two ways: both regarding how, in principle, Wales should be governed, and perceptions of the recent policy performance of the Welsh Assembly Government.[8]

Table 6.2 presents results for turnout levels across different categories of these five variables. It is immediately obvious that some of

Table 6.2 Reported referendum participation by political attitudes

Variable	% Reported turnout
Interest in politics	
Very interested	88
Fairly interested	71
Not very interested	57
Not at all interested	43
Don't know	19
Citizens' duty to vote	
Strongly agree	93
Agree	64
Neither agree nor disagree	27
Disagree	22
Strongly disagree	20
Don't know	7
Referendum importance	
A great deal	95
A fair amount	81
Not very much	60
None at all	34
Don't know	31
Constitutional preference	
No devolved government	78
NAW with fewer powers	59
Leave things as now	60
NAW with more powers	74
Independent Wales	75
Don't know	43
Assembly Gov't performance	
Positive evaluations	80
Neutral evaluations	62
Negative evaluations	83

Number of respondents = 2,569
Source: 2011 Welsh Referendum Study

these political factors offer greater empirical purchase on refer-endum turnout than the social background variables examined previously. Political interest, a sense of duty to vote and a sense of the importance of the referendum were all strongly related to turnout, in the expected directions: those with greater levels of political interest, a sense of a duty to vote and a belief in the import-ance of the referendum were all much more likely to participate than others. Interestingly, however, our other two political variables have little relationship to referendum turnout. Participation in the devolution referendum was not restricted only to those wanting greater self-government for Wales. Nor was it strongly related to views about the recent performance of the Welsh Assembly Government: those with positive and negative views were about equally likely to vote.

Thus, our initial exploration of individual-level data has suggested certain things about what shaped voter turnout in the 2011 Welsh referendum. Those more likely to vote were the older, more politic-ally engaged and those with a greater sense of duty to vote. They were also slightly more likely than average to be a Welsh speaker. Also interesting, however, are the 'dogs that didn't bark'. Some factors typically associated with voting turnout, such as income and social status, had little association with referendum participation. And both national identity and attitudes to devolution also appear to have been largely irrelevant.

Why did turnout differ?

The discussion above helps us to understand which people were more or less likely to vote in the 2011 Welsh referendum. But it offers far from the final word. The factors considered above do not exhaust all conceivable influences on referendum turnout; more-over, many of them are probably highly interrelated. Probing further, to attempt to understand the main factors shaping refer-endum participation, requires a multivariate analysis, which we conduct and report here.

What we are seeking to explain – whether an individual voted or not – is a dichotomy. The analysis here is therefore conducted using logistic regression. We specify separate models for the social back-ground and the political variables outlined above (with a control variable for the sex of the respondent added to the social background model). Two further sets of variables are also included in the analysis: whether an individual was a confirmed supporter of any particular party, and whether they reported having been contacted during the campaign period about the referendum by a party or one of the two main campaigning groups. A model is run including these variables, prior to a composite model that includes all the significant variables from the separate models. Table 6.3 reports summary results from this analysis, including goodness-of-fit statistics for the different models. (Full results are reported in an Appendix.)

Results from the sociological model confirm that age was significantly related to referendum participation, with younger voters much less likely to vote. But the generally limited association between social background factors and referendum turnout is also confirmed. Standard predictors of electoral participation, such as education level, social class, income and housing status, have only modest relationships with individuals' likelihood to have voted in the referendum (although the university-educated and middle class are a bit more likely to have voted, and those housed in private rented accommodation a bit less likely). The analysis also confirms that 'Welshness' had little association with referendum participation. Welsh speakers were little more likely than non-speakers to vote, while all national identity groups were more likely to vote than those (rather few survey respondents) unable to locate themselves on the Moreno national identity scale. In contrast to 1997, there is no indication of the referendum being disproportionately engaged with by those with a strongly Welsh identity.

The political attitudes model has a much better fit to the data, confirming that such factors help explain referendum

Table 6.3 Rival models of 2011 referendum participation

Model	McFadden R^2	% Correctly predicted	AIC[†]
Social background model	.14	73.0	2801.00
Political attitudes model	.36	81.6	2068.84
Party and campaign model	.04	68.7	3073.40
Composite model	.42	84.1	1929.21

† Smaller AIC figures indicate superior model performance

participation much more than social background variables do. Most of the findings are intuitive, and in line with those presented earlier. Those who believe strongly that voting is a civic duty were much likelier than others to participate; so also were those who believed that the referendum would have important consequences, and those with a generally high level of interest in politics. But also in line with our earlier findings, attitudes to the principle of devolution were not strongly associated with participation, and nor were attitudes to the policy performance of the Assembly government.

Our third model shows that confirmed supporters of the main parties, particularly Plaid Cymru and Labour, were much more likely than others to have voted. But being personally contacted by the campaigns seems to have made little difference to individuals' likelihood to vote. Finally, the composite model includes all significant variables from the earlier models: age, education, social class, housing status and national identity from the social background model; political interest, a duty to vote and referendum importance from the political attitudes model; whether or not someone was a supporter of a party. This model, unsurprisingly, obtains much the best fit of all the models. It confirms the robust relationship between individuals' likelihood to vote in the referendum and age. It also confirms that a sense of civic duty to vote, a general interest in politics and regarding the referendum as important were all strongly associated with participation in the referendum.

Some sense of the scale of these effects can be seen from figure 6.1. This presents the differences in the probabilities of an individual voting according to each category of the significant variables in our composite model.[9] Thus, we can see, for instance, that those 'strongly agreeing' that people have a duty to vote – even after controlling for other potential influences – were almost three times as likely to have participated in the referendum than those who chose the 'disagree' option on this question.

Overall, the results of our analysis suggest that no single factor wholly, or even mainly, shaped individuals' likelihood to vote in the 2011 Welsh referendum. As in many other contexts, in Wales younger voters proved much less willing to take part in the democratic process, while the more educated were a little more involved. Those who believe voting to be a civic duty, and that the referendum itself was important, were also notably more likely than others to participate. But the referendum did not attract participation only

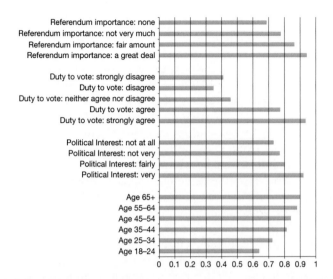

Figure 6.1 Effects of significant variables on predicted probabilities of voting in referendum

from those with a particular view of the National Assembly or a certain slant on the performance of the Assembly government. And being personally contacted by one of the campaigns or parties about the vote seemed to have had little impact on whether people chose to participate. Perhaps the most important finding of all is that, in the main, participation in the referendum does not appear to have been socially divisive. Voting turnout was not substantially skewed by social status, national identity or language: a Welsh referendum did not only attract the more affluent or only those voters identifying with Wales. Though overall turnout levels were low, this did not reflect significant elements of society excluding themselves from the referendum process.

Did turnout make a difference?

A final question we can explore concerning turnout in the 2011 Welsh referendum is whether it had any immediate consequences: did the low turnout actually affect the result of the referendum?

Given the decisive Yes victory, it is most unlikely that higher turnout could have changed the final referendum outcome from a

Yes to a No. (Thus, 2011 is very different from 1997, when turnout only a little higher might have produced a different result.) But it is possible that higher turnout might have produced a result distinctly different in tone. Perhaps the relative weakness of the No campaign, discussed in chapter four and in the following section of this chapter, may have failed to mobilize much of their potential support? If so, it is plausible that the referendum result appeared to give a much more decisive endorsement for enhancing the National Assembly's powers than public attitudes really warranted.

To investigate this, we take advantage of the fact that WRS interviewed the same respondents before and after the referendum. In the pre-referendum wave, respondents were asked about the likelihood that they would vote in the referendum and which way they would vote if they did so. The post-referendum wave asked respondents whether they had voted (and which way they had voted, for those who did participate). Our interest here is in those who did not vote. How likely was it that they might have voted, and what had their original voting intentions been? Results dealing directly with these questions are reported in table 6.4. They show that of those who originally stated that they were certain not to vote in the referendum, or unlikely to do so (the clear majority of whom, indeed, did not vote), most never formed a voting preference for the referendum. And the relatively small number who did have a view on the referendum split almost evenly. More interesting, though, are those who might have participated in the referendum (those scoring in the mid-range on the original intention to vote question), and those who originally indicated that they were certain or likely to

Table 6.4 Pre-referendum vote intention, by likelihood to vote, among non-voters

Pre-referendum likelihood to vote (0–10)	Pre-referendum vote intention			Number of respondents
	% Yes	% No	% Won't vote /don't know	
High (9–10)	49	26	25	178
Medium (5–8)	43	18	39	269
Low (0–4)	10	9	81	308

vote but did not ultimately do so. Among both these groups, the results show a clear pre-referendum lead for the Yes camp – and by a proportion closely approximating the referendum result.

These findings indicate that, whatever other effects it may have had, the low turnout in the 2011 Welsh referendum made no serious difference to the final outcome. There was not a substantial latent No vote which the relative weakness of the No campaign failed to mobilize. Even when we look at those voters who intended to vote, or considered doing so, but did not ultimately do so, Yes were well in the lead. A higher turnout would, in all likelihood, simply have extended the numerical advantage of Yes over No in a manner broadly proportional to what actually happened.

The impact of the campaign

In chapter four we examined the campaign for the 2011 Welsh referendum at some length. Here we will explore the impact that campaign had – on the numbers of voters who participated in the referendum, on how those who did participate voted and on their broader attitudes towards devolution and the National Assembly for Wales. This examination is facilitated by the manner in which the 2011 Welsh Referendum Study was conducted. Pre-referendum wave WRS interviews were carried out on a 'rolling' basis during the campaign. This enables us not only to compare individual voters before and after the referendum, but also to track any changes in the landscape of attitudes through the potentially crucial weeks immediately prior to the vote.

Campaign perceptions

We begin our exploration of the impact of the campaign by considering a simple question: to what degree did voters experience the campaign at all? For all the reasons discussed in chapter four, there was plenty of scope for many voters to avoid the referendum altogether. We therefore examine whether WRS respondents experienced any contact with the campaign, and what their reactions were to such contact.

The post-referendum wave of WRS fielded a range of questions about the campaign. One set asked respondents about whether or not they had been contacted by any of the parties or by a campaigning organization during the entire campaign period – and, if so, who contacted them and what form this contact took. As displayed in table 6.5, results from these questions show a campaign failing to connect with most voters: fewer than 10 per cent of WRS respondents recalled having been contacted at all. Of those who did recall contact, the Yes campaign achieved far greater levels of impact than the No campaign did, while among the parties, Plaid Cymru and Labour appear to have been the most active.

Among the fairly limited segment of the public with whom the campaigns achieved contact, a diversity of methods seems to have been used (see table 6.6). Leaflets, followed by social networks and street contacts, seem to have been the main method used by the Yes campaign; leaflets also appear to have been virtually the only grass-roots No activity to have registered at all. Although the web and social media were given substantial importance by the two campaigns, their ability to penetrate beyond the political cognoscenti into the wider population was evidently limited.

Another set of WRS questions probed respondents' reactions to the campaign as a whole: the level of information supplied, how it was covered in the media, the behaviour and visibility of the two sides, and which ran the best campaign. Results from this set of questions are presented in table 6.7. They show, in general, an

Table 6.5 Referendum campaign contact

Item	% Yes
Contacted by campaign or party?	10
Contacted by[†]	
Yes for Wales	5
True Wales	1
Conservative Party	1
Labour Party	3
Liberal Democrats	1
Plaid Cymru	3
Other	1

[†] Figures here sum to more than the 10 per cent contacted in total, as a few respondents reported being contacted by more than one organization or party
Number of respondents = 2,569
Source: 2011 Welsh Referendum Study (post-referendum wave)

Table 6.6 Forms of referendum campaign contact

Form of contact	% of all respondents reporting contact via this means from organization/party					
	Yes for Wales	True Wales	Conservative	Labour	Lib Dems	Plaid
Phone	1	<1	<1	<1	<1	1
Leaflets/direct mail	4	1	1	2	1	2
Home canvassing	<1	0	<1	1	0	1
Street contact	2	<1	<1	1	<1	1
E-mail	2	<1	0	1	<1	1
Social networks	2	0	<1	1	<1	1
Text message	<1	0	0	<1	0	<1

Number of respondents = 2,569
Source: 2011 Welsh Referendum Study (post-referendum wave)

Table 6.7 Campaign perceptions

Item	Strongly agree/ tend to agree	Neither agree nor disagree	Strongly disagree/ tend to disagree	Don't know
The referendum campaign gave me enough information to make an informed choice	27	22	44	8
During the referendum campaign, the two sides spent too much time criticizing one another	29	37	13	21
During the referendum campaign, the two sides did not talk about any of the issues that matter to me	37	31	16	16
The media coverage of the referendum made it difficult for me to understand what the referendum was really about	32	29	29	10
The Yes campaign were completely invisible; I didn't hear anything about them	37	20	36	7
The No campaign were completely invisible; I didn't hear anything about them	61	17	15	7

Number of respondents = 2,569
Source: 2011 Welsh Referendum Study (post-referendum wave)

electorate that was largely disengaged from the campaign – and to the extent that it was engaged, not very impressed. Even by the end of the campaign, barely a quarter indicated that they felt that they had been given enough information 'to make an informed choice'.[10] On two questions concerning the behaviour of the Yes and No campaigns, around half of all respondents either selected the mid-point 'Neither agree nor disagree' or the 'Don't know' options, indicating the campaigns failing even to generate a clear perception of their conduct among much of the public. And among those who did have a view, most were unfavourable. The news media escape only a bit more lightly – around a third of respondents agreed that their coverage made the referendum difficult to understand, slightly more than disagreed. And the two campaigns were hardly beacons of visibility to the voters. Almost two-fifths of voters agreed that the Yes campaign had been 'completely invisible'; more than three out of five thought this of the No campaign. On which of the two sides ran the best campaign, two clear and predictable messages emerge from the data. First, most people did not have a clear view. But of the minority who did offer an opinion, almost eighteen times as many nominated the Yes campaign than chose No.[11]

Party cues

In addition to asking voters about their direct experiences of the campaign, WRS probed voters' perceptions of the stances taken by the parties in the referendum. Given the strong evidence from many contexts, including Wales, that party cues can be a key factor shaping referendum behaviour, this is important to investigate. As we discussed previously, the leaders of the four main parties represented in the NAW supported a Yes vote in the referendum. But to what extent did this message get home to the voters – or even their party's core supporters?

WRS respondents were asked, for each of the four main parties in Wales, which way that party had recommended people vote in the referendum. Three of the four main parties officially endorsed a Yes vote; the Conservatives' Assembly group also supported this position, but the party as a whole was formally neutral – reflected by the fact that the Conservative Party was not even a registered participant in the referendum. Perceptions of the parties' stances might be taken as a measure of individuals' knowledge of what was occurring in the referendum, but it would probably be fairer to the electorate to interpret these data as indicating how clear and effective each party was in communicating its position. As a follow-up to the first question respondents were then asked whether they would describe each party as united or divided on the issue. Results from both questions for each of the main parties are displayed in table 6.8.

Table 6.8 Party cues in the referendum (%)

A. Which way do you think [PARTY] recommended people should vote in the referendum?

	Conservative	Labour	Lib Dems	Plaid
Yes	23	52	32	70
No	18	3	6	1
Did not make a recommendation	15	7	12	4
Don't know	44	39	49	25

B. Would you describe [PARTY] as united or divided on which way to vote in the referendum?

	Conservative	Labour	Lib Dems	Plaid
United	13	31	16	60
Divided	27	15	19	3
Neither united nor divided	14	11	13	6
Don't know	47	43	52	30

C. (Among own party supporters) Which way do you think [PARTY] recommended people should vote in the referendum?

	Conservative	Labour	Lib Dems	Plaid
Yes	28	66	57	97
No	16	3	2	0
Did not make a recommendation	19	4	8	0
Don't know	38	27	33	2
Number of respondents	367	805	96	137

Number of respondents = 2,569 (unless stated)
Source: 2011 Welsh Referendum Study

We see from the table that only Plaid Cymru established a clear line in the minds of most voters. A very narrow majority correctly perceived that Labour also supported a Yes vote, while slightly under a third did so for the Liberal Democrats. The Conservatives' ambiguous position on the referendum is reflected in disparate perceptions of their stance: around a quarter of respondents thought that the party supported a Yes (the stance of their Assembly group); just under a fifth thought that they supported a No (consistent both with their previous opposition to devolution and the continuing position of some Welsh Conservative MPs and many grass-roots members); just under 15 per cent opted for the No recommendation option (the party's official position); and more than two-fifths were – perhaps understandably – unclear as to the Tory position.

Similarly, Plaid Cymru was the only party whom the majority of WRS respondents saw as united on the referendum. For each of the others, significant proportions perceived the party as divided on the issue, or were simply unsure. These findings are probably best interpreted in the light of those from the previous section. In a context where the referendum campaign struggled to reach most voters, perceptions of what position the parties were taking, and how united they were on the issue, could draw only to a limited extent on the messages people received during the campaign itself. Longer-standing perceptions of the parties must also have mattered. Plaid has long been identified with the cause of greater Welsh political autonomy. Most people could therefore reliably expect that Plaid would be united behind support for greater powers for the Welsh Assembly. The other parties each had somewhat more ambiguous histories on the issue of devolution. With the referendum campaign struggling to connect to most people, many received only a very limited party cue as to how they should cast their ballot.

It is perhaps less important that a party convey its stance on an issue to all voters than that it communicates effectively with its own supporters. We examined perceptions of the parties' stances on the referendum among those identifying themselves as party supporters, for each of the four main parties. Findings on this comprise the third panel of table 6.8. They show that Labour and the Liberal Democrats were rather more successful at communicating to their core supporters than to the wider public. (For the Liberal Democrats, of greater concern was that the pool of such supporters had, by early 2011, shrunk to an alarmingly low level.) Plaid Cymru's supporters had, almost to a person, got the message. But many Conservatives remained, perhaps understandably, rather confused.

Changing votes or attitudes?

A final question to ask about the referendum campaign is whether it ultimately changed very much. Did it make an observable difference to the outcome of the vote, or have any broader impact on how people in Wales think about devolution? To examine these matters, we again take advantage of the design of WRS. That respondents to the pre-referendum wave were sampled on a 'rolling' basis through the four weeks prior to the vote allows us to isolate sub-samples from particular periods in the campaign and compare them with those at other time points.

First of all, we look at people's likelihood to vote in the referendum, who they intended to vote for and whether either changed substantially over the campaign. To do this we present a series of 'three-day rolling averages' for the twenty-eight days immediately prior to the referendum period. The first such averages are computed from those respondents interviewed in the first three full days of sampling. For the next averages, the first day's sample drops out and is replaced by that from the fourth day of sampling. This continues until the final rolling averages are compiled from the sampling in the last three days of the campaign period. With an average of 108 respondents gathered per day, this means that each three-day average is based on an average of 324 respondents. Such relatively small samples do produce greater 'margins of error' in sampling estimates; we should, therefore, expect to see some random turbulence in the results, presented in figures 6.2 and 6.3. What matters are not any such trendless fluctuations but any more systematic change.

As can clearly be seen in figure 6.2, beneath the random changes there is a modest upwards trend through the four weeks prior to the referendum in the proportion indicating that they were certain to vote. The campaign period appears to have had a slight impact in encouraging participation. The results presented in figure 6.3 also show – beneath the fluctuations – relatively modest changes across the campaign period. Nonetheless, the overall gap between Yes and No appears to have widened very slightly, while the numbers of

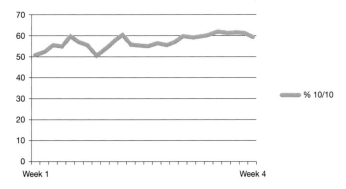

Figure 6.2 Intended turnout (rolling three-day average): % 'certain to vote'

those undecided or intending not to vote drifted downwards. There is certainly nothing here to suggest that the campaign saw the Yes advantage decline. Given the relative disparity of resources between the two sides, and the somewhat greater success the Yes side had in conveying their message, such a finding is hardly surprising. But the overall picture here is one of a campaign having rather limited impact.

But the referendum campaign might have had a wider impact. Beneath the immediate questions of whether people would vote in the referendum, and how they might vote, what about deeper changes in public attitudes? It is not impossible that the campaign, by enforcing some sustained attention to devolution, might have

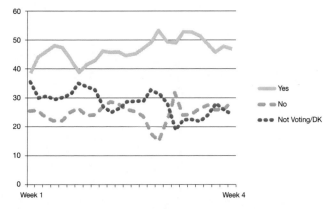

Figure 6.3 Referendum voting intention (rolling 3-day average) %

Table 6.9 Devolution attitudes (%) before and after the referendum

QUESTION	Referendum campaign first week	Referendum campaign final week	Post-referendum
Constitutional preference			
No devolution	16	16	16
NAW fewer powers	3	4	4
Leave things as they are	18	17	22
NAW more powers	42	40	38
Independence	8	11	9
Don't know	14	13	11
Influence over Wales – Has			
NAW	19	22	23
UK government	58	52	52
Local councils	7	7	8
EU	8	9	7
Don't know	8	11	10
Influence over Wales – Should have			
NAW	57	54	53
UK government	22	26	27
Local councils	10	8	10
EU	1	1	1
Don't know	10	11	10
Number of respondents	742	812	2,544

Source: 2011 Welsh Referendum Study

prompted change in attitudes to the issue. To consider this, we look at three questions which were asked both in the pre- and post-referendum WRS waves. The first is the multi-option constitutional preference question discussed in chapter three; the other two are the paired questions, also discussed in chapter three, asking respondents how important in running Wales they perceived different levels of government to be, and how important they desired those levels to be. The three panels of table 6.9 present results for each of these questions. For each one we present responses gathered from three time periods: those from the first week's sample in the WRS pre-referendum wave, right at the start of the final campaign period; those from the final seven days of the pre-referendum wave, gathered at the conclusion of the campaign; and those from the post-referendum wave, gathered after the vote.

These findings show little substantial change. On the constitutional preference question, there is a small increase over the three time points in the proportion favouring the 'No devolution' option, and a decline in those supporting the 'More powers' option. But such differences are within normal sampling variations. There is also a modest increase in the perceived importance of the National Assembly. In the context of a referendum campaign this makes sense, but again changes are within standard 'margins of error'. There is also a similarly modest decline in the proportion favouring the National Assembly being the most influential level of government. These findings certainly do not indicate that the referendum campaign engendered greater enthusiasm for devolution and the National Assembly. Very little change in this respect is evident.

Yes or no?

In this final main section of the chapter, we turn to perhaps the most important questions that the survey data can help us understand. Who voted Yes and No in the referendum, and why did they do so?

We begin by trying to find out what sorts of people voted Yes and No. Table 6.10 reports the percentage of WRS respondents (among those who voted) who voted Yes in the referendum, according to different categories of various social characteristics. We see that there were few differences in Yes voting across different age cohorts, except for rather lower levels of Yes voting among those aged sixty-five and older.[12] Nonetheless, even in this oldest age cohort a majority voted Yes. There were also few differences in voting patterns across different levels of education. For housing status, we see greatest levels of Yes voting among those who rent either publicly owned or housing association properties: this relationship likely reflects the paucity of Conservative voters among such individuals. There are also only modest differences across different categories of income. Yes and No in the 2011 Welsh referendum were not causes that divided people along lines of prosperity. Similarly, there are only very modest differences by social class category.

The social background differences which we can observe in levels of Yes voting are related to specifically Welsh characteristics. Those reporting a strongly, or even exclusively, Welsh sense of national identity were substantially more likely to have voted Yes in the referendum than those with a mainly or exclusively British identity. And those speaking the Welsh language were also more likely than

Table 6.10 Referendum vote by social characteristics

Variable	% Yes[†]
Age	
18–24	68
25–34	74
35–44	71
45–54	67
55–64	64
65+	56
Education	
No formal qualifications	61
GCSE/O level/equivalent	66
A level/equivalent	69
University or equivalent	68
Other qualifications	65
Don't know/refused	44
Housing status	
Owner occupiers	64
Council/hous. assoc. renters	72
Private renters	65
Don't know/refused	66

Variable	% Yes[†]
Household income	
< £10,000	70
£10,000–£14,999	74
£15,000–£19,999	71
£20,000–£29,999	64
£30,000–£39,999	62
£40,000–£59,999	71
£60,000+	70
Don't know/refused	56
Social class	
Middle class (ABC1)	64
Working class (C2DE)	67
National identity	
Welsh not British	85
More Welsh than British	84
Equally Welsh and British	63
More British than Welsh	48
British not Welsh	39
None of these/Don't know	55
Welsh language	
Fluent	88
Non-fluent	70
Non-Welsh speaker	59

† Among those who voted
Number of respondents = 1,766
Source: 2011 Welsh Referendum Study

non-speakers to have voted Yes – although a clear majority even among non-speakers voted Yes.

As with our examination of turnout, however, we can obtain far greater leverage in accounting for Yes and No referendum voting by examining political attitudes than from looking at social characteristics. As table 6.11 shows, there were few differences in Yes support across differing levels of political interest or a sense of duty to vote. However, those regarding the referendum as having important consequences for Wales were substantially more likely than others to vote Yes. And there are truly vast differences according to individuals' constitutional preferences. Those opposing devolution, wishing the National Assembly to have fewer powers or wishing for no change to devolution were, perhaps unsurprisingly, unlikely to vote Yes in the referendum; those wishing to see the NAW become more powerful, or desiring Welsh independence, overwhelmingly voted Yes. Similarly, those with positive perceptions of the recent performance of the Assembly Government were very strongly inclined to vote Yes; the rather lower number holding negative perceptions tended to vote No.

Also included in table 6.11 is a further variable not considered in our analysis of turnout. Much work on referendums indicates that

Table 6.11 Referendum vote by political attitudes

Variable	% Yes[†]
Interest in politics	
Very interested	65
Fairly interested	64
Not very interested	69
Not at all interested	73
Citizens' duty to vote	
Strongly agree	67
Agree	62
Neither agree nor disagree	67
Disagree	68
Strongly disagree	40
Referendum importance	
A great deal	86
A fair amount	78
Not very much	49
None at all	35
Don't know	57
Constitutional preference	
No devolved government	13
NAW with fewer powers	19
Leave things as now	27
NAW with more powers	96
Independent Wales	97
Don't know	71

Variable	% Yes[†]
Assembly Gov't performance	
Positive evaluations	91
Neutral evaluations	68
Negative evaluations	19
UK Gov't performance	
Positive evaluations	47
Neutral evaluations	57
Negative evaluations	75
Party supporter	
Labour	77
Conservative	29
Lib Dem	80
Plaid Cymru	97
Other	55
None	62

[†] Among those who voted
Number of respondents = 1,764
Source: 2011 Welsh Referendum Study

attitudes towards the government of the day can shape referendum voting;[13] analysis of sub-state elections has often indicated that voting decisions at the sub-state level can be influenced by attitudes towards the state-level government.[14] We therefore explore how referendum voting differed according to attitudes to the performance of the UK government.[15] We see that approval of the UK government was negatively correlated with the likelihood of casting a Yes vote; multivariate analysis below will explore whether this association is simply a function of Conservatives being much less inclined to vote Yes. And in line with work that has found party cues often to be important in shaping referendum voting, table 6.11 also presents evidence on how supporters of the different parties voted. Consistent with what we saw earlier, we find that parties had differing degrees of success in persuading their supporters how to vote in the referendum. Plaid Cymru supporters almost unanimously voted Yes. Both the Liberal Democrats and Labour mobilized somewhat fewer than four in five of their supporters to vote for something that their parties strongly endorsed. However, we should note that this represented an improvement for both parties on 1997, particularly the Liberal Democrats: in 1997, survey evidence indicated that a majority of their supporters voted against Welsh devolution, despite it having been the policy of their party and its predecessors for approximately a century!

Meanwhile, more than 70 per cent of Conservatives voted No: contrary to the stance of their Assembly group, but reflecting many Tories' long-standing antipathy to devolution.

To investigate these relationships further, we again run a series of multivariate models. We use logistic regression to explore differences between those choosing to vote Yes and those voting No. The first model incorporates the social characteristics used in table 6.10; the second draws on the political variables presented in table 6.11. Finally, we run a composite model incorporating those variables found to be significant in the first two models. As with our earlier analysis of referendum turnout, we present outline findings from the analysis in table 6.12; full details are in the Appendix.

The results confirm the limited ability of most social background variables to help explain referendum voting. Younger age cohorts are modestly more likely to have voted Yes than those in the reference category (those sixty-five and over); contrary to the True Wales argument that the Yes campaign was based on the interests of socio-economic and political elites, the Yes vote was actually stronger with those somewhat lower down the income scale. These relationships, however, are insufficiently strong to reach conventional levels of statistical significance. But the main social background variables to have any robust relationship with referendum voting are language – with fluent Welsh speakers having been significantly more likely to vote Yes – and national identity, with exclusive and mainly British identifiers being particularly likely to have voted No. In total, the

Table 6.12 Rival models of 2011 referendum voting

Model	McFadden R^2	% correctly predicted	AIC[†]
Social background model	.14	71.7	2090.02
Political model	.67	89.7	838.02
Composite model	.66	89.5	837.12

[†] Smaller AIC figures indicate superior model performance

modest model fit statistics indicate that social background variables do only a modest amount to help us account for why people voted Yes or No.

The model for the political variables has a very much better fit to the data. Attitudes towards the UK government, levels of interest in politics and a sense of duty to vote are all unrelated to referendum voting. So also, once other factors are controlled for, is a sense of the importance of the referendum. However, other variables are strongly related to voting choices. Conservative identifiers, even after other factors have been accounted for, were still significantly more likely than others to vote No; perhaps surprisingly, after controlling for other factors, Liberal Democrats were significantly more likely to vote Yes. But much the largest substantive effects come from the variables for evaluations of the performance of the Assembly Government and that for constitutional preference. These relationships are confirmed in the composite model, which includes the significant variables from the social background model (language and national identity) and from the political model (constitutional preferences, party supporters and WAG evaluations). Once all these factors are included together, only the political variables emerge as significant predictors of voting choices. And by far the strongest relationship is between vote choice and constitutional preference: that is, voting choices were most strongly related to how people thought Wales should be governed.

Once again, we can convey some sense of the substantive implications of these findings graphically (see figure 6.4). We can see that, even after accounting for all other factors, the probability of voting Yes in the referendum differed enormously according to constitutional preferences. The impact of the other significant variables in our composite model is notably smaller. This displays visually the point made immediately above: voting choices in the 2011 Welsh referendum were most strongly influenced by constitutional preferences.

Conclusions

In this chapter we have examined detailed evidence on individual voters, drawn from the 2011 Welsh Referendum Study, to explore three main issues in relation to the referendum. First, we considered turnout. We found that, although turnout was undoubtedly

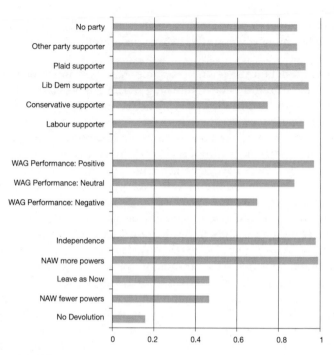

Figure 6.4 Effects of significant variables on predicted probabilities of voting yes in referendum

low, it was not heavily skewed towards particular social groups. Nor was participation in the referendum concentrated among supporters of devolution. Those choosing to vote tended to be those, often older voters, who believe that voting is a civic duty, and those thinking that the result of the referendum would have significant consequences for Wales. We found little evidence that the low turnout in the vote itself had a significant impact on the final result. Had turnout been higher than 35.6 per cent – had it been at 40, 45 or even 50 per cent – the final result would, in terms of the balance between Yes and No, probably have been very similar to that which ultimately prevailed.

Secondly, the chapter explored the effectiveness and impact of the referendum campaign. Our evidence suggested a campaign that struggled to register with many voters, to impress them or to have any substantial impact upon them. Few voters reported any direct contact with the campaigns. And few were impressed with what the campaigns delivered: particularly in terms of leaving them feeling engaged and informed about the issues. The campaign period appears to have had little impact on referendum voting patterns, nor made any notable difference to broader public attitudes to devolution. Such findings might be rather disappointing to those who worked hard during the campaign to try to sway the public. But our analysis also suggests that the final outcome of the referendum was not changed much by factors like the disparity between the strength of the Yes and No campaigns. The final outcome reflected longer-standing attitudes: the campaign period did little to alter things.

Finally, the chapter examined the choices made by those who voted. We found some differences in the social bases of Yes and No support. Unsurprisingly, those with a stronger identification with Wales were more likely to vote Yes. But the major factors shaping voting were more directly political. To some extent, voting choices were influenced by individuals' party attachments and by their perceptions of the effectiveness of the devolved institution. But most important seem to have been basic attitudes towards how Wales should be governed. We would suggest that some reasonably positive normative implications can be taken from this. Voting in the referendum was not primarily about the expression of group loyalties. The choice between Yes and No was not one that generally divided the more wealthy and privileged in society from others. Nor was the referendum widely used as a means to deliver a verdict on the UK government, as an expression of party loyalty or even mainly to deliver a verdict on the effectiveness of ministers in the previous Welsh Assembly Government. The most important factor shaping vote choice was arguably that most germane to the referendum: how people felt Wales should be governed. The significance of this finding is worth emphasizing. As stated earlier, analysis of public attitudes and voting behaviour in Wales has, in the past, probably tended to overplay social background factors, to the neglect of the political foreground. An illustration of this is the way that analyses of voting in previous devolution referendums did not explore the potential influence on voting behaviour of individuals' preferences between different constitutional options for Wales.[16] But in defence of past analysis, in a context where any form of home rule of Wales was a rather uncertain hypothetical construct, such preferences would have been distinctly difficult to form, still less have any independent impact on referendum voting. Our evidence indicates that, after more than a decade of experience with devolution as a daily, living reality, public preferences between different options for how Wales is governed have become more clearly defined. And these preferences are not mere artefacts of social location, party loyalty, attitudes to government performance or other potential influences.

Two final questions remain. First, what do our findings say about why Wales voted Yes? The main point is surely that, for most people who took part in the referendum, a Yes vote accorded with their views about how Wales should be governed. People were not, for the most part, greatly swayed by the campaign, or by a desire to use the referendum to deliver a verdict on the current UK government or the performance of the Assembly government. Nor did they use the referendum to express a 'tribal' loyalty within a deeply divided society. The outcome of the vote reflected the broad views about devolution, and how Wales should be governed, which had prevailed in Wales for some years prior to the referendum. As we saw in chapter three, enhanced devolution had been the most popular option for governing Wales in every major public opinion survey conducted in Wales throughout the decade prior to March 2011. When given the opportunity in the 2011 referendum, most of those voting chose this option. Referendums can often be dubious democratic tools. They frequently appear to produce results for reasons that have very little to do with what is ostensibly at stake. But in Wales, in March 2011, that was not what occurred. The most important factor shaping voting choices was the issue on the ballot. In that sense, and notwithstanding the many other problems with the referendum we have discussed previously, the referendum worked.

The final question we consider is to what extent March 2011 was a distinctly Welsh referendum. In one sense it obviously was. The referendum concerned only those registered to vote in Wales; its consequences were to be felt mainly in Wales. It was also very much Welsh in that, as we have just seen, most people voted on the basis of how Wales should be governed, rather than casting their ballot for reasons to do with any UK-level issues. In other senses, the Welsh experience was much less unique. Wales in early spring 2011 was simply one example of the growing global trend, across established and newer democracies, to use the direct democracy of referendums as a supplement to the institutions of representative democracy.

The particular type of referendum held in Wales in March 2011 – one concerned with a possible increase in the powers of an already established sub-state level of government – was distinctly unusual. But it was not unique, as we have mentioned earlier. Compared with other referendums, in the UK and elsewhere, the Welsh experience was disappointing in terms of the clarity of the question put, and the extent of public participation achieved. In some other respects, however, Wales in 2011 was one of the better examples of referendums. The vote did not divide society deeply, and vote choices appear to have been shaped mainly by opinions on the matter at hand, rather than more extraneous issues. But these are all respects in which Wales can be placed upon a spectrum, alongside other – better or worse – examples. There was little fundamentally unique about the Welsh experience. For better or worse, referendums are a growing feature of the political world. And Wales, in March 2011, contributed one more example to the genre.

7
The implications

And so it was all over. The referendum was done, and the people – well, some of them at least – had made their decision. As the Friday evening of 4 March moved well into night, the Yes campaign's celebration party in the Cardiff Millennium Centre began to wind down. Over the following days the temporary television studios, which had been constructed opposite the National Assembly in Cardiff Bay for the results shows, were dismantled; the campaign posters were taken down – where they had ever been erected in the first place; and the mainstream media and the blogosphere churned out instant analyses of what the referendum result meant. Campaigners from different parties who had united for the referendum went their separate ways and began working for the National Assembly election that was less than nine weeks away. And others who had taken a prominent role in the referendum campaign went back to the rest of their lives and got on with them.

There was no obvious or immediate change to life in Wales. There was certainly no Welsh equivalent of the tectonic shifts that the simultaneous Arab Spring was bringing to the societies of North Africa and the Middle East. Even the country's political life appeared remarkably unchanged. Indeed, as the party manifestos for the May election were published, observers could be forgiven for concluding that only the Welsh Conservatives had given serious thought to what might actually be done with the new legislative powers that the referendum had bestowed on the National Assembly. It was as if some superstitious desire not to tempt fate had stayed the hand of the pro-devolution parties, while the converts in the Tory Assembly group had simply been unable to conceive of the possibility that the Welsh electorate would refuse to share their new-found enthusiasm. Moreover, when Carwyn Jones's new minority government began its work after the electorate had eventually delivered its verdict, it was not the fascinating first months of the One Wales government that most observers were reminded of, but rather the lassitude of the 2003–7 Assembly. This was no brave new world.

So what had been the point of it all? What did it matter that Wales had voted Yes in the referendum? Would it have made any substantial difference to anything if there had never been a referendum, or if Wales had voted No? In this concluding chapter to the book, we consider the implications of the 2011 Welsh referendum. We will reflect upon what the campaign and the referendum result tell us about Welsh politics; what the Welsh experience in 2011 might have to contribute to our general understanding of referendums as a form of democratic political decision making; and about what further consequences the referendum outcome is likely to have for the government and politics of Wales, and possibly for the UK as a whole. Before we discuss that, however, we first consider a very basic question. What does it say about Wales and its politics that this referendum ever occurred?

Constitutional politics and the pathologies of one-partyism

For many of those involved in the referendum campaign, or trying to cover it in the news media, one of the most frustrating aspects of the entire experience was the difficulty that they encountered in explaining the nature of the choice before the voters of Wales. As we demonstrated in chapters one and two, the 2011 Welsh referendum was not a vote on a major issue of principle. It was not a referendum about whether or not Wales should have devolution (although some on the No side of the argument at times tried to make it so). The referendum was certainly not about independence for Wales – though, again, a few No voices suggested that a Yes victory would be a move down a 'slippery slope' heading inexorably in the direction of independence. Nor was the 2011 referendum even about a fundamental decision concerning the level or type of powers that the NAW should have. There was no issue of principle in terms of primary law-making powers: that had been decided by the UK Parliament when it passed the 2006 Government of Wales Act. It was not proposed that Wales should receive powers over taxation (the subject of the second question in Scotland's 1997 referendum), nor that the responsibilities of the National Assembly for Wales be broadened into new areas (such as had happened with policing and criminal justice for the Northern Ireland Assembly in

2010). Instead, the choice before voters was, as we have explained, between giving the National Assembly primary law-making powers in twenty policy areas almost immediately, or retaining the system under which legislative powers could be transferred to the Assembly, in piecemeal and tightly constrained fashion, over an indefinite time period.

This is not the most bizarre choice ever put before people in a referendum.[1] But it would be at least a little way along a spectrum of peculiarity. It is certainly some way distant from the sort of clear issues of principle which the House of Lords' Constitutional Committee recommended were most suitable for the use of referendums (see chapter one). How did Wales arrive at this rather strange constitutional juncture? The basic answer is that the referendum, as with much else over the preceding decade, was a legacy of the inadequacies of the 1998 Government of Wales Act. The Richard Commission, the 2006 Government of Wales Act, and ultimately the 2011 referendum all followed in a direct line of descent from the failure of the 1998 Act to establish a coherent and sustainable form of home rule for Wales within the UK.

Yet this answer, in many respects, simply raises more questions. Why was the 1998 Act so inadequate? Why were the remedies to it proposed by the Richard Commission not enacted as a package by the UK government? And why did the 2006 Government of Wales Act establish an untested and convoluted process for transferring powers to the National Assembly for Wales, while simultaneously providing for the referendum to abolish those structures that it was thereby putting in place? As we indicated in chapter two, to arrive at remotely satisfactory answers to these questions one has to look further back into history, and also take into account some of the long-term structural imbalances in Welsh political life. Wales has long witnessed one-party domination in its politics: first with the Liberals as the hegemonic force, then – after an inter-war interregnum – Labour becoming dominant. Such is not, generally, a healthy form of democratic politics. And the development of devolution in Wales constitutes, we would suggest, one of the clearest illustrations of the pathologies of one-partyism. As we have demonstrated, all the major decisions on the models of devolution to be pursued have been made within the Labour Party; the decisions made have reflected the internal politics and balance of forces within that party. Indeed it was not until after the 1997 referendum that any serious attempt was made to involve other parties or wider civil society in a general discussion about how devolved government might operate. Moreover, even after a broad-based process did eventually generate a blueprint for effective devolved government – through the work of the Richard Commission – the progress of this agenda has been limited and conditional on satisfying various constituencies with the Labour Party. Indeed, had it not been for the way that a semi-proportional voting system at the devolved level has, on occasion, empowered other political actors, progress would have almost certainly been more limited. As we have already seen, the establishment of the Richard Commission itself was the result of the Labour–Liberal Democrat coalition agreement of 2000. And as was discussed in chapter four, the timing of the referendum on a move to Part IV of the 2006 Act was a condition of the coalition agreement between Labour and Plaid Cymru in 2007.

Beguiled by the deliberations of American constitution makers as outlined in the remarkable *Federalist Papers* – a staple of undergraduate courses – students of politics may well have a tendency to idealize the thought processes and motivations that lie behind foundational moments in the development of a political system. In reality, of course, politics is always more complicated and messy than that. Pragmatic concerns must inevitably play a central role at all major junctures – yes, even in America's Federal Convention of 1787 or, for that matter, Scotland's equivalent two centuries later. It will not do, therefore, to indulge in facile condemnation of those dramatis personae most centrally involved in the constitutional journey on which devolved Wales has embarked on the basis of their failure to live up to some impossible ideal. But equally, we should not shy away from recognizing the ways in which one-party dominance has impacted, and arguably distorted, the political development of contemporary Wales. There can certainly be no understanding as to why Wales ended up having the constitutionally unnecessary referendum that occurred in March 2011 unless we first confront the structural reality of party dominance.

Campaigners and voters: what the referendum tells us about politics in Wales

The 2011 Welsh referendum was probably unnecessary. Constitutionally it might even be termed frivolous. But it doesn't necessarily follow from this, and nor is it true, that the referendum was of no consequence. Perhaps the people of Wales should not have been asked to make the choice placed before them. But they were, and what happened matters in several respects.

One of the respects in which the referendum matters is for what the campaign and vote tell us about the nature of contemporary Welsh politics. We suggest that several significant lessons can be drawn here. A first lesson is simply the extent to which devolution has become accepted across the political, socio-economic and cultural elites of Wales. There was no substantial body of people within such elites who were ready and willing to voice opposition to a Yes vote in the referendum. This may be, as some from the No camp suggested, because those opposed to advancing devolution were fearful of the consequences of such public opposition. It may be that they wished to avoid association with what increasingly looked like a lost cause. But a more plausible explanation may be the rather simpler one that the principle of devolution is no longer a matter of widespread controversy. We have discussed at various points in the book the process by which that has come to be the case. And we should certainly note that, as we will discuss further below, support for the principle of devolution does not mean that there is no room for future disagreement on the details of what it should look like. But the basic point stands: to an extent that was very difficult to imagine in the 1990s, it has become widely accepted among social and political elites that Wales will and should have a significant degree of self-government.

A second important lesson from the referendum concerns how it was fought. If the holding of this referendum reflected, more than anything else, the enduring influence of one-partyism in Welsh politics, the conduct of the campaign demonstrated the growing acceptance and practice of a somewhat more pluralistic form of politics. It was noticeable that the different parties, and particularly the two most substantial contributors of time and effort to the Yes cause, Labour and Plaid Cymru, were able to work together far more easily in the cause of promoting devolution than they had managed in 1979 or even in 1997. Inevitably, there were some tensions, both in the national Yes campaign and at times at the local level. But these were the exception rather than the rule. Even the Conservatives, while in general making a rather modest contribution to the campaign, played a very different role from 1997 when they were the hostile 'other' against which the Yes forces were campaigning.

Of course the referendum offered rather favourable circumstances for cross-party cooperation: there was an obvious incentive to seek the broadest possible coalition of support behind the Yes campaign. Circumstances over the following few years will likely push in the opposite direction, with a single-party Labour government in Cardiff having at least some political incentive to pursue an antagonistic relationship with the parties controlling power in London, amidst a UK-wide context of growing competition for increasingly scarce resources. But the broad direction of travel since the creation of the National Assembly, through its various periods of coalition and minority government, has been towards the parties becoming more ready to consider working together in various ways. The relative harmony that prevailed within the Yes camp in the run-up to the referendum stands as an exemplar of the new political culture to which the National Assembly and its semi-proportional electoral system are slowly giving rise.

A third lesson about contemporary Welsh politics comes from how people voted in the referendum. The result strongly confirmed the changes in public attitudes since the 1997 referendum which research had long been pointing to. Continuing opponents of devolution had often questioned the public endorsement given to devolution in 1997, arguing – with considerable justification – that in only slightly different circumstances the result would have been a No, and that a margin of fewer than 7,000 votes on a 50.1 per cent turnout indicated very limited enthusiasm for devolution among the Welsh people. Surveys subsequent to 1997 had identified steadily declining opposition to devolution, particularly among those groups that had been most heavily opposed, and growing support from 2001 onwards for taking devolution further. But this evidence was often viewed sceptically or even dismissed outright. Such arguments can have little remaining credibility. The referendum result confirmed that devolution is no longer problematic to most people in Wales. It also confirmed that support for devolution has grown most in those areas where it was originally weakest, as attitudes have become more homogenous across Wales.

Though there is little remaining room for reasonable doubt about the breadth of public support for devolution in Wales, somewhat more questionable may be the depth of those attitudes. Do the devolved institutions enjoy the 'diffuse support' that many scholars consider necessary for their legitimacy to be regarded as wholly secure?[2] Here, our knowledge is unavoidably limited by the circumstances under which devolution has operated. We have limited experience of the sort of context identified as important by many scholars who have studied institutional legitimacy.[3] What would happen if Wales were ever to pass through an extended period where those in authority in Cardiff were closely associated with deeply unpopular policies or actions? Would people respond to this by seeking only to challenge those in power within the devolved institutions? Or would they begin to question the worth of those institutions themselves? But such circumstances seem likely to remain hypothetical: as we have seen, the public in Wales tend to associate the devolved bodies with positive policy developments, and lay most blame going on government in London. And until or unless circumstances provide devolution with such an ultimate test, the 2011 referendum has surely settled the issue of the public acceptance of devolution in Wales. Devolution increasingly looks like the settled will of the Welsh people.

Neges Cymru: what Wales tells us about referendums

March 2011 was far from being Wales's first experience of a referendum. And considered from a global perspective, Wales contributed but one more example to the increasingly frequent use of referendums as a form of democratic political decision making. Yet, while they occur with steadily increasing frequency across the democratic world, referendums remain rather less well understood than do elections. Can the experience of Wales in 2011 contribute anything to our broader understanding of how direct democracy does, or should, work?

There are several areas in which the Welsh experience may offer some valuable lessons. A first, unsurprisingly, is that of public participation. It is well established that turnout rates in elections have been declining in recent times within many established democracies, including the UK. It is also well established that participation levels in referendums tend to be lower than in elections (except in those instances where a referendum is held simultaneous to an election). It is rather less well established under what circumstances – other than under a system of compulsory voting – referendum turnout rates are likely to be higher or lower. But the experience of Wales indicates fairly clearly that engaging with and motivating the electorate is likely to be more difficult if the referendum is framed around a specific question that is difficult for the public to comprehend. The main lesson that Wales might be said to offer on turnout is that if you wish to engage most of the public in a referendum, you need to present them with clear alternatives so that the consequences of a Yes or a No vote can be readily understood. It is likely also to help engage people in the process if those alternatives constitute different sides of some sort of principled difference. Such was not the case in Wales. Indeed, as we have suggested previously, much about the 2011 Welsh referendum might almost have been designed to elicit a low level of public participation. In this respect, Wales in 2011 offers a useful negative role model to the rest of the democratic world: it was an example of How Not To Do It.

More positive lessons can be drawn, however, when we consider those who did vote. The experience of Wales in 2011 shows that it is possible for the majority of people who vote in a referendum to do so on the basis of their views on the issue at stake, and to do so in a reasonably considered manner. There are abundant less positive examples across the world. In addition to those unhappy cases where voting is actually coerced or fraudulent, there are also plenty of instances where referendum votes appear to have been cast primarily in line with tribal, racial, religious or other affiliations; where the referendum seems to have become a form of 'second order' national election, used to issue a verdict on an unpopular national government or leader; or where a highly effective campaign, perhaps underpinned by substantial financial resources unavailable to the other side, has managed to change voting intentions significantly prior to the vote, often by playing on matters of marginal relevance to the decision actually being made in the referendum.

On the whole, Wales managed to avoid following these negative examples. Most of those who voted seem to have done primarily on the basis of their views on matters directly relevant to the question on the ballot. Moreover, their behaviour reflected a state of public opinion on devolution that had been pretty settled for almost a decade, rather than one that had been swayed by a slick campaign run over a few weeks. Why was Wales able to achieve this? A key point is surely that while the specific question on the ballot was rather difficult to understand, it related to a broader issue that had been a matter of public discussion in Wales – though only rarely at the forefront of public consciousness – for a long period of time. People had been given ample time to develop some sort of general attitude towards the issue, namely whether or not more powers should be invested at the devolved level. And the lengthy process of preparation for the referendum itself helped many people work out how the rather confusing specific question on the ballot related to their more general attitude. In sum, the experience of Wales suggests that giving people time to learn about and think through the issues matters for the basis on which they will cast their vote.

In this respect the contrast with the other referendum in 2011 in which the people of Wales were able to vote – the UK-wide ballot on the possible adoption of the alternative vote (AV) for UK general elections – is rather stark. Although electoral reform has been an issue of interest to a certain cognoscenti for many decades, it has rarely been a matter of widespread public debate. And the short campaign period leading up to the referendum gave rather little time in which to engage and educate the public about the wider issues at stake, and their relationship to the specific question on the ballot paper. In these circumstances, and especially given that the ballot was taking place on the same day as devolved and local elections, it is rather unsurprising that many people in the AV referendum appear to have cast their votes based on something other than a settled view on the core issue on the ballot – on the basis of their party affiliation, or their attitudes towards leading political figures, such as the then highly unpopular Liberal Democrat leader and deputy prime minister, Nick Clegg.

A final potential lesson of some broader applicability from Wales concerns the constitutional provisions, laws and other regulations that govern the conduct and media coverage of referendums. In a healthy democracy these will provide for a substantial degree of neutrality. That is, the different sides in the referendum will be given equal opportunity to establish, organize and conduct their campaigns – rather than, as has occurred sometimes in less healthy political systems, one side being systematically harassed and obstructed by the forces of the state. In a healthy democracy the machinery and personnel of the state should stand aside from active involvement in the referendum – rather than seeking, by fair means or foul, to ensure the government's preferred outcome. And in a healthy democracy, both sides will be given ample opportunities to communicate with the voters – rather than the population being bombarded with messages from state-sponsored media 'encouraging' them to vote in only one direction. The details of how such neutrality will be sought may differ: for instance, different places take different positions on the extent to which donations and spending on a referendum should be restricted in an attempt to ensure that highly motivated individuals or groups with substantial resources are prevented from dominating the referendum campaign. But the broad outlines of what laws regulating conduct in referendums, of which as the UK's Political Parties, Elections and Referendums Act (PPERA) of 2000 is one instance, should be seeking to achieve are fairly clear.

However, Wales in 2011 demonstrated at least one type of context in which well-intentioned attempts to ensure neutrality in referendums can become problematic. What happens when, as in Wales in 2011, one side in the referendum campaign is too weak to attract substantial numbers of active supporters or to build an effective campaigning organization? Part of the answer to this question almost certainly lies one stage farther back in the process: one should try to ensure that referendums are only held on issues where there are principled differences and strong alternative cases to be made. But if one does have a referendum for which only one side has developed a serious organization, how should this be dealt with? The UK's provisions under PPERA were shown to be deficient in these circumstances. PPERA provides that the lead campaign organizations on both sides should be provided with money to support their organization, should be entitled to a free mail-shot to all registered voters, and should be entitled to some free broadcasting time as well to help them communicate their message to the public. But if these provisions are appropriate – if there is accepted to be a public good, worthy of support from public money, in a referendum campaign being able to communicate its message to the public – then it surely cannot be right that one side should lose all these entitlements if their opponents do not seek, or do not properly qualify for, official recognition as a lead campaign organization? It is bizarre that the provision of this public good be made contingent on the strength, and the behaviour, of their opponents. A similar problem arises with media coverage. It is certainly proper that public service broadcasters should seek to inform the public about the issues at stake in a referendum, and that they should at all times seek to do so with neutrality, rather than propagating one or other cause. But if there is – as there surely is – a public good in one side to the referendum being provided with the time and space to communicate their arguments in their own way to the public, then this good surely cannot be conditional on their opponents also being both willing and able to do the same? If one side to a referendum campaign is too weak or poorly organized to advocate their cause in this way, it cannot be right that they thereby scupper their opponents' ability to do so. In these respects, the experience of Wales in 2011 indicated at least some ways in which laudable attempts to ensure neutrality and fairness in referendums can have unforeseen, and largely negative, consequences.

A settled constitution?

Following the result of the March 2011 referendum, the National Assembly for Wales now enjoys primary legislative powers across twenty areas of public policy as specified by the terms of Schedule 7 of the 2006 Government of Wales Act. More colloquially, Wales has a law-making parliament. However low-key the referendum campaign, however narrow the question on the ballot paper and however underwhelming initial political responses to the result, this is surely a momentous development. Quite how momentous remains to be seen. Much depends, of course, on what Wales's political class and broader society make of the new possibilities that now exist. But this is not simply a Welsh story. There is a wider transformation of territorial government within the United Kingdom within which Welsh developments, including the 2011 referendum, must be placed. And the ultimate significance of developments in Wales will be shaped as much by this broader process as by decisions in Wales. Thus, while our final reflections on the likely impact of the referendum initially focus on Wales, we conclude by considering the wider UK picture.

Since 1997, many have referred to one or another of Wales's various devolutionary dispensations as a 'settlement'. This is wholly inappropriate. As was discussed in chapter two, Welsh devolution has been characterized by almost constant constitutional upheaval, such that the term 'settlement' has been more aspirational than accurate. However, the principal author of the 2006 Act, Peter Hain, argued that this was legislation to establish the parameters of devolved government for a generation. It is worth asking, therefore, to what extent we can expect the move to Part IV to herald a period of stability? In our estimation: not at all. There are several major issues that the 2006 Act, and the referendum it caused, simply did not address. But failing to deal with them did not make them go away.

Some issues would probably have found their place on to the political agenda even if the move to Part IV had not taken place. But the referendum result makes them even more salient. Thus far, the National Assembly has been a spending institution with no significant power to raise its own money. This was always something of an anomaly, and it has come under increasing scrutiny in recent times. This is partly because of developments outside Wales. The way in which the 'unionist' parties have chosen to couch the case for giving meaningful tax powers to the Scottish Parliament in terms of 'accountability' makes it difficult to resist extending the same argument, and powers, to Wales.[4] Why, after all, should Scotland's law-making Parliament be financially 'accountable' but Wales's law-making National Assembly not?

Another factor here is the significant squeeze on public spending that the UK government is seeking to implement between 2011 and 2015. The UK Treasury has historically opposed devolving tax powers. But in a harsh financial climate, the hope that fiscal devolution might impose greater financial discipline on former clients now appears to trump traditional concerns about loss of control. But there are also specifically Welsh factors at work. Another outcome of the One Wales coalition deal was the Holtham Commission process which addressed the funding of devolved government.[5] This confirmed that Wales was indeed underfunded (in terms of relative need) by the Barnett formula – an argument that Plaid Cymru, in particular, had long advanced. But the most important long-term impact of Holtham may be that its final report, like the Richard Commission Report, becomes a reference point for future debate, and a yardstick against which any concrete proposals will be measured. However politically inconvenient, the quality and clarity of thinking contained within Holtham is such that its conclusions cannot be ignored.

Another issue already in the ether prior to the referendum was scrutiny. The Richard Commission pointed to the relatively small size of the National Assembly and questioned whether so few backbenchers could properly scrutinize primary legislation or hold to account a government operating on the basis of such powers. They recommended increasing the size of the Assembly to eighty members. This was a compelling case; one that has never been addressed properly, let alone refuted. Proponents of the status quo have pointed to the possibility of adopting more effective working practices in the Assembly. They may well have a case that resources will now be freed up by the disappearance of the time-consuming LCO system. But there remain fundamental constraints imposed by the small numbers of Assembly Members. Few will be eager to make the case for more politicians, but the enhanced status of the Assembly may embolden some to take this issue more seriously.

The scope of the National Assembly's powers is another issue that, though not directly relevant to the referendum, may be affected by its result. Powers over police and criminal justice are obvious possibilities to be devolved, given the fine dividing line between them and those areas of social policy for which the National Assembly is already responsible. Will a National Assembly that now enjoys greater legitimacy after the March referendum result feel emboldened to demand an expansion of its areas of competence?

Even more fundamental is the question of a Welsh legal jurisdiction. First Minister Carwyn Jones has consistently argued since 2007 that a move to Part IV would inevitably lead to the establishment of a separate Welsh jurisdiction.[6] The kernel of his argument has not changed in the interim: 'I'm not aware of any other part of the world where two primary lawmaking institutions exist within the same jurisdiction, passing laws in the same areas of responsibility.'[7] One might argue that this logic applied once Part III of the 2006 Act came into force: the moment the National Assembly became a primary law-making institution. But this argument is greatly strengthened by the coming into force of Part IV. That the argument has such a powerful advocate is also significant.

This leads to another potential issue that one can confidently expect to form part of the Welsh political agenda in the coming years. That the framework established by Part IV of the 2006 Act will prove more adequate than that created by Part III was not questioned by any serious commentator on devolution during the referendum campaign. Given the manifest failings of the latter, this is hardly surprising. But remaining largely unquestioned was the adequacy of the Part IV model of devolving power compared to other alternatives. That this was unquestioned is hardly surprising. The referendum was a take-it-or-leave-it proposition: no alternative to the Part IV model was on offer. But we can reasonably expect this now to change: especially given that one obvious alternative is operating in another part of the United Kingdom, namely Scotland.

As previously mentioned in chapter two, the model of devolution established by Part IV is closer to that proposed for Scotland by the 1978 Scotland Act than that which was finally established two decades later by its 1998 successor. The latter is a reserved powers model of devolution: meaning that the Scottish Parliament has general legislative competence in all areas not specifically reserved to Westminster or otherwise debarred by the United Kingdom's international treaty obligations. The new Welsh model, like the 1978 Scotland model, is a conferred powers model of devolution: the National Assembly can only legislate in areas where powers have been conferred upon it by Schedule 7 of the 2006 Act. This difference may seem esoteric, but it may yet prove consequential. To understand why one must ask why the basic design of the Scottish model was altered between 1978 and 1998.

This was actually a fairly late change to the proposed scheme of Scottish devolution.[8] The Scottish Constitutional Convention's various reports assumed that the conferred powers model would be the basis of the division of powers between London and Edinburgh.[9] The intervention of the Constitution Unit – and in particular its 1996 publication *Scotland's Parliament: Fundamentals for a New Scotland Act* – appears to have proven decisive.[10] Reviewing arguments voiced in Scotland in the 1970s but largely ignored at the time; the views of civil servants who had worked on the 1970s legislation; and evidence from the operation of the Stormont Parliament (which had been founded on a reserved powers model), the report concluded that a conferred powers model would likely cause unnecessary complexity and confusion. A memorandum from the Scottish Law Commission from 1975 is quoted with evident approval:

> It is of central importance to select the best method of ensuring legal clarity on the scope of devolution. This ... can in our opinion be best achieved, and probably only achieved, by specifying the powers to be retained by the United Kingdom government and, subject to the reservation of ultimate sovereignty to parliament, conferring upon the Assembly residual legislative competence.[11]

Lack of clarity was not likely to prove a legal problem alone. The report's authors were evidently worried about the political implications of the frustrations and conflicts that would surely result. Thus, they strongly advocated the reserved powers model.

This case was sufficiently compelling that Tony Blair's government was persuaded to adopt the reserved powers model as the basis for the Scotland Act 1998. This raises the question of why, only a few years later, the same government adopted the conferred powers model for a future Welsh legislative parliament? Even by 2005, the drawbacks and political frustrations associated with the complex and confusing division of powers between Cardiff and London were only too apparent. Why not adopt the more straightforward system that had already proved its value in Scotland? The answer, it seems, was concerns about a Welsh jurisdiction. In the only substantial attempt made to justify adopting the Scotland 1978 model rather than its 1998 successor (examples they refer to specifically), Peter Hain and Rhodri Morgan argued that extending general legislative competence to the National Assembly would inevitably give rise to a situation where courts in Wales would have to operate 'fundamentally different legal principles' from those in England.[12] This in turn would necessitate the establishment of different legal institutions – and a distinctive system of legal education – in and for Wales. As the government did not intend to establish a separate legal jurisdiction for Wales, this was not acceptable. Hence the more constrained conferred powers model.

This is a curious argument. Even under Part IV of the 2006 Act we can expect that, across twenty areas of public policy, courts will soon be applying rather different laws in Wales (we leave it for others to judge the extent to which they embody different legal principles). This will necessitate changes to legal education. Moreover, there have already been considerable institutional changes as the legal system has responded to – indeed, anticipated – the impact of devolution.[13] Hain and Morgan appear to have been engaged in an attempt to head off developments that are anyway inevitable. It is inconceivable that these arguments will not elicit more critical attention now that the Part IV system has been enacted.[14]

To summarize, there is clearly a substantial agenda of further potential constitutional change to be reckoned with. Not all of this is directly attributable to the referendum result. But the referendum has brought much of this agenda into sharper focus. The

UK government's decision to establish a Commission to consider the future of Welsh devolution in the wake of the Yes result provides an obvious route by which some or all of these issues might be considered.[15] We cannot anticipate how such a Commission will address these issues, nor how various political actors will respond to any Commission proposals. But it requires no great political insight to predict that the role of a referendum (or even referendums) in approving any further changes will form an important part of the debate. The Holtham Commission has already declared that the Scottish precedent of 1997 indicates that a referendum would be needed before tax powers are devolved to Wales; then Justice Secretary Jack Straw made an (unscripted) suggestion that the establishment of a Welsh jurisdiction should be subject to another referendum.[16] As we have seen earlier, the UK's practice with regards to referendums has been so flexible that precedents can be identified for almost any decision ultimately taken concerning their use (or non-use). But one might reasonably hope that the March 2011 experience of holding a referendum on a technical question of little apparent relevance to the daily lives of the electorate will serve as a salutary warning to those quick to demand a poll before change can be enacted.

Ultimately, however, much will depend on the wider political context across the United Kingdom as a whole. The UK is entering a crucial period. In Scotland, following the sweeping SNP victory in the May 2011 devolved election, the Scottish government is (at the time of writing) preparing for a referendum on independence towards the end of its five-year term. It remains to be seen whether or not the UK government will seek to assuage Scottish opinion in the interim by devolving further powers above and beyond that envisaged by the current Scotland Bill. If it does choose to do so, it is quite possible that there will be spillover effects for the other devolved territories. And while we may safely assume that Wales will not feature much in the debate that precedes the Scottish referendum, its result will be enormously consequential for all the nations of the UK, Wales certainly not excepted.

Less dramatic, but perhaps equally consequential in its potential effect on Wales, is the commission that that the current Conservative–Liberal Democrat coalition administration in London has pledged to establish in order to 'consider' the West Lothian question.[17] The outcome of the 2011 referendum has meant that

the ambiguities inherent in the previous devolutionary dispensations of secondary powers and attenuated primary powers have now
been swept away. It should now be quite clear: the West Lothian
question applies fully to Wales. Thus, any attempts to address the
question by constraining or curtailing the role of non-English MPs
in the scrutiny of legislation that applies only to England will inevitably affect Welsh MPs. Even if the government shies away from any
fundamental changes for now, it is hard to envisage that the West
Lothian question can remain unanswered indefinitely. Any UK
general election result that reprises those of 1964 or February 1974
– when the Conservatives had a majority of seats in England but
Labour formed a government on the basis of its strength elsewhere
– will likely provoke a full-blown constitutional crisis.

Herein lies one of the most striking, yet apparently unnoticed,
consequences of the March referendum. Since the so-called Acts of
Union of the sixteenth century, Wales has been an integral part of
the English core of what was eventually to become the United
Kingdom of Great Britain and Northern Ireland. While that position may have begun to change with the establishment of the Welsh
Office in 1964, and while the establishment of the National Assembly
heralded an even more momentous change, it is the creation of a
Welsh legislative parliament that signals the definitive rupture.
Wales is still, of course, part of the United Kingdom, but it is now
clearly a constituent national unit in its own right, rather than an
addendum to an 'England and Wales' unit. By extension, the referendum was also the moment at which the English polity emerged,
or more accurately re-emerged, as an incubus within the UK state
– a development that we may plausibly anticipate will have significant consequences. To repeat our argument: the referendum held
in Wales on 3 March 2011 may well have been unnecessary, but it
does not follow that it was inconsequential. And its consequences
will continue to affect not only Wales, but also the remainder of the
United Kingdom.

Appendix 1
The 2011 Welsh Referendum Study

The 2011 Welsh Referendum Study was funded by a grant from the Economic and Social Research Council of the United Kingdom (Grant RES-000–22–4496). The co-directors of the Study were Professor Roger Scully and Professor Richard Wyn Jones.

Survey fieldwork for the study was conducted by YouGov, via the internet. The pre-referendum wave of the study included 3,029 respondents; 2,569 of these (or 84.8 per cent) also participated in the post-referendum wave. All data used in the analysis were weighted for representativeness of the registered adult electorate in Wales, using YouGov's standard weighting factors which adjust for a range of demographic and attitudinal factors, including age, gender, region, social class, newspaper readership and past vote.

WRS data, as well as further details on the study, are available to download at: *http://www.aber.ac.uk/en/interpol/research/research-projects/welshelectionstudy/aboutthestudy/*.

Appendix 2
Full details on all referendum polls discussed in chapter three

Poll	% Yes	% No	% DK/NR	% 'Yes' lead
BBC/ICM, June 2007[a]	47	44	9	3
BBC/ICM, February 2008[b]	49	42	9	7
National Assembly/GfK NOP, June–July 2008[c]	46	32	22	14
All Wales Convention/GfK NOP, Nov–Dec 2008[d]	49	35	16	14
BBC/ICM, February 2009[e]	52	39	9	13
IWP-WGC/YouGov, July 2009[f]	44	36	21	8
All Wales Convention/GfK NOP, July 2009[g]	47	37	16	10
IWP-WGC/YouGov, October 2009[h]	42	37	21	5
ITV Wales/YouGov, November 2009[i]	51	30	20	21
ITV Wales/YouGov, January 2010[j]	49	32	20	17
BBC/ICM, February 2010[k]	56	35	10	21
ITV Wales/YouGov, March 2010[l]	53	31	16	22
NAW/YouGov, March 2010[m]	50	34	17	16
IWP-WGC/YouGov, May 2010[n]	51	32	18	19
ITV Wales/YouGov, June 2010[o]	55	28	17	27
ITV Wales/YouGov, July 2010[p]	48	34	19	14
ITV Wales/YouGov, August 2010[q]	48	32	21	16
ITV Wales/YouGov, September 2010[r]	49	30	20	19
ITV Wales/YouGov, October 2010[s]	52	29	20	23
ITV Wales/YouGov, November 2010[t]	48	30	22	18
BBC/ICM, November 2010[u]	57	24	18	33
Western Mail/Beaufort, November 2010[v]	60	28	13	32
ITV Wales/YouGov, Dec 2010[w]	46	25	29	21
ITV Wales/YouGov, Jan 2011[x]	49	26	26	23

Poll	% Yes	% No	% DK/NR	% 'Yes' lead
WRS/YouGov, 3–10 Feb 2011ʸ	54	27	19	27
WRS/YouGov, 11–17 Feb 2011ᶻ	52	30	18	22
WRS/YouGov, 11–17 Feb 2011ᴬ	53	29	18	24
ITV Wales/YouGov, 21–3 Feb 2011ᴮ	58	29	13	29
Media Wales/RMG, 25–8 Feb 2011ᶜ	49	22	28	27
ITV Wales/YouGov, 24 Feb–1March 2011ᴰ	61	28	12	33
BBC/ICM, 1 November–2 March 2011ᴱ	60	26	13	34

[a] Telephone poll conducted by ICM for BBC Wales. Number of respondents = 1,001. Question asked: 'If there were to be a referendum on turning the National Assembly for Wales into a full law-making Welsh Parliament with tax-raising powers, how would you vote?'

[b] Telephone poll conducted by ICM for BBC Wales. Number of respondents = 1,210. Question asked: 'If there were to be a referendum on turning the National Assembly for Wales into a full law-making Welsh Parliament, how would you vote?'

[c] Telephone poll conducted by GfK NOP for the National Assembly Commission. Number of respondents = 2,538. Question asked: 'If there were to be a referendum tomorrow on giving the National Assembly for Wales full law-making powers (similar to those held by the Scottish Parliament) how would you vote?'

[d] Telephone poll conducted by GfK NOP, as part of work to support the All-Wales Convention. Number of respondents = 1,650. Question asked: 'If there were to be a referendum tomorrow on giving the National Assembly for Wales full law-making powers in these areas [specified in previous questions], how would you vote?'

[e] Telephone poll conducted by ICM for BBC Wales. Number of respondents = 1,000. Question asked: 'If there were to be a referendum on turning the National Assembly for Wales into a full law-making Welsh Parliament, how would you vote?'

[f] Internet poll conducted by YouGov for Institute of Welsh Politics, Aberystwyth University and Wales Governance Centre, Cardiff University. Number of respondents = 1,023. Question asked: 'If there were to be a referendum tomorrow on giving the National Assembly for Wales full law-making powers how would you vote?'

[g] Telephone poll conducted by GfK NOP, as part of work to support the All-Wales Convention. Number of respondents = 1,553. Question asked: 'If there were to be a referendum tomorrow on giving the National Assembly for Wales full law-making powers in these areas [specified in previous questions], how would you vote?'

[h] Internet poll conducted by YouGov for Institute of Welsh Politics, Aberystwyth University and Wales Governance Centre, Cardiff University. Number of respondents = 1,078. Question asked: 'If there were to be a referendum tomorrow on giving the National Assembly for Wales full law-making powers how would you vote?'

[i] Internet poll conducted by YouGov for ITV Wales. Number of respondents = 1,080. Question asked: 'If there were to be a referendum tomorrow on giving the National Assembly for Wales increased law-making powers how would you vote?'

[j] Internet poll conducted by YouGov for ITV Wales. Number of respondents = 1,137. Question asked: 'If there were to be a referendum tomorrow on giving the National Assembly for Wales increased law-making powers how would you vote?'

[k] Telephone poll conducted by ICM for BBC Cymru-Wales. Number of respondents = 1,000. Question asked: 'You may have seen or heard that Assembly Members have voted in favour of holding a referendum on giving the National Assembly full law-making powers. If there were to be a referendum, how would you vote?'

[l] Internet poll conducted by YouGov for ITV Wales. Number of respondents = 1,131. Question asked: 'If there were to be a referendum tomorrow on giving the National Assembly for Wales increased law-making powers how would you vote?'

[m] Internet poll conducted by YouGov for NAW Commission. Number of respondents = 1,002. Question asked: 'If there were a referendum held tomorrow on increasing the law-making powers of the National Assembly for Wales how would you vote?'

[n] Internet poll conducted by YouGov for IWP-WGC. Number of respondents = 1,475. Question asked: 'If there were to be a referendum held tomorrow on giving the National Assembly for Wales increased law-making powers how would you vote?'

[o]. Internet poll conducted by YouGov for ITV Wales. Number of respondents = 1,001. Question asked: 'If there were to be a referendum tomorrow on giving the National Assembly for Wales increased law-making powers how would you vote?'

[p] Internet poll conducted by YouGov for ITV Wales. Number of respondents = 1,002. Question asked: 'If there were to be a referendum tomorrow on giving the National Assembly for Wales increased law-making powers how would you vote?'

[q] Internet poll conducted by YouGov for ITV Wales. Number of respondents = 1,007. Question asked: 'If there were to be a referendum tomorrow on giving the National Assembly for Wales increased law-making powers how would you vote?'

[r] Internet poll conducted by YouGov for ITV Wales. Number of respondents = 1088. Question asked: 'If there were to be a referendum tomorrow on giving the National Assembly for Wales increased law-making powers how would you vote?'

[s] Internet poll conducted by YouGov for ITV Wales. Number of respondents = 1,012. Question asked: 'If there were to be a referendum tomorrow on giving the National Assembly for Wales increased law-making powers how would you vote?'

[t] Internet poll conducted by YouGov for ITV Wales. Number of respondents = 1,018. Question asked: 'If there were to be a referendum tomorrow on giving the National Assembly for Wales increased law-making powers how would you vote?'

[u] Telephone poll conducted by ICM for BBC Cymru-Wales. Number of respondents = 1,000. Question asked: 'If there were to be a referendum tomorrow on giving the National Assembly for Wales increased law-making powers how would you vote?'

[v] Face-to-face poll conducted by Beaufort Research. Number of respondents = 1,012. Question asked: 'Do you want the Assembly now to be able to make laws on all matters in the 20 subject areas it has powers for?'

[w] Internet poll conducted by YouGov for ITV Wales. Number of respondents = 1,005. Question asked: 'And in this referendum on giving the National Assembly for Wales increased law-making powers how will you vote?'

[x] Internet poll conducted by YouGov for ITV Wales. Number of respondents = 1,113. Question asked: 'And in this referendum on giving the National Assembly for Wales increased law-making powers how will you vote?'. (NB. Results for this poll, unlike in YouGov polls prior to 2011, were weighted by likelihood to vote.)

[y] Internet poll conducted by YouGov for the Welsh Referendum Study (first week of rolling pre-referendum wave). Number of respondents = 634. Question asked: 'And in this referendum on giving the National Assembly for Wales increased law-making powers how will you vote?' Results weighted by likelihood to vote.

[z] Internet poll conducted by YouGov for the Welsh Referendum Study (second week of rolling pre-referendum wave). Number of respondents = 727. Question asked: 'And in this referendum on giving the National Assembly for Wales increased law-making powers how will you vote?' Results weighted by likelihood to vote.

[A] Internet poll conducted by YouGov for the Welsh Referendum Study (third week of rolling pre-referendum wave). Number of respondents = 694. Question asked: 'And in this referendum on giving the National Assembly for Wales increased law-making powers how will you vote?' Results weighted by likelihood to vote.

[B] Internet poll conducted by YouGov for ITV Wales (for use in S4C programme *Y Byd ar Bedwar*). Number of respondents = 1,003. Question asked: 'And in this referendum on giving the National Assembly for Wales increased law-making powers how will you vote?'. Results weighted by likelihood to vote.

[C] Telephone poll conducted by RMG for Media Wales. Number of respondents = 1,000. Question asked: 'Do you intend to vote Yes or No?' [following previous question 'Do you intend to vote in the upcoming referendum for further law-making powers for the National Assembly?']

[D] Internet poll conducted by YouGov for ITV Wales. Number of respondents = 1,036. Question asked: 'And in this referendum on giving the National Assembly for Wales increased law-making powers how will you vote?' (Results weighted by likelihood to vote.)

[E] Telephone poll conducted by ICM for BBC Cymru-Wales. Number of respondents = 1,003. Question asked not stated.

Appendix 3
Models of referendum participation and vote choice

Below are listed full results (including logistic regression coefficient and robust standard errors) for the multivariate analysis discussed and reported in chapter six.

A. Models of Referendum Participation

i. Social background model

Variable	Coefficient (standard error)
Female (Reference category: male)	−.25 (.12)
Age group	
(Reference category: 65+)	
18–24	−2.48 (.30)**
25–34	−1.90 (.26)**
35–44	−1.42 (.26)**
45–54	−1.08 (.25)**
55–64	−.52 (.24)
Education level	
(Reference category: no qualifications)	
GSCE or equivalent	.31 (.25)
A level or equivalent	.25 (.26)
University or equivalent	.77 (.22)*
Other qualifications	.11 (.23)
Middle class	.36 (.14)*
Household income	
(Reference category: < £10k p.a.)	
£10k–£14,999	.18 (.23)
£15k–£19,999	.00 (.22)
£20k–£29,999	.11 (.19)

£30k–£39,999	−.02 (.22)
£40k–£59,999	.05 (.22)
£60k plus	.31 (.31)
Housing status	
(Reference category: home owner)	
Council/HA renter	.52 (.26)
Private renter	−.50 (.18)*
Welsh language	
(Reference category: non-speaker)	
Fluent speaker	.55 (.24)
Non-fluent speaker	.26 (.15)
National identity	
(Reference category: none)	
Welsh not British	.94 (.24)**
More Welsh than British	.89 (.23)**
Equally Welsh and British	1.02 (.22)**
More British than Welsh	.63 (.26)
British not Welsh	.50 (.23)
Constant	.69 (.32)
Number of respondents	2,569
McFadden R^2	.14
% correctly predicted	73.0
AIC#	2,801.00

* $p < .01$; ** $p < .001$.

ii. Political attitudes model

Variable	Coefficient (standard error)
Political interest	
(Reference category: not at all interested)	
Very interested	1.20 (.33)**
Fairly interested	.32 (.25)
Not very interested	.29 (.28)
Duty to vote?	
(Reference category: neither agree nor disagree)	
Strongly agree	3.14 (.22)**
Agree	1.44 (.20)**
Disagree	−.36 (.32)

Strongly disagree	−.34 (.42)
Referendum importance	
(Reference category: none at all)	
A great deal	2.03 (.43)**
A fair amount	1.28 (.25)**
Not very much	.54 (.25)
Constitutional preference	
(Reference category: don't know)	
No devolution	.82 (.35)
NAW fewer powers	.18 (.45)
Leave things as they are	.45 (.32)
NAW more powers	.69 (.32)
Independence	.81 (.43)
WAG performance	
(Reference category: neutral)	
Positive	.06 (.20)
Negative	.51 (.25)
Constant	−2.67 (.32)**
Number of respondents	2,569
McFadden R^2	.36
% correctly predicted	81.6
AIC#	2,068.84

* p < .01; ** p < .001.

iii. Party and campaign model

Variable	Coefficient (standard error)
Contacted during campaign	.38 (.23)
Party supporter	
(Reference category: none)	
Labour	.69 (.14)**
Conservative	.50 (.18)*
Lib Dems	.68 (.34)
Plaid Cymru	2.85 (.51)**
Other	.71 (.41)
Constant	.36 (.08)**

Number of respondents	2,569
McFadden R^2	.04
% correctly predicted	68.7
AIC#	3,073.40

* p < .01; ** p < .001.

iv. Composite model

Variable	Coefficient (standard error)
Age group	
18–24	−2.07 (.37)**
25–34	−1.15 (.30)**
35–44	−.98 (.29)*
45–54	−.61 (.28)
55–64	−.29 (.27)
Education level	
(Reference category: no qualifications)	
GSCE or equivalent	.23 (.31)
A level or equivalent	.16 (.31)
University or equivalent	.42 (.27)
Other qualifications	−.35 (.28)
Middle class	.17 (.17)
Housing status	
(Reference category: home owner)	
Council/HA renter	.51 (.28)
Private renter	−.61 (.24)
National identity	
Welsh not British	.78 (.33)
More Welsh than British	.67 (.31)
Equally Welsh and British	.74 (.29)
More British than Welsh	.57 (.35)
British not Welsh	.42 (.30)
Political interest	
(Reference category: not at all interested)	
Very interested	1.51 (.33)**
Fairly interested	.42 (.25)
Not very interested	.30 (.26)

Duty to vote?

Strongly agree	3.12 (.24)**
Agree	1.40 (.22)**
Disagree	−.37 (.39)
Strongly disagree	−.36 (.42)

Referendum importance

A great deal	1.87 (.41)**
A fair amount	1.27 (.24)**
Not very much	.46 (.22)

Party supporter

Labour	−.18 (.19)
Conservative	−.42 (.25)
Lib Dems	.38 (.44)
Plaid Cymru	1.75 (.77)
Other	.85 (.50)
Constant	−1.94 (.45)**
Number of respondents	2,569
McFadden R^2	.42
% correctly predicted	84.1
AIC#	1,929.21

* $p < .01$; ** $p < .001$.

B. Models of referendum voting

i. Social background model

Variable	Coefficient (standard error)
Female (Reference category: male)	−.12 (.14)

Age group
(Reference category: 65+)

18–24	.35 (.36)
25–34	.60 (.29)
35–44	.52 (.24)
45–54	.33 (.23)
55–64	.31 (.19)

Education level
(Reference category: no qualifications)

GSCE or equivalent	.26 (.29)
A level or equivalent	.61 (.32)
University or equivalent	.50 (.26)
Other qualifications	.43 (.27)
Middle class	−.36 (.16)

Household income
(Reference category: < £10k p.a.)

£10k–£14,999	.61 (.24)
£15k–£19,999	.44 (.27)
£20k–£29,999	−.04 (.20)
£30k–£39,999	.07 (.26)
£40k–£59,999	.31 (.22)
£60k plus	.38 (.31)

Housing status
(Reference category: home owner)

Council/HA renter	.15 (.27)
Private renter	−.14 (.25)

Welsh language
(Reference category: non-speaker)

Fluent speaker	.90 (.30)*
Non-fluent speaker	.04 (.16)

National identity
(Reference category: none)

Welsh not British	.75 (.34)
More Welsh than British	.76 (.33)
Equally Welsh and British	−.15 (.30)
More British than Welsh	−1.34 (.33)**
British not Welsh	−1.24 (.31)**
Constant	.10 (.38)
Number of respondents	1,851
McFadden R^2	.14
% correctly predicted	71.7
AIC#	2,090.02

* $p < .01$; ** $p < .001$.

ii. Political model

Variable	Coefficient (standard error)
Political interest	
(Reference category: not at all interested)	
Very interested	.03 (.62)
Fairly interested	−.65 (.60)
Not very interested	−.09 (.61)
Duty to vote?	
(Reference category: neither agree nor disagree)	
Strongly agree	.02 (.46)
Agree	−.03 (.50)
Disagree	−1.16 (.71)
Strongly disagree	−1.55 (.76)
Referendum importance	
(Reference category: none at all)	
A great deal	1.13 (.53)
A fair amount	1.01 (.40)
Not very much	.59 (.39)
Constitutional preference	
(Reference category: don't know)	
No devolution	−2.80 (.49)**
NAW fewer powers	−3.70 (.60)**
Leave things as they are	−1.46 (.44)*
NAW more powers	4.73 (.80)**
Independence	3.16 (.88)**
WAG performance	
(Reference category: neutral)	
Positive	1.14 (.34)**
Negative	−1.52 (.34)**
Party supporter	
Labour	.30 (.30)
Conservative	-1.39 (.37)**
Lib Dems	1.48 (.48)*
Plaid Cymru	.62 (.72)
Other	-.15 (.51)

UK govt performance
(Reference category: neutral)

Positive	.62 (.37)
Negative	.15 (.35)
Constant	.44 (.54)
Number of respondents	1,851
McFadden R^2	.67
% correctly predicted	89.7
AIC#	838.02

* p < .01; ** p < .001.

iii. Composite model

Variable	Coefficient (standard error)
Welsh language	
(Reference category: non-speaker)	
Fluent speaker	.19 (.49)
Non-fluent speaker	−.28 (.25)
National identity	
Welsh not British	−.04 (.60)
More Welsh than British	.51 (.55)
Equally Welsh and British	.11 (.51)
More British than Welsh	−.66 (.55)
British not Welsh	−.43 (.53)
Constitutional preference	
(Reference category: don't know)	
No devolution	−2.47 (.46)**
NAW fewer powers	−3.13 (.59)**
Leave things as they are	−1.27 (.41)*
NAW more powers	4.88 (.79)**
Independence	3.35 (.89)**
WAG performance	
(Reference category: neutral)	
Positive	1.35 (.36)**
Negative	−1.31 (.34)**

Party supporter

Labour	.24 (.28)
Conservative	−1.22 (.35)*
Lib Dems	1.51 (.45)*
Plaid Cymru	.51 (.75)
Other	−.00 (.51)
Constant	.92 (.55)
Number of respondents	1,851
McFadden R^2	.66
% correctly predicted	89.5
AIC#	837.12

* p < .01; ** p < .001.

Notes

1: The Road to the Referendum

1   House of Lords Select Committee on the Constitution, *Referendums in the United Kingdom*, HL Paper 99.

2   The Select Committee's members included the chair, Lord Goodlad (a former government chief whip, shadow leader of the House of Commons and high commissioner to Australia), Lord Irvine of Lairg (a former Lord Chancellor), Baroness Jay of Paddington (a former leader of the House of Lords), Lord Lyell of Markyate (a former Attorney General), Lord Norton of Louth (a distinguished professor of politics), Baroness Quin (a former Minister for Europe), Lord Rodgers of Quarry Bank (a former cabinet minister and co-founder of the SDP), Lord Wallace of Tankerness (Advocate General for Scotland, and former deputy first minister of Scotland) and Lord Woolf (former Master of the Rolls and Lord Chief Justice).

3   Even in Switzerland there is considerable variation in terms of the level of engagement achieved. In November 2004, for example, a referendum asked voters to decide whether or not to allow stem-cell research and whether or not to renew the government's mandate to impose taxes. Turnout was 36 per cent. See *http://www.electionguide.org/country-news.php?ID=207*.

4   The academic literature on the Sunday closing referendums is very limited. For analysis of local referendum results from the 1960s, see H. Carter and J. G. Thomas, 'The referendum on the Sunday opening of licensed premises in Wales as a criterion of a culture region', *Regional Studies*, 3 (1969), 61–71. These local polls are now probably best remembered for the result in Dwyfor in 1996. Having become 'wet' for the first time in 1989, the 1996 result saw Dwyfor revert to 'dry' status on a 9 per cent turnout.

5   *Referendums in the United Kingdom*, paras 109–10, p. 49.

6   Lawrence LeDuc, 'Referendums and initiatives: the politics of direct democracy', in L. LeDuc, R. Niemi and P. Norris (eds), *Comparing Democracies 2: New Challenges in the Study of Elections and Voting* (London: Sage, 2002).

7   David Butler and Iain McLean, 'Referendums', in B. Taylor and K. Thomson (eds), *Scotland and Wales: Nations Again?* (Cardiff: University of Wales Press, 1999).

8   John Allswang, *The Initiative and Referendum in California, 1898–1998* (Stanford: Stanford University Press, 2000).

[9] The 1975 UK referendum is a prime example of the use of a referendum to resolve a divisive issue splitting a governing party. For a general discussion of the issues surrounding the 1975 referendum, see Hugo Young, *This Blessed Plot: Britain and Europe from Churchill to Blair* (London: MacMillan, 1998), especially chapter 8; for a more specific discussion of the referendum itself, see David Butler and Uwe Kitzinger, *The 1975 Referendum* (London: Macmillan, 1976).

[10] Harold Clarke and Allan Kornberg, 'The politics and economics of constitutional choice: voting in Canada's 1992 national referendum', *Journal of Politics*, 56 (1994), 940–62; Jon H. Pammett and Lawrence LeDuc, 'Sovereignty, leadership and voting in the Quebec referendums', *Electoral Studies*, 20 (2001), 265–80; Harold Clarke, Allan Kornberg and Marianne Stewart, 'Referendum voting as political choice', *British Journal of Political Science*, 34 (2004), 345–55.

[11] Richard Wyn Jones and Dafydd Trystan, 'The 1997 Welsh referendum vote', in B. Taylor and K. Thomson (eds), *Scotland and Wales: Nations Again?* (Cardiff: University of Wales Press, 1999), pp. 65–93.

[12] See Clarke and Kornberg, 'The politics and economics of constitutional choice'; Simon Hug and Pascal Sciarini, 'Referendums on European integration: do institutions matter in the voter's decision?', *Comparative Political Studies*, 33 (2000), 3–36.

[13] Shaun Bowler and Todd Donovan, *Demanding Choices: Opinion, Voting, and Direct Democracy* (Ann Arbor: University of Michigan Press, 1998).

[14] Bo Sarlvik, Ivor Crewe, James Alt and Anthony Fox, 'Britain's membership of the EEC: a profile of electoral opinions in the spring of 1974 – with a postscript on the referendum', *European Journal of Political Research*, 4 (1976), 83–113; Roy Pierce, Henry Valen and Ola Listhaug, 'Referendum voting behavior: the Norwegian and British referenda on membership in the European Community', *American Journal of Political Science*, 27 (1983), 43–63.

[15] Mark Franklin, Cees van der Eijk and Michael Marsh, 'Referendum outcomes and trust in government: public support for Europe in the wake of Maastricht', *West European Politics*, 18 (1995), 101–17.

[16] Jack Vowles, 'The politics of electoral reform in New Zealand', *International Political Science Review*, (1995), 95–115.

[17] 'Labour will establish a directly elected council [*sic*] for Wales with function, power and finance to enable it to be an effective force in the life of Wales': Labour Party, *Policies for a Brighter Future for Wales* (1974), p. 2. Note that the nomenclature of Council was soon to be replaced by that of assembly.

[18] For overviews of the history of devolution, see Vernon Bogdanor, *Devolution in the United Kingdom* (updated edn; Oxford: Oxford Paperbacks, 2001); James Mitchell, *Devolution in the UK* (Manchester: Manchester University Press, 2009).

[19] H. M. Drucker and Gordon Brown, *The Politics of Nationalism and Devolution* (London: Longman, 1980), p. 94.

[20] For the most comprehensive account of what is termed as 'The clamour for a referendum', see John Gilbert Evans, *Devolution in Wales: Claims*

and Responses, 1937–1979 (Cardiff: University of Wales Press, 2006), pp. 150–63.

21 *Devolution and Democracy: a Statement by the Executive Committee for Consideration at a Special Delegate Conference, Llandrindod Wells, 22nd June, 1974*, The Labour Party in Wales, part 1.8; *Western Mail*, 24 June 1974.

22 Iain McLean and Alistair McMillan, *State of the Union: Unionism and the Alternatives in the United Kingdom since 1707* (Oxford: Oxford University Press, 2005), p. 127.

23 Iain McLean and Tom Lubbock, 'The curious incident of the guns in the night time: Curragh, Larne and the UK constitution', *Nuffield College Working Papers*, 2007–W4 (8 June 2007), available at *www.nuff.ox.ac.uk/ politics/papers*. Also compare Iain McLean and Alistair McMillan, 'Professor Dicey's contradictions', *Public Law* (autumn 2007), 435–43, with Vernon Bogdanor, 'The consistency of Dicey: a reply to McLean and MacMillan', *Public Law* (spring 2008), 19–20.

24 Cf. Rivka Weill, 'Dicey was not a Diceyan', *Cambridge Law Journal*, 62 (2003), 474–94. Weill offers an ingenuous argument to the effect that Dicey was more consistent in his position on referendums than is usually allowed. She argues that Dicey was increasingly drawn to the idea that some statutes – the Act of Union with Ireland among them – should rightly be regarded as enjoying entrenched, constitutional status and that these should not be overturned by simple parliamentary majority but (in the absence of a House of Lords with veto power) should rather be subject to the popular will. The problem with Weill's position is that it overlooks Dicey's support for what can only be fairly described as acts of treason and sedition. *Pace* Weill, in his position on Ireland, Dicey stands revealed not as some unlikely tribune of popular sovereignty but rather as a diehard adherent of an *ancien régime*.

25 In a parliamentary debate on devolution in 1975, Neil Kinnock famously couched his opposition in the language of class emancipation: 'If I had to use a label of any kind, I should have described myself as a "unionist" … I believe that the emancipation of the class which I have come into this house to represent … can best be achieved in a single nation and in a single economic unity, by which I mean a unit where we can have … the combined strength of working-class people throughout the whole of the United Kingdom brought to bear against any bully, any Executive, any foreign power, any bureaucratic arrangement, be it in Brussels or in Washington': House of Commons Debates, 3 February 1975, column 1031.

26 An important source here is the Constitution Unit report on the prospects for Scottish devolution in the late 1990s, which drew extensively on interviews with members of the Cabinet Office 'Constitution Unit' responsible for the 1970s devolution legislation. See Constitution Unit, *Scotland's Parliament: Fundamentals for a New Scotland Act* (London: Constitution Unit, 1996), and especially p. 29.

27 The referendum was effectively conceded a week after the introduction of the Scotland and Wales Bill in November 1976 as it had become clear that there was no prospect of securing a Second Reading without it.

The guillotine motion was defeated in February 1977. The history of these events is well covered in the volumes cited in n. 18 above. From a specifically Welsh perspective, see also the various contributions by David Foulkes, J. Barry Jones and R. A. Wilford (eds), *The Welsh Veto: the Wales Act 1978 and the Referendum* (Cardiff: University of Wales Press, 1983).

[28] For striking evidence of the lack of enthusiasm around Harold Wilson's cabinet table, see Bernard Donoghue, *Downing Street Diary: With Harold Wilson in No. 10* (London: Jonathan Cape, 2005), pp. 284–7. As for his successor, James Callaghan's biographer, Kenneth O. Morgan, reports that he viewed devolution as a 'necessary evil, to placate Scottish nationalists and Plaid Cymru', and that he 'ploughed the sands of Celtic devolution in the later 1970s without enthusiasm or great commitment': Kenneth O. Morgan, *Callaghan: a Life* (Oxford: Oxford University Press, 1997), p. 510.

[29] Vernon Bogdanor, 'The 40 per cent clause', *Parliamentary Affairs*, 33 (1979), 249–63.

[30] Mari James and Peter D. Lindley, 'The parliamentary passage of the Wales Act 1978', in David Foulkes, J. Barry Jones and R. A. Wilford (eds), *The Welsh Veto: the Wales Act 1978 and the Referendum* (Cardiff: University of Wales Press, 1983), pp. 34–61 (p. 35).

[31] See, inter alia, J. Barry Jones and R. A. Wilford, 'The referendum campaign: 8 February–1 March 1979', in David Foulkes, J. Barry Jones and R. A. Wilford (eds), *The Welsh Veto: the Wales Act 1978 and the Referendum* (Cardiff: University of Wales Press, 1983), pp. 118–52 (118–20). This essay represents the best overview of the 1979 referendum campaign as a whole.

[32] On the internal politics within Plaid Cymru, see Rhys Evans, *Gwynfor Evans: a Portrait of a Patriot* (Talybont: Y Lolfa, 2008).

[33] This point is well made by Geoffrey Evans and Dafydd Trystan, 'Why was 1997 different?', in B. Taylor and K. Thomson (eds), *Scotland and Wales: Nations Again?* (Cardiff: University of Wales Press, 1999), pp. 95–117.

[34] The 'Gang of Six' were Leo Abse, Donald Anderson, Neil Kinnock, Ifor Davies, Alfred Evans and Ioan Evans.

[35] The most accessible English-language version of this trope is the final chapter of Gwyn A. Williams's *When Was Wales: a History of the Welsh* (London: Penguin, 1985).

[36] Kenneth O. Morgan, 'Foreword', in David Foulkes, J. Barry Jones and R. A. Wilford (eds), *The Welsh Veto: the Wales Act 1978 and the Referendum* (Cardiff: University of Wales Press, 1983), p. ix.

[37] Richard Wyn Jones, 'In the shadow of 1979', *Planet: the Welsh Internationalist*, 194 (spring 2009), 8–15.

[38] For accounts of this period, see the varying perspectives contained in, inter alia, Kevin Morgan and Geoff Mungham, *Redesigning Democracy: the Welsh Labour Party and Devolution* (Bridgend: Seren, 2000); Leighton Andrews, *Wales Says Yes* (Bridgend: Seren, 1999); Denis Balsom and J. Barry Jones (eds), *The Road to the National Assembly for Wales* (Cardiff: University of Wales Press, 1999); Richard Wyn Jones and Bethan Lewis,

'The 1997 Welsh devolution referendum', *Politics*, 19 (1999), 37–46. Comparisons with Scotland are developed in David McCrone and Bethan Lewis, 'The Scottish and Welsh devolution campaigns', in B. Taylor and K. Thomson (eds), *Scotland and Wales: Nations Again?* (Cardiff: University of Wales Press, 1999), pp. 17–40; Linsday Paterson and Richard Wyn Jones, 'Does civil society drive constitutional change? The cases of Scotland and Wales', in B. Taylor and K. Thomson (eds), *Scotland and Wales: Nations Again?* (Cardiff: University of Wales Press, 1999), pp. 169–97.

39 Part of the 'normalization' of Plaid Cymru was the growing acceptance of public bilingualism as well as the rapid expansion of Welsh-medium education.

40 The passage of the 1994 Local Government (Wales) Act led to the abolition of the two-tier system of local government that had replaced Wales's thirteen historic counties in 1974. In 1979, the upper layer of eight county councils had been the site of tenacious opposition to devolution. While we cannot assume that this would still have been the case had they survived until 1997, their abolition is widely regarded as having removed a potential roadblock to reform. In addition, the relatively small size of the twenty-two unitary authorities created by the 1994 legislation helped strengthen the case for an elected, all-Wales level of government.

41 As minister of state in the Privy Council Office, it was John Smith who shepherded Labour's devolution proposals through Parliament in the late 1970s. The phrase 'motive force' is taken from Constitution Unit, *Scotland's Parliament*, p. 27.

42 This point is emphasized in Hywel Francis, *History on our Side: Wales and the 1984–85 Miners' Strike* (Cardigan: Parthian Books, 2009).

43 Ron Davies, *Devolution: a Process Not an Event* (Cardiff: Institute of Welsh Affairs, 1999), p. 4.

44 A scholarly analysis of Davies is long overdue. In the interim, see John Osmond's inevitably dated *Welsh Europeans* (Bridgend: Seren, 1996).

45 The case against a referendum was laid out in the policy statement on the party's Assembly proposals adopted by the Labour Party in Wales at its annual conference in Llandudno in May 1995: 'The Commission feels that there is no scope for a referendum as the clearly laid out policy of the Labour Party will leave no room for doubt in the elector's minds. The choice they need to make will be clear': Labour Party Wales, *'Shaping the Vision': an Outline of Labour Party Wales Proposals* (Cardiff: Wales Labour Party, 1995), p. 6.

46 On the referendum decision as viewed through the prism of UK and Scottish Labour politics, see journalist Peter Jones's blow-by-blow account in 'Labour's referendum plan: sell-out or act of faith?', *Scottish Affairs*, 18 (1997), 1–17.

47 Interview with Dave Hill, March 1999.

48 We discuss the terms 'executive' and 'legislative' devolution more fully in chapter two.

49 *Report of the Richard Commission* (2004), p. 262. The report is available at *http://www.richardcommission.gov.uk/*.

[50] Ted Rowlands, 'Annex 8: letter to the chair', *Report of the Richard Commission*, p. 305, emphasis added.

[51] See 2006 Government of Wales Act 93(1): 'an Assembly Measure may make any provision that could be made by an Act of Parliament'.

[52] See, for example, his remarks in the Commons second reading debate: House of Commons Debates, 9 January 2006, col. 45. Peter Hain was Secretary of State for Wales from October 2002 to January 2008 and then again, following an interregnum under Paul Murphy, from June 2009 until Labour's defeat at the May 2010 UK general election.

[53] Anonymous sources.

[54] On the 2003 National Assembly election, see Richard Wyn Jones and Roger Scully, 'Minor tremor but several casualties: the 2003 Welsh election', *British Elections and Parties Review*, 14 (2004), 191–210.

[55] Indeed, given that – partly due to the peculiar circumstances of the 1918 UK election – Labour did not stand candidates in one-quarter of all the Welsh seats, 2007 was in reality Labour's worst ever result in a devolved or parliamentary election in Wales. The year 2007 was also the first time in which Labour's vote share in Wales had not been higher than its vote share in Scotland at a devolved or UK election since 1924.

[56] Roger Scully and Anwen Elias, 'The 2007 Welsh Assembly election', *Regional and Federal Studies*, 18 (2008), 103–9.

[57] The 'One Wales Agreement' is reproduced as an appendix to John Osmond's useful account of the extraordinary interregnum that followed the 2007 National Assembly election, *Crossing the Rubicon: Coalition Politics Welsh Style* (Cardiff: Institute of Welsh Affairs, 2007).

[58] Anonymous sources.

2: The unlikely survival of the platypus: constitution building in Wales

[1] Cited in Vernon Bogdanor, 'Devolution and the constitution,' *Parliamentary Affairs*, 31 (1978), 252–67 (252).

[2] Gwilym Prys Davies, *A Central Welsh Council* (Aberystwyth: Undeb Cymru Fydd/New Wales Union, 1963).

[3] Prys Davies, now Lord Prys Davies, remains a stalwart of what might be termed (without prejudice) the Welsh nationalist wing of the Labour Party. Students of Welsh politics are fortunate in having two volumes of Davies's political memoirs/reflections to draw upon. They are *Llafur y Blynyddoedd* (Dinbych: Gwasg Gee, 1991) and *Cynhaeaf Hanner Canrif: Gwleidyddiaeth Gymreig 1945–2005* (Llandysul: Gomer, 2008).

[4] On Labour's commitment to a Secretary of State the classic account is Kenneth O. Morgan, 'The red dragon and red flag: the cases of Jim Griffiths and Aneurin Bevan', *Modern Wales: Politics, Places and People* (Cardiff: University of Wales Press, 1995), pp. 443–53. On Griffiths's battles with Whitehall, see Ted Rowlands, 'Whitehall's last stand: the establishment of the Welsh Office, 1964', *Contemporary Wales*, 16 (2004), 39–52. On Griffiths more generally, see J. Beverley Smith (ed.), *James*

Griffiths and his Times (Labour Party Wales and the Llanelli Constituency Labour Party, 1978).

[5] See *NUM (South Wales Area) Minutes of the Area Annual Conference held at the Pavilion, Porthcawl, on 10th, 11th, 12th and 15th May 1954*, pp. 449–54. For Griffiths's key speech see pp. 453–4.

[6] The commission draft recommendations were published in 1961 with the final report submitted the following year. See *Report and Proposals of the Local Government Commission for Wales, Presented to the Minister of Housing and Local Government. December, 1962* (London: HMSO, 1963).

[7] *Report on WCL Annual Conference 1966*. Motion approved 21 May 1966.

[8] *Draft White Paper, Local Government in Wales*, April 1967 (Cledwyn Hughes papers, NLW). See especially paras 46–58. The 'New' here is a reference to the previous Council for Wales (initially known as the Council for Wales and Monmouthshire), a nominated body with purely advisory functions that was established in 1948. The most detailed account of the council's activities is E. L. Gibson, *A Study of the Council for Wales and Monmouthshire, 1948–1966* (unpublished LLB, University College of Wales, Aberystwyth, 1968).

[9] *Draft White Paper, Local Government in Wales*, paras 57, 55.

[10] Ibid., para. 54.

[11] *Strengthening of the Welsh Office and the Welsh Council: Memorandum by the Secretary of State for Wales*, 26 March 1968, para. 3. This position was premised on the argument that: 'the present executive responsibilities of the Secretary of State are not wide enough to give him real authority in Wales. Thus he controls less than 3 per cent of the Central Government staff now located in Wales, deals with only a small proportion of Government Spending there and is responsible for only a small proportion of the appointments made and honours given': ibid., para. 7.

[12] Ibid., para. 10.

[13] Ibid., para. 12. The following paragraph – para. 13 – set out three possible configurations for membership, one of which was a 'wholly directly elected Council'.

[14] Ibid., para. 16.

[15] Ibid., paras 17–20

[16] The following paragraph draws heavily on Duncan Tanner, 'Richard Crossman, Harold Wilson and devolution, 1966–70: the making of government policy', *Twentieth Century British History*, 17 (2006), 545–78.

[17] The note of condescension in Crossman's treatment of Cledwyn Hughes is unmistakable. Commenting on the Welsh Secretary's efforts to reform local government in Wales, introducing an elected Welsh Council in the process, part of Crossman's diary entry for 30 November 1966 reads: 'What made me furious was the discovery that the little Secretary of State for Wales wanted to publish his own White Paper on Local Government reform and to legislate on it for Wales in this Parliament, before our Royal Commission in England and Scotland had reported. That seems to me to be absolute nonsense and I said so with considerable brutality': Richard Crossman, *The Diaries of a Cabinet*

Minister: Vol. 2, Lord President of the Council and Leader of the House of Commons 1966–1968 (London: Hamilton, 1976), p. 142. It should be noted, however, that Crossman subsequently relented and became much more supportive of Hughes's devolutionary ambitions. Tanner ('Richard Crossman, Harold Wilson and devolution, 1966–70') provides the authoritative account.

[18] Emyr Price, *Yr Arglwydd Cledwyn o Benrhos* (Penygroes: Cyhoeddiadau Mei, 1990), pp. 57–8.

[19] Later, at least, it seems that Thomas was aware of the ways in which the establishment of the Welsh Office had created a bureaucratic momentum that was inimical to the interests of anti-devolutionists. It is this realization that surely underlies his comment to (then journalist) John Osmond in 1973 that 'Our greatest mistake was to have set up the Welsh Office.' Cited in John Osmond, *Creative Conflict: the Politics of Welsh Devolution* (Llandysul and London: Gomer and Routledge and Kegan Paul, 1978), p. 106.

[20] Tanner, 'Richard Crossman, Harold Wilson and devolution, 1966–70', pp. 567–70.

[21] Ibid., p. 570.

[22] While the idea of establishing a Royal Commission had long been in circulation, a key influence on Wilson's eventual decision to take such a step was then Home Secretary James Callaghan. He had in turn been influenced by one of his junior ministers, Elystan Morgan – formerly a high-profile member of Plaid Cymru who had defected to Labour in 1965 and had been elected as Member of Parliament for Cardiganshire the following year. Morgan recalls that the idea of urging Callaghan to act as advocate for the establishment of a Royal Commission was originally hatched during conversations with John Morris – later Secretary of State for Wales – while the two were on a joint family holiday in the summer of 1968. Interview with Lord Elystan Morgan, 6 July 2007. See also Gwilym Prys Davies, *A Central Welsh Council*, pp. 91–3.

[23] Richard Crossman, *The Diaries of a Cabinet Minister: Vol. 3, Secretary of State for Social Services, 1968–1970* (London: Hamilton, 1977), p. 235.

[24] The terms of reference were, in fact, the source of considerable difficulty and controversy for the Royal Commission itself. See, inter alia, *Royal Commission on the Constitution, 1969–73: Volume 1: Report, Cmnd. 5460*, pp. 5–7 and, especially, compare p. 10 with *Royal Commission on the Constitution 1969–73, Volume II: Memorandum of Dissent, Cmnd. 5460–1* (London: HMSO, October 1973), pp. vii, 1–2.

[25] The phrase 'deeply concerned' comes from a letter that George Thomas sent to Harold Wilson while the latter was holidaying in the Isles of Scilly on 25 August 1969 (a copy can be found in George Thomas's papers at the National Library of Wales). It presaged a wholesale assault by the Secretary of State and his allies against the proposals that were being developed by the Welsh Council. The whole episode is briefly discussed in J. Barry Jones, 'The British Labour Party as a centralising force', University of Strathclyde: Centre for the Study of Public Policy no. 32 (1979). Although this is not made clear in the text, Barry

Jones was in fact a key participant in that he played the key role in the group that had been established by Emrys Jones. See also Alan Butt Philip, *The Welsh Question: Nationalism in Welsh Politics 1945–70* (Cardiff: University of Wales Press, 1975), especially p. 288; John Gilbert Evans, *Devolution in Wales: Claims and Responses, 1937–1979* (Cardiff: University of Wales Press, 2006), pp. 125–8.

26 The only substantive difference between Hughes's Welsh Council proposals and the proposals that Labour was eventually to recommend to the Royal Commission was that the latter accepted that the council comprise only directly elected members.

27 See part II, section 7. Available online at *http://www.psr.keele.ac.uk/area/uk/man/lab70.htm#dem.*

28 *Labour's Programme for Britain: Annual Conference* (London: Labour Party, 1972); *Labour's Programme for Britain: Annual Conference 1973* (London: Labour Party, 1973).

29 House of Commons, Standing Committee D, 1971–2, vol. V, col. 2890, 16 March 1972.

30 *Western Mail,* 1 December 1973. See also *Western Mail,* 3 December 1973 for an account of another speech by Thomas, this time to a party meeting in Llandudno, arguing a similar case.

31 *Western Mail,* 7 November 1973.

32 Labour Party, *Policies for a Brighter Future for Wales* (1974), p. 2

33 *Report of the Royal Commission on the Constitution 1969–1973, Cmnd. 5460* (London: HMSO, October 1973), especially paras 1125–53, see also paras 733–826.

34 Ibid. paras 1154–73; as well as *Memorandum of Dissent, Cmnd. 5460–1.*

35 *Western Mail,* 7 March 1974. Emphasis added.

36 Gwilym Prys Davies has pointed out that no preparatory work had been undertaken ('ni wnaed dim gwaith rhagbaratoawl') on Labour's devolution proposals by Welsh Office civil servants prior to the February 1974 general election, which further inhibited any rapid developments. See his *Llafur y Blynyddoedd,* p. 97. The sheer volume of work that had to be undertaken at the official level in central government – where the bulk of the work was ultimately undertaken – is also a key theme in the retrospective offered in Constitution Unit, *Scotland's Parliament: Fundamentals for a New Scotland Act* (London: Constitution Unit, 1996), pp. 24–31.

37 Office of the Lord President of the Council, *Devolution within the United Kingdom: Some Alternatives for Discussion* (London: HMSO, 1974).

38 James G. Kellas, *The Scottish Political System* (Cambridge: Cambridge University Press, 1989), pp. 145–7.

39 *Devolution and Democracy: a Statement by the Executive Committee for Consideration at a Special Delegate Conference, Llandrindod Wells, 22nd June, 1974,* The Labour Party in Wales, part 1.8.

40 As cited in *The Labour Party, Welsh Office, Speakers' Notes on Devolution,* January 1976, p. 4.

41 *Devolution and Democracy,* parts 2.12 and 2.13.

42 Ibid., part 3.2.

43 *Democracy and Devolution: Proposals for Scotland and Wales, Cmnd. 5732* (London: HMSO, 1974).

44 Ibid., paras 27–33

45 *Our Changing Democracy: Devolution to Scotland and Wales, Cmnd. 6348* (London: HMSO, November 1975); *Devolution to Wales and Scotland: Supplementary Statement, Cmnd. 6585* (London: HMSO, August 1976); *Devolution: Financing the Devolved Services, Cmnd. 6890* (London: HMSO, July 1977).

46 *Democracy and Devolution*, para. 31. The change in nomenclature appears to have been influenced by the Kilbrandon Commission's use of 'Assembly' to describe a devolved body with executive powers. Kilbrandon reserved the term Council for a body with advisory powers only. No mention was made in the White Paper of the Assembly's internal organization.

47 Ibid., para. 30

48 Ibid.

49 *Wales Will Win with Labour* (Cardiff: Wales Labour Party, 1974), p. 4. Interestingly, the manifesto also implied that whole fields of policy would be devolved to the Assembly in which it would exercise executive responsibilities. This – if viable – would have represented a more expansive version of empowerment than was eventually allowed under the terms of the Wales Act 1978, in which the putative Assembly's executive powers were to be derived from the specific derogation of powers to ministers, and particularly the Secretary of State for Wales, as allowed for under the terms of existing primary legislation. It is unclear whether this was a deliberate attempt by the framers of Labour's Welsh manifesto to push for a more expansive version of executive devolution, or was rather a reflection of uncertainty and/or misunderstanding on their part of the government's intentions. See here Prys Davies, *Llafur y Blynyddoedd*, pp. 114–15.

50 *Our Changing Democracy*, para. 188. Cf. paras 43–4.

51 Ibid., para. 189.

52 Prys Davies, *Llafur y Blynyddoedd*, p. 120.

53 Ibid., paras 175, 196.

54 Ibid., paras 196–7.

55 Any hint is indeed very subtle. Note in particular the strikingly passive formulation of the most relevant passage: 'The Commission may take the view that some of the duties now falling to the Welsh Office could, with advantage, be progressively transferred to the Welsh Council and that this would be especially necessary if it is decided that the Central Government should legislate broadly allowing the various UK regions a wide area of discretionary powers': *Evidence of the Labour Party in Wales to the Commission on the Constitution*, p. 16. It is noteworthy also that this passage was reprinted in the *Speaker's Notes on Devolution* issued by the Labour Party in Wales in January 1976 (see p. 5), a document clearly designed to cement party unity by stressing the continuity of official party policy.

56 See, for example, remarks by Gwynoro Jones in the *Western Mail* of 10 December 1973, and by John Morris in the *Western Mail* on 17 January

1974. In a similar vein, a document on the party's devolution policy presented to a meeting of the Wales Labour Party Executive Committee on 13 January 1975 lamented the way in which the debate about powers 'has been bedevilled by sterile arguments as to whether an assembly should have "Legislative" powers, "Executive' powers" etc.': *Devolution, Procedures for Exercising Powers*, presented to a meeting of the Executive Committee, 13 January 1975, Wales Labour Party papers, NLW, p. 2.

57   For example, compare *Our Changing Democracy*, paras 30 and 175.

58   For example, in ibid., paras 201 and 206.

59   Reported in the *Western Mail*, 17 January 1974.

60   Lord Morris's views on this matter have been conveyed through personal correspondence. Gwilym Prys Davies's most recent assessment of the speech's significance can be found in *Cynhaeaf Hanner Canrif*, pp. 108–9. In truth, few other observers have accorded any particular significance to the speech – indeed it has scarcely been noticed. One partial exception is John Osmond's *Creative Conflict*, which mentions the speech as part of an abortive debate within the Labour Party in Wales about the proposed assembly's legislative powers (p. 148). Attempts to evaluate recent claims about the significance of the speech are hampered by the fact that it was, in John Morris's own words, 'ddim yn hollol glir' (not totally clear); that it was not formally scripted; that the journalist whose report of the speech is our only source for its contents (namely Osmond himself) was not present at the meeting at which it was made, and that the *Western Mail* report itself is notably vague.

61   The best summary of the various schemes is provided in the government's own 1974 consultation document *Devolution within the United Kingdom*, esp. pp. 7–16

62   See the *Report of the Royal Commission on the Constitution*, paras 1154–73, also paras 827–919. See in addition the *Memorandum of Dissent*, paras 208–76.

63   *Llafur y Blynyddoedd*, p. 123. John P. Mackintosh, *The Devolution of Power: Local Democracy, Regionalism and Nationalism* (London: Penguin, 1968) was a key text for Labour devolutionists.

64   *Western Mail*, 29 April 1974; see also, inter alia, reports in the same newspaper on 15 and 18 May 1974. The Wales TUC supported the Kilbrandon proposal for legislative devolution, endorsing every significant element of that plan except proportional representation and the abolition of the post of Secretary of State (although it reversed its position on the latter issue at a subsequent General Council meeting on 19 June 1974). See 'Devolution for Wales', Wales TUC Policy Document, presented to General Council Meeting on 19 June 1974.

65   Osmond, *Creative Conflict*, p. 144.

66   *The National Labour Party commitment to the policy put forward in Wales on the matter of a Welsh Assembly and Devolution* (no date given, but probably 1975), p. 3. See also Labour Party in Wales, *Speaker's Notes on Devolution*.

67   So, for example, Gwilym Prys Davies quotes an angry letter received by the Welsh Office from Cliff Prothero, Emrys Jones's predecessor as Secretary of the Welsh Council of Labour, arguing that the party had

gone beyond the terms of its original commitment to an elected Council. See *Cynhaeaf Hanner Canrif*, pp. 111–12.

68 In addition to sources cited below, this section draws heavily on Richard Wyn Jones and Bethan Lewis, 'The Wales Labour Party and Welsh civil society: aspects of the constitutional debate in Wales', paper presented to the 1998 Annual Conference of the Political Studies Association; Wyn Jones and Lewis, 'The 1997 Welsh devolution referendum', *Politics*, 19 (1999), 37–46.

69 John Prescott and Tom Pendry, *Alternative Regional Strategy: a Framework for Discussion* (London: Labour Party, 1982).

70 Labour Party, *Local Government Reform in England and Wales*, Labour Party Consultative Paper (London: Labour Party, 1986).

71 The phrase 'nominal commitment' is used by Morgan and Mungham to describe Labour's position in the 1992 general election. Kevin Morgan and Geoff Mungham, 'Unfinished business: Labour's devolution policy', in J. Barry Jones and Denis Balsom (eds), *The Road to the National Assembly for Wales* (Cardiff: University of Wales Press, 2000), pp. 28–49 (p. 34). The description of the powers of the proposed Assembly – an obvious code for executive devolution – are taken from the manifesto itself, available at *http://www.politicsresources.net/area/uk/man/lab92.htm*.

72 See, for example, Rhodri Morgan, *Variable Geometry UK* (Cardiff: Institute of Welsh Affairs, 2000); Ieuan Wyn Jones interviewed in the *Guardian*, 25 February 2003 (see *http://www.guardian.co.uk/politics/2003/feb/25/wales.comment*).

73 See, inter alia, John Osmond, 'A constitutional convention by other means: the first year of the National Assembly for Wales', in Robert Hazell (ed.), *The State and the Nations: the First Year of Devolution in the United Kingdom* (Exeter: Imprint, 2001), pp. 37–77; Robert Hazell, Meg Russell, Jeremy Croft, Ben Seyd and Roger Masterman, 'The constitution: rolling out the new settlement', *Parliamentary Affairs*, 54 (2001), 190–205 (191); Laura McAllister, 'The Richard Commission – Wales's alternative constitutional convention?', *Contemporary Wales*, 17 (2004), 128–39.

74 Interview with Wayne David MEP, 6 March 1998.

75 'Labour scupper all party talks on assembly', *Western Mail*, 23 June 1992.

76 This is the obvious inference to be drawn from Morgan and Mungham, *Redesigning Democracy*, pp. 100–7.

77 Wales Labour Party, *Shaping the Vision. A Report on the Powers and Structure of the Welsh Assembly* (Cardiff: Wales Labour Party, 1995), para. 4.4 on p. 5. For Labour's plans for Welsh devolution in the run-up to the 1997 UK general election see, in addition, Wales Labour Party, *A Welsh Assembly. The Way Forward. Wales Labour Party Policy Commission Interim Report* (Cardiff: Wales Labour Party, 1993); Wales Labour Party, *Shaping the Vision. A Consultation Paper on the Powers and Structure of the Welsh Assembly* (Cardiff: Wales Labour Party, 1994); Wales Labour Party, *Preparing for a New Wales: a Report on the Structure and Workings of the Welsh Assembly* (Cardiff: Wales Labour Party, 1996).

[78] The definitive account is Paul Chaney, Fiona Mackay and Laura McAllister, *Women, Politics and Constitutional Change* (Cardiff: University of Wales Press, 2007).

[79] The quote comes from a speech made by Tony Blair in Edinburgh on 28 June 1996.

[80] This basic truth has been widely recognized in the academic literature. See, inter alia, Rawlings, *Delineating Wales: Constitutional, Legal and Administrative Aspects of National Devolution* (Cardiff: University of Wales Press, 2003), pp. 26–9; James Mitchell, *Devolution in the United Kingdom* (Manchester: Manchester University Press, 2009), p. 159; Prys Davies, *Cynhaeaf Hanner Canrif*, p. 127.

[81] Cited in Rawlings, *Delineating Wales*, p. 28

[82] Welsh Office National Assembly Advisory Group, *National Assembly for Wales: Have your Say on How it Will Work: a Consultation Paper* (Cardiff: Welsh Office, 1998). See also Martin Laffin and Alys Thomas, 'Designing the National Assembly for Wales', *Parliamentary Affairs*, 53 (2003), 557–76.

[83] As well as his magnum opus, *Delineating Wales*, see also Richard Rawlings, *Three Faces of the National Assembly for Wales* (Swansea: University of Wales Swansea, 2002).

[84] For an insider account, see McAllister, 'The Richard Commission', 128–39.

[85] In fairness, it must be pointed out that it was the smaller partner that brought the bulk of the policy proposals to the joint policy statement that was the agreed basis of the new 'partnership' government. Labour's 1999 manifesto had been a particularly anaemic affair. It is also clear that the Welsh coalition agreement was closely modelled on the agreement that had previously been reached by Labour and the Liberal Democrats in Scotland soon after that country's first devolved election.

[86] Our point here is not to claim that other parties had not made various suggestions about Wales's constitutional status and development at different times. Rather, the point is that the basic architecture legislated for in the 1970s, and again in the late 1990s, was very much a Labour Party model, shaped by debates internal to the Labour Party.

[87] Commission on the Powers and Electoral Arrangements of the National Assembly for Wales, *Report of the Richard Commission* (Cardiff: National Assembly for Wales, 2004). On the latter point, see David Melding, 'Terrific twins of Welsh constitutional thought', *Agenda: the Journal of the Institute of Welsh Affairs*, 42 (2010), 29.

[88] As already discussed in the previous chapter, one commissioner, the former Labour MP Ted Rowlands, did append a rather opaque note to the final report expressing doubts about the timing of the proposed move to extend primary legislative powers to the Assembly and insisting, in particular, on the need for a referendum. But he did not call into question the direction of travel that was recommended. Neither did Rowlands seek to produce a minority report or disassociate himself in

any way from the Commission's recommendations. Thus, the consensus view that the Commission's report was unanimous seems fully justified.

89   *Report of the Richard Commission*, p. 241.
90   Ibid., pp. 261–2.
91   Ibid., pp. 243–4.
92   See, in particular, the Wales Monitoring Reports on the Constitution Unit website from March 2004, June 2004, September 2004, December 2004, April 2005 and January 2006, all available at *www.ucl.ac.uk/constitution-unit*. See also Alan Trench, 'Rhodri's retreat', *Agenda: the Journal of the Institute of Welsh Affairs* (summer 2004), 40–1.
93   With regard to the latter, para. 26 of *Better Governance for Wales* makes the point in the following terms: 'One option would be to grant the Assembly enhanced Order making powers to make new legal provision for Wales in defined fields within the responsibilities currently devolved to it, including a power to amend or repeal relevant earlier legislation in these fields. This would in effect apply the principle of framework legislation retrospectively': Welsh Labour Party, *Better Governance for Wales* (August 2004), p. 8.
94   Ibid., para. 29, p. 8.
95   Ibid., para. 9, p. 5.
96   *Britain Forward Not Back, Wales Labour Party Manifesto* (Cardiff: Wales Labour Party, 2005), p. 108.
97   Alan Trench, 'Introduction: the dynamics of devolution', in A. Trench (ed.), *The Dynamics of Devolution: State of the Nations 2005* (Exeter: Imprint Academic, 2005), pp. 1–22 (p. 15).
98   Ibid., p. 17.
99   John Osmond, 'Wales: towards 2007,' in A. Trench (ed.), *The Dynamics of Devolution: State of the Nations 2005*, p. 43.
100 Wales Office, *Better Governance for Wales, Cm 6582* (London: The Stationery Office, 2005).
101 It is surely no coincidence that the proposal to legislate immediately for primary powers was dealt with in only one sentence (on p. 4) of the seven-page Wales Office press release that accompanied the publication of the White Paper. It is not mentioned at all in press release's bullet point summary of the White Paper proposals (on p. 2). See 'White Paper takes forward Welsh devolution', Wales Office Press Release, 15 June 2005.
102 The ability of Westminster to refuse an Assembly request for a referendum raised the ire of some devolutionists. And the requirement for an Assembly super-majority represented a de facto Labour veto. But, as Peter Hain pointed out, in reality it would always be very difficult to win a referendum without overwhelming support in the Assembly, as demonstrated by a two-thirds majority. Moreover, any decision by Westminster to refuse a referendum request backed by two-thirds of the Assembly would surely increase support for Cardiff at the expense of London. Westminster would have little to gain and much to lose in provoking such a confrontation. See Richard Wyn Jones, 'Route map to power', interview with the Right Hon. Peter Hain, Secretary of State for

Wales, *Agenda: the Journal of the Institute of Welsh Affairs* (winter 2005/
2006), 24–8.

[103] Anonymous sources.

[104] So, for example, when Peter Hain was challenged on the dangers of
'double scrutiny' by one of the present authors before Part III came
into force he maintained that 'the orders themselves are going to be in
pretty general terms': Wyn Jones, 'Route map to power', 26.

[105] With regards to the former, it should be noted that in July 2005, Peter
Hain suggested publicly that active consideration was then being given
to incorporating a mechanism in the Bill that would allow an increase
in the size of the Assembly at some future point – presumably after the
unlocking of primary powers. Evidently nothing came of the suggestion. The venue for his remarks was a joint Institute of Welsh Politics/
UCL Constitution Unit conference on 'The White Paper and the future
of Welsh devolution' at Cardiff's Millennium Centre Cardiff in July
2005.

[106] Welsh Office, *Better Governance for Wales, Cm 6562*, p. 29.

[107] See 'Route map to power', 24–8.

[108] Ibid. See also Commission on Boundary Differences and Voting
Systems, *Putting Citizens First: Boundaries, Voting and Representation in
Scotland* (Edinburgh: Stationery Office, January 2006), paras 4.55–4.61,
pp. 42–5.

[109] Contrast Peter Hain's oral evidence to the House of Commons Welsh
Affairs Committee on 10 November 2005, especially Q. 245 (available at
*http://www.publications.parliament.uk/pa/cm200506/cmselect/cmwelaf/
uc551-iv/uc55102.htm*) with Lord Steel's intervention in a Lords' debate
on the Bill on House of Lords Debates, 22 March 2006, col. 263.
Contrast also Peter Hain's comments to the Welsh Grand Committee
meeting on 23 June 2005 (House of Commons Debates, 23 June 2005,
col. 5), with Electoral Reform Society, *Much Better Governance for Wales*
(Cardiff: Electoral Reform Society Wales, 2005).

[110] See *Public Attitudes to Dual Candidacy in the Elections to the National Assembly
for Wales, Occasional Paper No. 5*, Bevan Foundation, January 2006.

[111] See, respectively, *The Electoral Commission's Response* (Cardiff: Electoral
Reform Society Wales, 2005) and oral evidence to the House of
Commons Welsh Affairs Committee on 18 October 2005 by Richard
Wyn Jones and Roger Scully, especially Q. 61 (available at *http://www.
publications.parliament.uk/pa/cm200506/cmselect/cmwelaf/uc551-i/
uc55102.htm*)

[112] See the BBC's report on Elis-Thomas's remarks 'Call to end election
"ping-pong"', 23 June 2006 (available at *http://news.bbc.co.uk/1/hi/
wales/5108196.stm*).

[113] Interview with Peter Hain conducted by Richard Wyn Jones on 13 July
2007 for the S4C television series *Datganoli*.

[114] Anonymous sources.

[115] Anonymous sources.

[116] On one-partyism in Wales, see Ian McAllister's still unsurpassed paper
'The Labour Party in Wales: the dynamics of one-partyism', *Llafur*, 3
(1980), 79–89. More generally see T. J. Pempel (ed.), *Uncommon*

Democracies: the One-Party Dominant Regimes (Ithaca, NY: Cornell University Press, 1990).

[117] As recalled in Tim Williams, 'Yes, we have no bananas', *Western Mail*, 12 August 2002.

[118] The decline of this sense of constitutional self-confidence is traced in Michael Foley, *The Politics of the British Constitution* (Manchester: Manchester University Press, 1999).

3: The evolution of public attitudes

[1] Denis Balsom, 'Public opinion and Welsh devolution', in David Foulkes, J. Barry Jones and R. A. Wilford (eds), *The Welsh Veto: the Wales Act 1978 and the Referendum* (Cardiff: University of Wales Press, 1983), pp. 197–215 (p. 199).

[2] Richard Rose, 'The United Kingdom as a multi-national state', *University of Strathclyde Occasional Paper* (1970), no. 6.

[3] Andrew Edwards and Duncan Tanner, 'Defining or dividing the nation? Opinion polls, Welsh identity and devolution, 1966–1979', *Contemporary Wales*, 18 (2006), 54–71 (58–9).

[4] See ibid., 63–5 for an interesting discussion, drawing on important archival evidence of internal civil service discussions, of the process through which the Royal Commission survey question emerged.

[5] The British Election Study findings in Wales were 25 per cent support for 'Keeping things much as they are at present'; 36 per cent for 'Keeping things much the same, but making sure that the needs of the region are better understood at the centre'; 29 per cent supporting 'More decisions to be made in the region', and only 11 per cent endorsing 'Let the region take over complete responsibility for running its own affairs' (number of respondents = 124).

[6] The small sample sizes demand that we interpret these findings with caution, but the overall trend is sufficiently strong to reach conventional levels of statistical significance. Combining all the cases from the three BES and two BSA surveys into a single file, and regressing constitutional preference on the year of survey (with constitutional preference coded '1' for no change, '2' for assembly, and '3' for independence) yields an unstandardized coefficient for year of survey of .049 (standard error .005), t-value = 9.30 (p < .000).

[7] A Beaufort Research Poll for the BBC in October 1994 produced the following results: For elected assembly 51 per cent; against 16 per cent; undecided 33 per cent (number of respondents = 1,000). Another Beaufort Poll for the BBC in September 1996 found: For elected assembly 55 per cent; against 28 per cent; undecided 17 per cent (number of respondents = 1,000).

[8] Denis Balsom, 'The three-Wales model', in J. Osmond (ed.), *The National Question Again* (Llandysul: Gomer, 1985).

[9] Richard Wyn Jones and Dafydd Trystan, 'The 1997 Welsh referendum vote', in B. Taylor and K. Thomson (eds), *Scotland and Wales: Nations Again?* (Cardiff: University of Wales Press, 1999), pp. 65–93.

[10] These surveys included both academic studies and other polls for the news media, the National Assembly for Wales Commission and the All-Wales Convention. They were conducted using three different types of survey method: face to face, telephone and internet. They were conducted by four different survey companies: the National Centre for Social Research, YouGov, GfK NOP and ICM. And they included six different forms of question wording/response categories. (Richard Wyn Jones and Roger Scully, 'What happened in the 2010 election? Why?', paper presented to Public Seminar on the 2010 General Election, Cardiff (2010).)

[11] The Electoral Commission, *Wales Votes? Public Attitudes towards Assembly Elections* (London: The Electoral Commission, 2002); The Electoral Commission, *Wales – Poll Position. Public Attitudes towards Assembly Elections* (London: The Electoral Commission, 2006); *All Wales Convention Report* (Cardiff: All Wales Convention, 2009), ch. 5.

[12] The 1997 Welsh referendum study found 36 per cent of male respondents chose the 'No devolution' option on the standard constitutional preference question, and 42 per cent of female respondents selected that option. Research conducted by NOP for the Electoral Commission in 2006 indicated that while 23 per cent of men now endorsed the 'No devolution' constitutional preference, only 18 per cent of women did so.

[13] G. R. Boynton and Gerhard Loewenberg, 'The development of public support for Parliament in Germany, 1951–59', *British Journal of Political Science*, 3 (1973), 169–89; Kendall Baker, Russell Dalton and Kai Hildebrandt, *Germany Transformed: Political Culture and the New Politics* (Cambridge: Cambridge University Press, 1981).

[14] For example, a survey conducted after the 2010 UK general election found that of the slightly more than 40 per cent of respondents in Wales who perceived the National Health Service to have improved since 2005, some 47 per cent attributed this improvement mainly down to the actions of the Welsh Assembly Government, compared to only 16 per cent who gave most credit to the UK government. But among the smaller proportion who perceived the NHS to have declined over the previous five years, only 14 per cent attributed this to the devolved authorities, while around twice as many accorded most blame to government in London. (See Wyn Jones and Scully, 'What happened in the 2010 election?')

[15] See, for example, Reinhardt Bendix, *Nation-building and Citizenship* (New York: John Wiley and Sons, 1965).

[16] Roger Scully, 'Has devolution made the people of Wales more Welsh?', paper presented to the Department of Politics and International Relations, Swansea University, February 2010.

[17] Our argument here is broadly consistent with that of Rebecca Davies, who has argued that the political implications drawn by many people in

Wales from their national identities have changed significantly in recent decades. See Rebecca Davies, 'Banal Britishness and reconstituted Welshness: the politics of national identities in Wales', *Contemporary Wales*, 18 (2006), 106–21.

[18] Roger Scully and Richard Wyn Jones, 'The legitimacy of devolved government in Scotland and Wales', paper presented to the Annual Conference of the American Political Science Association, Boston (2008), p. 27.

[19] The only reported research on public attitudes that offered a substantially different picture from the published polls discussed here was that apparently conducted by the group True Wales and reported on their website (see *www.truewales.org.uk/en/true_wales_campaign.html* and *www. truewales.org.uk/en/true_wales_media.html*). This research claimed to have found, in surveys conducted in a number of towns across Wales (including Abertillery, Barry, Brecon, Carmarthen, Cowbridge, Merthyr and Penarth), much higher levels of support than indicated in any of the published national polls for either the abolition of the Assembly or for its powers to remain at the current level. However, the reports on this research on the True Wales website did not give any details regarding the sample sizes (except for Penarth, where the sample size was reported as being fifty); the precise question wordings used or the answer options given to respondents; the method of interview, or any details regarding how the sample was selected and/or weighted to ensure representativeness of the wider population. (All such details were available for all the polls and surveys reported in the main text.) Thus, it is impossible to evaluate seriously the quality of the True Wales research.

4: From coalition agreement to polling day

[1] The vote was split into two sections with the trade unions and affiliates approving the deal by a margin of 95.8 per cent to 4.2 per cent, while the constituency, county parties and women's forums voted in favour by a margin of 61 per cent to 39 per cent; *http://news.bbc.co.uk/1/hi/wales/6275036.stm.*

[2] The Plaid Cymru vote was 92 per cent in favour of the One Wales coalition agreement; *http://news.bbc.co.uk/1/hi/wales/6278848.stm.*

[3] The texts of two agreements may be compared in John Osmond, *Crossing the Rubicon: Coalition Politics Welsh Style* (Cardiff: Institute of Welsh Affairs). Cf. pp. 75–95 and pp. 96–127.

[4] Text in Osmond, *Crossing the Rubicon*, pp. 98–9.

[5] While John Osmond reports that the original idea came from Peter Hain, based on an original suggestion by Edwina Hart (ibid., p. 37), Cynog Dafis suggests that the idea eminated from within Plaid Cymru, with Adam Price credited as its author. Interview with Cynog Dafis, 11 May 2011.

[6] David Butler and Iain McLean describe the 1997 Welsh referendum as 'perhaps, the most unsatisfactory ... of UK referendums'

('Referendums', in B. Taylor and K. Thomson (eds), *Scotland and Wales: Nations Again?* (Cardiff: University of Wales Press, 1999),p. 8. We should note that we do not concur with this judgement: even on the most negative reading it seems implausible to rate the 1997 Welsh experience as more unsatisfactory than the 1973 Northern Ireland referendum, which was boycotted by a substantial majority of the Catholic population. However, concerns about government neutrality were voiced by the Committee on Standards in Public Life, and these influenced the drafting of PPERA. (See *The Funding of Political Parties in the United Kingdom*, London: The Stationery Office, 1998).

7   *All-Wales Convention Report* (November 2009), para. 1.1.6, pp. 9–10.

8   In addition to Sir Emyr Jones Parry (chair), the members of the All-Wales Convention were Alex Aldridge (the Labour party nominee), Joan Asby, Shan Ashton, Nick Bennett, Aled Edwards, Rhodri Evans, Meryl Gravel, Efa Gruffydd Jones (from April 2009), Laura Hayes (until 12 January 2009), Rob Humphreys (the Liberal Democrat nominee), Sally Hyman, John Jones, Harry Ludgate, Paul O'Shea, Marc Phillips (the Plaid Cymru nominee – who served until 20 October 2009), Paul Valerio (the Conservative nominee) and Shereen Williams. They were referred to collectively as the 'Executive Committee of the All-Wales Convention', implying that there was a wider convention process at work – presumably on the lines of the Scottish Constitutional Convention. In the event, however, the All-Wales Convention was essentially a repeat of the Richard Commission model.

9   *All-Wales Convention Report*, para. 6.2.16, p. 100.

10 Ibid., para. 6.2.2, p. 98. Beyond the referendum recommendation itself, the stress on 'rule of law' is perhaps the most interesting and potentially significant feature of the All-Wales Convention report, introducing a new register to the devolution debate in Wales.

11 Ibid., para. 6.2.4, p. 98.

12 This figure is taken from ibid., para. 1.3.5, p. 11.

13 Richard Wyn Jones, 'In the shadow of 1979', *Planet: the Welsh Internationalist*, 194 (spring 2009), 8–15.

14 Interview with Mark Drakeford, 4 July 2011; Dafydd Elis-Thomas, 'Second constitution', *Agenda: the Journal of the Institute of Welsh Affairs* (summer 2006), 16–18.

15 *All-Wales Convention Report*, para. 5, p. 4.

16 Researchers attached to Cardiff University's Wales Legislation Online became persistent critics. As one of many possible examples, see the submission made by David Lambert and Elizabeth Smith to the National Assembly's Subordinate Legislation (later Constitutional Affairs) Committee in February 2010. (*http://www.assemblywales.org/bus-home/bus-third-assembly/bus-committees/bus-committees-perm-leg/bus-committees-legislation-dissolved/bus-committees-third-sleg-home/bus-committes-third-sleg-current_inquiries/inquiry-si/bus_leg_slc_sis-1.htm*). The Assembly's committees themselves became very effective critics. See, for example, National Assembly for Wales Legislation Committee No. 4, *Report on the National*

Assembly for Wales (Legislative Competence) (Environment) Order 2009 (www. assemblywales.org/cr-ld7575-e.pdf).

17 Interview Rachel Banner, 6 March 2011.

18 Martin Shipton, *Poor Man's Parliament? Ten Years of the Welsh Assembly* (Bridgend: Seren, 2011), pp. 238–40.

19 Carwyn Jones won outright victory in the first round of voting, clinching 52 per cent of the overall Electoral College vote. The college itself was split into three sections, each accounting for a third of the total. One section was made of elected members, the second of individual party members and the third of unions and affiliated organizations. Carwyn Jones's margin of victory was remarkably consistent across all three. See *http://www.walesonline.co.uk/news/wales-news/2009/12/01/carwyn-jones-victorious-91466-25299305/* and *http://www.bbc.co.uk/blogs/thereporters/ betsanpowys/2009/12/its_carwyn.html.*

20 Anonymous sources.

21 Gary Owen, Rhodri Morgan and Peter Hain, *Joint Statement in Response to the All-Wales Convention Report* (Welsh Labour Party, 24 November 2011). While Hain's name appears last on the list of signatories (defying alphabetical order), he seems universally regarded as the joint statement's instigator.

22 In fact, several sections of the 'One Wales agreement' are directly relevant here. In addition to the general commitment to collective responsibility, the final section bound both parties to the following: 'in order to provide consistency across portfolios and the need to engage the two parties of the coalition government, both the First Minister and the Deputy First Minister will be engaged in policy presentation'. Even more starkly, 'It is essential that both the First Minister and the Deputy First Minister are kept fully and promptly informed across the range of Government business.'

23 Anonymous sources.

24 *http://news.bbc.co.uk/1/hi/wales/wales_politics/8376640.stm.* The multiple entries for 24 November 2009 on the blog of the BBC Wales political editor give a flavour of events as they unfolded. See *http://www.bbc. co.uk/blogs/thereporters/betsanpowys/2009/11/.*

25 *http://www.bbc.co.uk/blogs/thereporters/betsanpowys/2009/11/first_minis- ters_statement.html.*

26 The statement in full is available at *http://www.cynulliadcymru.org/bus- home/bus-third-assembly/bus-chamber/bus-chamber-third-assembly-rop.htm?act =dis&id=154061&ds=11/2009#2.*

27 The full statement read as follows: 'The Assembly Government once again reaffirms its commitment to the One Wales agreement in relation to a referendum on Part Four powers. Both parties recognise the diffi- culties which would be created for a purposeful and united "yes" campaign, if that were attempted to be held during the run up to a General Election. Both recognise that a successful "Yes" campaign will rest on mobilising support from all political parties in Wales, and from those who have no political affiliation. Otherwise, all options for the timing of a referendum remain open. Nothing has been ruled in or

ruled out, including, if it proved practical, a referendum in the autumn': *http://www.bbc.co.uk/blogs/thereporters/betsanpowys/2009/11/peace_in_ our_time.html.*

28 In private it appears that Carwyn Jones did initially ask Ieuan Wyn Jones to consider delaying the referendum until after the May 2011 National Assembly election. When the latter refused he did not, however, press the case. Rather, once it became clear that the terms of the coalition agreement on the timing of the referendum were not (re)negotiable, he determined to use the 'political capital' he had accrued through his comfortable victory in the battle to succeed Rhodri Morgan in order to ensure that his own party adopted a more unified and positive approach to the now inevitable referendum. (Anonymous sources).

29 Relatedly, the events of 24 November represent one of the few moments at which the often-difficult relationship that existed between Hain and Morgan emerged into public view. Herein, surely, lies the origin of Rhodri Morgan's otherwise utterly inexplicable decision to sign the joint statement. Informants report that meetings between the First Minister and the Secretary of State were characterized by a tendency to talk past each other. With Morgan also tending to shy away from direct confrontation, it is suggested that he signed the statement without realizing its potential implications.

30 Peter Hain's comments on 4 February 2011, just a few weeks before the referendum, make clear his continuing resentment at this turn of events: 'Clearly the Plaid Cymru insistence on holding the referendum before May 2011 is the reason we have a referendum on March 3rd. We wouldn't have had one otherwise.' See *http://www.bbc.co.uk/news/ uk-wales-12351404.*

31 Interview with Cynog Dafis, 11 May 2011.

32 The importance of the 1979 experience in shaping the subsequent attitudes and trajectory of Plaid Cymru is explored in depth in Richard Wyn Jones, *Rhoi Cymru'n Gyntaf: Syniadaeth Plaid Cymru. Cyfrol 1* (Caerdydd: University of Wales Press, 2007), pp. 181–260.

33 This tension emerged into public view in the aftermath of the referendum when a public spat between Peter Hain and Carwyn Jones led to the latter proclaiming that 'I am the leader of the Welsh Labour party.' This was countered in a briefing to journalist Adrian Masters by a 'Labour source' who 'pointedly told me that Ed Miliband is the UK party leader and Carwyn Jones speaks on matters devolved to Wales.' See *http://adrianmastersitv.wordpress.com/2011/03/08/labours-coalition- split/.*

34 The role of the term *crachach* in the vocabulary of contemporary Welsh politics deserves study. In its original Welsh meaning it carries both class connotations (suggesting gentry or petty gentry) as well as connotations of character (snobbish and conceited). As a loan word in English language political discourse it often seems to be used to refer (dismissively) to any Welsh speaker prominent in public life.

35 Another indication of Labour's continuing internal tensions around the referendum is that, in this initial period, officials at Transport

House were insisting that, despite his status as a recently retired First Minister, Morgan was not, in fact, representing the Labour Party at steering committee meetings but was rather attending in a 'personal capacity'! (Anonymous sources.)

[36] The Conservative group in the Assembly were represented by Paul Davies AM and, for a brief period, a researcher working for the group.

[37] Interview Leighton Andrews, 25 May 2011.

[38] At the same time, future Assembly Member Mick Antoniw was made Yes for Wales treasurer. He had also worked on the Carwyn Jones's leadership campaign.

[39] See *http://www.walesonline.co.uk/news/columnists/2010/06/08/it-s-either-forward-or-back-there-s-no-other-option-91466–26606976/*.

[40] It was left to the broadcasters themselves to link two potential spokesmen, Bill Hughes and former Welsh Conservative chairman Sir Eric Howells, to the True Wales organization, and it was they who were to fly the flag for the No campaign in the Welsh-language TV debate broadcast from Holyhead on S4C on 23 February. Without wishing to appear uncharitable, we will simply observe that Hughes and Howells did not prove to be the most coherent or knowledgeable proponents of their cause.

[41] Until mid-December 2010 the BBC's coverage of the forthcoming referendum conformed to the usual editorial guidelines requiring impartial coverage of 'contentious' subjects (see *http://www.bbc.co.uk/editorial-guidelines/guidelines*). Moving into the campaigning period proper a more specific set of referendum guidelines were applied (to be found at *http://downloads.bbc.co.uk/guidelines/editorialguidelines/pdfs/Referendum Guidelines_2010.pdf*). We are grateful to Rhys Evans for guidance on this issue.

[42] House of Commons Debates, 24 July 1997, column 1050.

[43] Interview Rachel Banner, 6 March 2011.

[44] Sadly, one suggested element of the launch event and subsequent campaign – a video of the choir Only Men Aloud singing 'Vote Yes' to the tune of 'Go West' by the Pet Shop Boys – did not materialize due to copyright considerations, thus depriving connoisseurs of camp of what would surely have been the highlight of the 2011 referendum.

[45] Roger Lewis, speech at 'Yes for Wales' launch meeting, Cardiff, 4 January 2011.

[46] Interview Daran Hill, 7 April 2011.

[47] Interview Roger Lewis, 23 May 2011.

[48] The programme may be viewed at *http://www.bbc.co.uk/news/uk-wales-12248111*.

[49] Interview Len Gibbs, 21 May 2011. It is worth noting that the audience figures for the three-set-piece debates were substantially higher than for the leaders' debates in the May 2011 Assembly election.

[50] Interview Cathy Owens, 8 April 2011.

[51] Interview Rob Humphreys, 5 May 2011.

[52] Interviews with Meilyr Ceredig (21 March 2011), Lisa Francis (18 March 2011) and Rebecca Williams (11 March 2011).

[53] Much of the attention in the Aberystwyth debate was, in the event, grabbed by the former (Labour) leader of Cardiff Council, Russell Goodway. Goodway declared himself to be 'undecided' on the referendum, although he struck a decidedly sceptical note about the Yes campaign throughout. Shortly before polling day, however, Goodway announced his intention to vote Yes. See *http://www.walesonline.co.uk/ news/welsh-politics/welsh-politics-news/2011/02/28/former-cardiff-council-leader-russell-goodway-will-vote-yes-in-assembly-referendum-91444-28247445/*.

[54] While True Wales spent £3,785, the Yes Campaign in Ceredigion spent £4,711, *http://www.electoralcommission.org.uk/party-finance/party-finance-analysis/campaign-expenditure/welsh-referendum-expenditure*.

[55] The speech is available at *http://www.truewales.org.uk/en/news.html*.

[56] See True Wales statement of 19 January 2011 under the heading 'Statement on the refusal of taxpayers' money and lead campaign status' at *http://www.truewales.org.uk/en/news.html*.

[57] To arrive at this figure we have assumed that the mail-shots would have cost no more than £150,000 to deliver and that the Electoral Commission would have supported the two lead campaigns up to a total of around £70,000. With regards the latter figure, it is true that the Electoral Commission envisaged that their total support for both campaigns could have amounted to £140,000 (see Electoral Commission, *Report on the referendum on the law-making powers of the National Assembly for Wales, 3rd March 2011*, p. 31, available at *http://www.electoralcommission.org.uk/ elections/upcoming-elections-and-referendums/wales/referendum*). Nonetheless, before the route to lead status was closed to them the Yes campaign had privately estimated that, given the restrictions on its use, they were in reality unlikely to have qualified for more than some £35,000 of public funding. Perhaps generously, we have assumed that the No campaign could have qualified for a similar amount.

[58] This is the Electoral Commission's figure for the final cost of the referendum. See Electoral Commission, *Report on the referendum on the law-making powers of the National Assembly for Wales*, p. 58. It is the case that, by January 2011, True Wales was arguing that the referendum should take place at the same time as the Assembly election scheduled for May, which would have led to some saving on the projected £5 million figure. This was, however, a reversal of their previous position whereby the group had demanded an 'immediate referendum'. See, for example, the True Wales response to the publication of the All-Wales Convention report (especially under the sub-heading 'Referendum now') published on its website on 21 November 2009, *http://www.true-wales.org.uk/en/all_wales_convention.html*.

[59] True Wales statement, 24 January 2011, 'Why we did not apply for lead campaign status under the Political Parties, Elections and Referendums Act', at *http://www.truewales.org.uk/en/news.html*. The reference to the church hierarchy may strike some readers as unexpected. In fact, the alleged machinations of the church were a particular bugbear for some True Wales activists due to the role of the Archbishop of Wales, Barry Morgan, as chair of Cymru Yfory. Their concerns were summed up in

the text on a True Wales poster on prominent display at the Newbridge launch meeting which read 'True Wales demands: root and branch reform of all tiers of government; an end to the undemocratic influence of the church hierarchy and voluntary sector on the political process.'

[60] True Wales, 'Why we did not apply for lead campaign status'.

[61] In addition to the restrictions on what public funding could be used for, another problem was that the Electoral Commission would not be in a position to release any funds before February (although receipts from the middle of December 2010 could be submitted for backdated payment). This state of affairs further underlines the gross inadequacies of the PPERA framework, something to which we return in the concluding chapter.

[62] Interview Daran Hill, 7 April 2011.

[63] Interview Len Gibbs, 21 May 2011.

[64] See chapter three, n. 19.

[65] See, for example, Pippa Norris and John Curtice, 'Getting the message out: a two-step model of the role of the internet in campaign communication flows during the 2005 British general election', *Journal of Information Technology and Politics*, 4 (2008), 3–13.

[66] Anonymous sources.

[67] Interview Lee Waters, 7 April 2011.

5: The referendum result

[1] The applicability and relevance of the concept of swing in the context of the 2011 referendum is discussed in more detail below.

[2] David Butler and Austin Ranney (eds), *Referendums Around the World: the Growing Use of Direct Democracy* (Washington, DC: American Enterprise Institute Press, 1994), pp. 14–16.

[3] The turnout levels in the March 1979 devolution referendums of 63.8 per cent in Scotland and 58.8 per cent in Wales compared with participation levels of 76.8 per cent in Scotland and 79.4 per cent in Wales at the following May general election. In 1997, the September devolution referendum turnout rates of 60.4 per cent for Scotland and 50.1 per cent for Wales were again much lower than in the May general election of that year: 71.3 per cent in Scotland and 73.5 per cent in Wales.

[4] Andrew Dowling, '*Autonomistes, Catalanistes* and *Independentistes*: politics in contemporary Catalonia', *International Journal of Iberian Studies*, 22 (2009), 185–200.

[5] Mark Franklin, *Voter Turnout and the Dynamics of Electoral Competition in Established Democracies since 1945* (Cambridge: Cambridge University Press, 2004).

[6] Results in the 1979 referendum were declared in the eight 'preserved counties' of Wales. The 2011 results were aggregated from the current twenty-two authorities into these eight areas in order to conduct the correlation. Given that parliamentary and National Assembly

constituency boundaries in 2010 and 2011 are contained within the preserved counties but not within the current local authority boundaries, these results were also aggregated to the level of the preserved counties before being correlated with 2011 referendum turnout at this level.

[7] See, for example, David Denver, James Mitchell, Charles Pattie and Hugh Bochel, *Scotland Decides: the Devolution Issue and the Scottish Referendum* (London: Frank Cass, 2000), pp. 127–32. One factor that has consistently been an influence on turnout in general elections in the UK is unlikely to have been anything more than an indirect influence on turnout rates in the referendum: this is the marginality of a constituency. For reasons that are self-evident, marginal seats tend to attract the most intense efforts by the parties to mobilize their support. But in the context of a nationwide referendum, notions of local marginality are rendered irrelevant. Local marginality could only plausibly be expected to have an impact through the indirect means of it having caused particular areas to have become far more politically well organized and active. However, even this is impossible to test for 2011 in Wales given that we do not have data on the referendum results available at constituency-level.

[8] The rural, socio-economic and Welsh identity and language measures reported in table 5.3 (and later in table 5.7) were drawn from the StatsWales website *http://statswales.wales.gov.uk/index.htm*. All measures used were as defined by StatsWales, and were for the nearest available date to March 2011.

[9] It was remarkable that the three final polls produced *exactly* the same result given that all such surveys are subject to random sampling error. Mathematical sampling theory suggests that even a series of perfectly conducted polls should produce some random variation around the true figures that they are attempting to estimate.

[10] We emphasize that we use the term 'bias' here in the technical sense: to mean that the methodology of the surveys was tending to produce estimates that were wrong in a particular direction. We are not suggesting that any survey company was deliberately seeking to overstate Yes support in the referendum.

[11] Figures for the 1997 polls were taken from David McCrone and Bethan Lewis, 'The Scottish and Welsh referendum campaigns', in B. Taylor and K. Thomson (eds), *Scotland and Wales: Nations Again?* (Cardiff: University of Wales Press, 1999), p. 36.

[12] Richard Wyn Jones and Roger Scully, 'Devolution in Wales: what does the public think?', *Briefing Paper 7, ESRC Programme on Devolution and Constitutional Change* (2004), available at *http://www.devolution.ac.uk/Briefing_papers.htm*. Richard Wyn Jones and Roger Scully, 'A settling will? Wales and devolution, five years on', *British Elections and Parties Review*, 13 (2003), 86–106.

[13] For the purposes of this comparison, Ynys Môn, Gwynedd, Conwy, Flintshire, Denbighshire and Wrexham were counted as being in north Wales. Powys, Ceredigon, Carmarthen and Pembrokeshire were

counted as constituting mid and west Wales. All other local authorities were included in south Wales.

[14] Denis Balsom, 'The three-Wales model', in J. Osmond (ed.), *The National Question Again* (Llandysul: Gomer, 1985).

6: The people's choice: explaining voting in the referendum

[1] The potential hazards in drawing ecological inferences have long been understood. (For an excellent general discussion of the problem, and ways in which it can be addressed, see Wendy K. Tam Cho and Charles F. Manski, 'Cross-level/ecological inference', in Janet M. Box-Steffensmeier, Henry E. Brady and David Collier (eds), *The Oxford Handbook of Political Methodology* (Oxford: Oxford University Press, 2008).) To give a contemporary, political example of the problems that can arise: the BNP have often secured their best electoral results in the UK in areas with relatively high black and minority ethnic populations. We would surely not wish to infer from this that the BNP were therefore drawing the bulk of their support from such populations.

[2] For a full description of the 2011 Welsh Referendum Study, see the Appendix at the end of the book.

[3] For a major contemporary discussion of factors shaping voter turnout (and other forms of political participation) in the UK, see Harold D. Clarke, David Sanders, Marianne C. Stewart and Paul F. Whiteley, *Performance Politics and the British Voter* (Cambridge: Cambridge University Press, 2009), ch. 7.

[4] See, for example, Robert Johns, David Denver, James Mitchell and Charles Pattie, *Voting for a Scottish Government: the Scottish Parliament Election of 2007* (Manchester: Manchester University Press, 2010), ch. 8.

[5] Richard Wyn Jones and Dafydd Trystan, 'The 1997 Welsh referendum vote', in B. Taylor and K. Thomson (eds), *Scotland and Wales: Nations Again?* (Cardiff: University of Wales Press, 1999), pp. 65–93.

[6] The analysis in this section draws on survey data. Surveys typically over-state turnout levels in elections and referendums, for several reasons. Some people genuinely misremember; others prefer not to admit having not voted and offer a more 'socially-desirable' response. It is also true that people who agree to respond to social surveys are also more likely to vote. Internet-based surveys, like the 2011 Welsh Referendum Study, appear particularly prone to overstating turnout levels. (For an invaluable discussion on this point, within a wider comparison of different survey methods, see David Sanders, Harold D. Clarke, Marianne C. Stewart and Paul Whiteley, 'Does mode matter for modeling political choice? Evidence from the 2005 British Election Study', *Political Analysis*, 15 (2007), 257–85.) The official turnout figure in the referendum of 35.6 per cent compares with a reported turnout figure in the WRS post-referendum wave of 68.7 per cent. But the key point is that our analysis is seeking to uncover factors that distinguish voters from non-voters, not to estimate absolute levels of turnout.

7   On the importance of a sense of civic duty for shaping likelihood to vote, see Andre Blais, *To Vote or Not to Vote: the Merits and Limits of Rational Choice* (Pittsburgh: University of Pittsburgh Press, 2000).

8   Perceptions of the performance of the Welsh Assembly Government were measured via an index created from answers to a set of questions on key policy issues. Respondents were asked whether they perceived standards to have improved or declined since the previous NAW election in 2007 in four areas: the NHS, education, law and order, and the standard of living. Those perceiving either improvement or decline were then asked to whom they attributed primary responsibility for such changes. Respondents believing that improvements in any area were down to the Assembly Government were given a score of +1 for that policy; those believing that WAG was mainly to blame for any decline were given a score of –1 for that policy. All other respondents were coded 0 for the respective policy area. Two dummy variables are then created for the empirical analysis. The first is coded '1' for those with an overall positive rating of the WAG policy record, and 0 for all other respondents; the second is coded '1' for all those with a negative rating of the WAG policy record, 0 otherwise.

9   The predicted probabilities reported in figure 6.1 (and in figure 6.4) were computed using the CLARIFY software developed by Tomz, Wittenberg and King. (See Michael Tomz, Jason Wittenberg and Gary King, *CLARIFY: Software for Interpreting and Presenting Statistical Results Version 2.0.* (Cambridge, MA: Harvard University, 1 June 2000), *http://gking.harvard.edu*; Gary King, Michael Tomz and Jason Wittenberg, 'Making the most of statistical analysis: improving interpretation and presentation', *American Journal of Political Science*, 44 (2000), 347–61.) Results are calculated holding all other variables in the logistic regression equation at their mean values.

10 As a comparison, an almost identical question was used in the 2005 British Election Study. When asked whether they felt that 'The election campaign gave me enough information to make a good choice between the parties', more than two out of five respondents strongly agreed (2.3 per cent) or agreed (39.6 per cent), 30.1 per cent neither agreed nor disagreed, and slightly less than 30 per cent either disagreed (25.1 per cent) or strongly disagreed (2.9 per cent). Source: British Election Study 2005, post-election wave face-to-face sample; number of respondents = 4,070.

11 To the question 'Which of the two sides do you think ran the best referendum campaign?', 33.7 per cent chose the Yes campaign, 1.9 per cent chose the No campaign, 42.8 per cent chose Neither, and 21.6 per cent selected the Don't Know option. WRS post-referendum wave; number of respondents = 2,569.

12 This finding is very much in line with all survey evidence on public attitudes, which has long shown older age cohorts to have the lowest levels of enthusiasm for devolution in Wales.

13 See, for example, Sara Binzer Hobolt, *Europe in Question: Referendums on European Integration* (Oxford: Oxford University Press, 2008).

[14] Richard Wyn Jones and Roger Scully, 'Devolution and electoral politics in Scotland and Wales', *Publius*, 36 (2006), 115–34; Charlie Jeffery and Arjan Schakel, 'Are regional elections really "second-order" elections?', unpublished paper.

[15] Our measure of attitudes to the UK government was drawn from two WRS questions, which asked respondents to rate the performance over the previous year of Conservative ministers in the UK government, and Liberal Democrat ministers in the UK government, on a five-point scale running from very good to very bad. Responses to the two questions were then averaged. Two dummy variables were then created: one was coded '1' for those with an average positive response to the performance of Conservative and Liberal Democrat UK ministers, and 0 otherwise; the second was coded '1' for those with an average negative response, 0 otherwise.

[16] Wyn Jones and Trystan, 'The 1997 Welsh referendum vote'.

7: The implications

[1] There are plenty of examples of strange referendums. Some would count among their number Wales's local referendums on Sunday drinking. In some instances it is not so much the question that is odd as the structure of the choice. To give but one example of the latter: a referendum on school reform in Munich in 2010, rather than asking citizens to choose between two options, asked citizens to cast separate votes on two contradictory proposals – thus making it possible to vote Yes on both of them! (We thank Johannes Blumenberg for informing us about this case.)

[2] For the classic discussion of 'diffuse support', see David Easton, *A Systems Analysis of Political Life* (New York: Wiley, 1965).

[3] See, for example, Gregory Caldeira and James Gibson, 'The legitimacy of the Court of Justice in the European Union: models of institutional support', *American Political Science Review*, 89 (1995), 356–76.

[4] *http://www.commissiononscottishdevolution.org.uk/*.

[5] The commission's report is available at *http://wales.gov.uk/icffw/home/report/?lang=en*.

[6] See *http://www.ukcle.ac.uk/resources/directions/previous/issue16/wales/*.

[7] Cited in *http://www.ukcle.ac.uk/resources/directions/previous/welsh-politics/welsh-politics-news/2011/03/23/wales-needs-a-distinctive-legal-jurisdiction-91466-28385237/*.

[8] The next three paragraphs draw on Richard Wyn Jones, 'Seiliau cyfansoddiadol y ddeddfwrfa Gymreig', Darlith Flynyddol y Coleg Cymraeg Cenedlaethol, Eisteddfod Genedlaethol Wrecsam a'r Fro 2011 (Caerfyrddin: Y Coleg Cymraeg Cenedlaethol, 2011).

[9] Scottish Constitutional Convention, *Towards Scotland's Parliament* (Edinburgh: Scottish Constitutional Convention, 1990); Scottish Constitutional Convention, *Scotland's Parliament; Scotland's Right* (Edinburgh: Scottish Constitutional Convention, 1995).

10 The Constitution Unit, *Scotland's Parliament: Fundamentals for a New Scotland Act* (London: Constitution Unit, 1996), especially pp. 35–9.

11 Cited ibid., p. 39.

12 Peter Hain and Rhodri Morgan, 'Memorandum to the House of Commons Select Committee on Welsh Affairs, 10 November 2005', *Government of Wales Act: Explanatory Notes* (2005), pp. 58–9 (*www.legislation.gov.uk/ukpga/2006/32/pdfs/ukpgaen_20060032_en.pdf*).

13 For an authoritative recent overview, see Sir David Lloyd Jones, 'The machinery of justice in a changing Wales', Law Society Wales Office Annual Lecture 2010 (available from *http://www.lawsociety.org.uk/about-lawsociety/how/workinwales/news.page*).

14 It should be noted that the Richard Commission (on p. 250 of the report) favoured the reserved powers model for Wales.

15 *http://www.walesoffice.gov.uk/2011/07/19/next-steps-for-commission-on-devolution-in-wales-outlined/*.

16 For Holtham, see the *Final Report. Fairness and Accountability: a New Funding Settlement for Wales* (Cardiff: Welsh Assembly Government, July 2010), pp. 119–21. Straw was speaking on 3 December 2009. His speech is available from *http://webarchive.nationalarchives.gov.uk/+/http://www.justice.gov.uk/news/speech031209a.htm*. That Straw departed from his original script in voicing his support for referendum has been confirmed to the authors by a single anonymous source. See also Alan Trench's commentary at *http://devolutionmatters.wordpress.com/2009/12/03/jack-straw-a-welsh-legal-jurisdiction-and-yet-another-referendum/*.

17 The UK coalition agreements are available from *http://www.cabinetoffice.gov.uk/news/coalition-documents*. The pledge referred to is on p. 27 of the *Programme for Government*.

Bibliography

Official documents

Report and Proposals of the Local Government Commission for Wales, Presented to the Minister of Housing and Local Government. December, 1962 (London: HMSO, 1963).

Strengthening of the Welsh Office and the Welsh Council: Memorandum by the Secretary of State for Wales (26 March 1968).

'Devolution and other aspects of governance: an attitudes survey', *Royal Commission on the Constitution Research Paper 7* (London: HMSO, 1973).

Report of the Royal Commission on the Constitution 1969–1973, Cmnd. 5460 (London: HMSO, October 1973).

Royal Commission on the Constitution 1969–73, Volume II: Memorandum of Dissent, Cmnd. 5460–1 (London: HMSO, October 1973).

Office of the Lord President of the Council, *Devolution within the United Kingdom: Some Alternatives for Discussion* (London: HMSO, 1974).

Democracy and Devolution: Proposals for Scotland and Wales, Cmnd. 5732 (London: HMSO, 1974).

Our Changing Democracy: Devolution to Scotland and Wales, Cmnd. 6348 (London: HMSO, November 1975).

Devolution to Wales and Scotland: Supplementary Statement, Cmnd. 6585 (London: HMSO, August 1976).

Devolution: Financing the Devolved Services, Cmnd. 6890 (London: HMSO, July 1977).

Committee on Standards in Public Life, *The Funding of Political Parties in the United Kingdom* (London: The Stationery Office, 1998).

Welsh Office National Assembly Advisory Group, *National Assembly for Wales: Have your Say on How it Will Work: a Consultation Paper* (Cardiff: Welsh Office, 1998).

Wales Office, *Better Governance for Wales, Cm 6582* (London: The Stationery Office, 2005).

Commission on Boundary Differences and Voting Systems, *Putting Citizens First: Boundaries, Voting and Representation in Scotland* (Edinburgh: Stationery Office, January 2006).

All Wales Convention Report (Cardiff: All Wales Convention, 2009).

Final Report. Fairness and Accountability: a New Funding Settlement for Wales (Cardiff: Welsh Assembly Government, July 2010).

Labour Party publications and policy documents

Labour's Programme for Britain: Annual Conference (London, 1972).

Labour's Programme for Britain: Annual Conference 1973 (London, 1973).

Devolution and Democracy: a Statement by the Executive Committee for Consideration at a Special Delegate Conference, Llandrindod Wells, 22nd June, 1974 (1974).

Wales Will Win with Labour (Cardiff, 1974).

Policies for a Brighter Future for Wales (1974).

The National Labour Party commitment to the policy put forward in Wales on the matter of a Welsh Assembly and Devolution (no date given, but probably 1975).

Speaker's Notes on Devolution (January 1976).

Local Government Reform in England and Wales, Labour Party Consultative Paper (London, 1986).

A Welsh Assembly. The Way Forward. Wales Labour Party Policy Commission Interim Report (Cardiff, 1993).

Shaping the Vision. A Consultation Paper on the Powers and Structure of the Welsh Assembly (Cardiff, 1994).

Shaping the Vision. A Report on the Powers and Structure of the Welsh Assembly (Cardiff, 1995).

'Shaping the Vision': an Outline of Labour Party Wales Proposals (Cardiff, 1995).

Preparing for a New Wales: a Report on the Structure and Workings of the Welsh Assembly (Cardiff, 1996).

Better Governance for Wales (August 2004).

Britain Forward Not Back, Wales Labour Party Manifesto (Cardiff, 2005).

Secondary works

Allswang, John, *The Initiative and Referendum in California, 1898–1998* (Stanford: Stanford University Press, 2000).

Andrews, Leighton, *Wales Says Yes* (Bridgend: Seren, 1999).

Baker, Kendall, Russell Dalton and Kai Hildebrandt, *Germany Transformed: Political Culture and the New Politics* (Cambridge: Cambridge University Press, 1981).

Balsom, Denis, 'Public opinion and Welsh devolution', in David Foulkes, J. Barry Jones and R. A. Wilford (eds), *The Welsh Veto: the Wales Act 1978 and the Referendum* (Cardiff: University of Wales Press, 1983), pp. 197–215.

Balsom, Denis, 'The three-Wales model', in J. Osmond (ed.), *The National Question Again* (Llandysul: Gomer, 1985).

Balsom, Denis and J. Barry Jones (eds), *The Road to the National Assembly for Wales* (Cardiff: University of Wales Press, 1999).

Bendix, Reinhardt, *Nation-building and Citizenship* (New York: John Wiley and Sons, 1965).

Bevan Foundation, *Public Attitudes to Dual Candidacy in the Elections to the National Assembly for Wales, Occasional Paper No. 5* (January 2006).

Blais, Andre, *To Vote or Not to Vote: the Merits and Limits of Rational Choice* (Pittsburgh: University of Pittsburgh Press, 2000).

Bogdanor, Vernon, 'Devolution and the constitution', *Parliamentary Affairs*, 31 (1978), 252–67.

Bogdanor, Vernon, 'The 40 per cent clause', *Parliamentary Affairs*, 33 (1979), 249–63.

Bogdanor, Vernon, *Devolution in the United Kingdom* (updated edn; Oxford: Oxford Paperbacks, 2001).

Bogdanor, Vernon, 'The consistency of Dicey: a reply to McLean and MacMillan', *Public Law* (spring 2008).

Bowler, Shaun and Todd Donovan, *Demanding Choices: Opinion, Voting, and Direct Democracy* (Ann Arbor: University of Michigan Press, 1998).

Boynton, G. R. and Gerhard Loewenberg, 'The development of public support for Parliament in Germany, 1951–59', *British Journal of Political Science*, 3 (1973), 169–89.

Butler, David and Uwe Kitzinger, *The 1975 Referendum* (London: Macmillan, 1976).

Butler, David and Iain McLean, 'Referendums', in B. Taylor and K. Thomson (eds), *Scotland and Wales: Nations Again?* (Cardiff: University of Wales Press, 1999).

Butler, David and Austin Ranney (eds), *Referendums Around the World: the Growing Use of Direct Democracy* (Washington, DC: American Enterprise Institute Press, 1994).

Butt Philip, Alan, *The Welsh Question: Nationalism in Welsh Politics 1945–70* (Cardiff: University of Wales Press, 1975).

Caldeira, Gregory and James Gibson, 'The legitimacy of the Court of Justice in the European Union: models of institutional support', *American Political Science Review*, 89 (1995), 356–76.

Carter, H. and J. G. Thomas, 'The referendum on the Sunday opening of licensed premises in Wales as a criterion of a culture region', *Regional Studies*, 3 (1969), 61–71.

Chaney, Paul, Fiona Mackay and Laura McAllister, *Women, Politics and Constitutional Change* (Cardiff: University of Wales Press, 2007).

Clarke, Harold and Allan Kornberg, 'The politics and economics of constitutional choice: voting in Canada's 1992 national referendum', *Journal of Politics*, 56 (1994), 940–62.

Clarke, Harold, Allan Kornberg and Marianne Stewart, 'Referendum voting as political choice', *British Journal of Political Science*, 34 (2004), 345–55.

Clarke, Harold D., David Sanders, Marianne C. Stewart and Paul F. Whiteley, *Performance Politics and the British Voter* (Cambridge: Cambridge University Press, 2009).

Commission on the Powers and Electoral Arrangements of the National Assembly for Wales, *Report of the Richard Commission* (Cardiff: National Assembly for Wales, 2004).

The Constitution Unit, *Scotland's Parliament: Fundamentals for a New Scotland Act* (London: Constitution Unit, 1996).

Crossman, Richard, *The Diaries of a Cabinet Minister: Vol. 2, Lord President of the Council and Leader of the House of Commons 1966–1968* (London: Hamilton, 1976).

Crossman, Richard, *The Diaries of a Cabinet Minister: Vol. 3, Secretary of State for Social Services, 1968–1970* (London: Hamilton, 1977).

Davies, Rebecca, 'Banal Britishness and reconstituted Welshness: the politics of national identities in Wales', *Contemporary Wales*, 18 (2006), 106–21.

Davies, Ron, *Devolution: a Process Not an Event* (Cardiff: Institute of Welsh Affairs, 1999).

Denver, David, James Mitchell, Charles Pattie and Hugh Bochel, *Scotland Decides: the Devolution Issue and the Scottish Referendum* (London: Frank Cass, 2000).

Donoghue, Bernard, *Downing Street Diary: With Harold Wilson in No. 10* (London: Jonathan Cape, 2005).

Dowling, Andrew, '*Autonomistes, Catalanistes* and *Independentistes*: politics in contemporary Catalonia', *International Journal of Iberian Studies*, 22 (2009), 185–200.

Drucker, H. M. and Gordon Brown, *The Politics of Nationalism and Devolution* (London: Longman, 1980).

Easton, David, *A Systems Analysis of Political Life* (New York: Wiley, 1965).

Edwards, Andrew and Duncan Tanner, 'Defining or dividing the nation? Opinion polls, Welsh identity and devolution, 1966–1979', *Contemporary Wales*, 18 (2006), 54–71.

The Electoral Commission, *Wales Votes? Public Attitudes towards Assembly Elections* (London: The Electoral Commission, 2002).

223

The Electoral Commission, *Wales – Poll Position. Public Attitudes towards Assembly Elections* (London: The Electoral Commission, 2006).

Evans, Geoffrey and Dafydd Trystan, 'Why was 1997 different?', in B. Taylor and K. Thomson (eds), *Scotland and Wales: Nations Again?* (Cardiff: University of Wales Press, 1999), pp. 95–117.

Evans, John Gilbert, *Devolution in Wales: Claims and Responses, 1937–1979* (Cardiff: University of Wales Press, 2006).

Evans, Rhys, *Gwynfor Evans: a Portrait of a Patriot* (Talybont: Y Lolfa, 2008).

Foley, Michael, *The Politics of the British Constitution* (Manchester: Manchester University Press, 1999).

Foulkes, David, J. Barry Jones and R. A. Wilford (eds), *The Welsh Veto: the Wales Act 1978 and the Referendum* (Cardiff: University of Wales Press, 1983).

Francis, Hywel, *History on our Side: Wales and the 1984–85 Miners' Strike* (Cardigan: Parthian Books, 2009).

Franklin, Mark, *Voter Turnout and the Dynamics of Electoral Competition in Established Democracies since 1945* (Cambridge: Cambridge University Press, 2004).

Franklin, Mark, Cees van der Eijk and Michael Marsh, 'Referendum outcomes and trust in government: public support for Europe in the wake of Maastricht', *West European Politics*, 18 (1995), 101–17.

Gibson, E. L., *A Study of the Council for Wales and Monmouthshire, 1948–1966* (unpublished LLB, University College of Wales, Aberystwyth, 1968).

Hazell, Robert, Meg Russell, Jeremy Croft, Ben Seyd and Roger Masterman, 'The constitution: rolling out the new settlement', *Parliamentary Affairs*, 54 (2001), 190–205.

Hobolt, Sara Binzer, *Europe in Question: Referendums on European Integration* (Oxford: Oxford University Press, 2008).

Hug, Simon and Pascal Sciarini, 'Referendums on European integration: do institutions matter in the voter's decision?', *Comparative Political Studies*, 33 (2000), 3–36.

James, Mari and Peter D. Lindley, 'The parliamentary passage of the Wales Act 1978', in David Foulkes, J. Barry Jones and R. A. Wilford (eds), *The Welsh Veto: the Wales Act 1978 and the Referendum* (Cardiff: University of Wales Press, 1983), pp. 34–61.

Johns, Robert, David Denver, James Mitchell and Charles Pattie, *Voting for a Scottish Government: the Scottish Parliament Election of 2007* (Manchester: Manchester University Press, 2010).

Jones, J. Barry, 'The British Labour Party as a centralising force', University of Strathclyde: Centre for the Study of Public Policy no. 32 (1979).

Jones, J. Barry and R. A. Wilford, 'The referendum campaign: 8 February–1 March 1979', in David Foulkes, J. Barry Jones and R. A. Wilford (eds), *The Welsh Veto: the Wales Act 1978 and the Referendum* (Cardiff: University of Wales Press, 1983), pp. 118–52.

Jones, Peter, 'Labour's referendum plan: sell-out or act of faith?', *Scottish Affairs*, 18 (1997), 1–17.

Kellas, James, G., *The Scottish Political System* (Cambridge: Cambridge University Press, 1989).

King, Gary, Michael Tomz and Jason Wittenberg, 'Making the most of statistical analysis: improving interpretation and presentation', *American Journal of Political Science*, 44 (2000), 347–61.

Laffin, Martin and Alys Thomas, 'Designing the National Assembly for Wales', *Parliamentary Affairs*, 53 (2003), 557–76.

LeDuc, Lawrence, 'Referendums and initiatives: the politics of direct democracy', in L. LeDuc, R. Niemi and P. Norris (eds), *Comparing Democracies 2: New Challenges in the Study of Elections and Voting* (London: Sage, 2002).

McAllister, Ian, 'The Labour Party in Wales: the dynamics of one-partyism', *Llafur*, 3 (1980), 79–89.

McAllister, Laura, 'The Richard Commission – Wales's alternative constitutional convention?', *Contemporary Wales*, 17 (2004), 128–39.

McCrone, David and Bethan Lewis, 'The Scottish and Welsh devolution campaigns', in B. Taylor and K. Thomson (eds), *Scotland and Wales: Nations Again?* (Cardiff: University of Wales Press, 1999), pp. 17–40.

Mackintosh, John P., *The Devolution of Power: Local Democracy, Regionalism and Nationalism* (London: Penguin, 1968).

McLean, Iain and Alistair McMillan, *State of the Union: Unionism and the Alternatives in the United Kingdom since 1707* (Oxford: Oxford University Press, 2005).

McLean, Iain and Alistair McMillan, 'Professor Dicey's contradictions', *Public Law* (autumn 2007), 435–43.

McLean, Iain and Tom Lubbock, 'The curious incident of the guns in the night time: Curragh, Larne and the UK constitution', *Nuffield College Working Papers*, 2007–W4 (8 June 2007), available at *www.nuff.ox.ac.uk/politics/papers*.

Melding, David, 'Terrific twins of Welsh constitutional thought', *Agenda: the Journal of the Institute of Welsh Affairs*, 42 (2010).

Mitchell, James, *Devolution in the United Kingdom* (Manchester: Manchester University Press, 2009).

Morgan, Kenneth O., 'Foreword', in David Foulkes, J. Barry Jones and R. A.

Wilford (eds), *The Welsh Veto: the Wales Act 1978 and the Referendum* (Cardiff: University of Wales Press, 1983).

Morgan, Kenneth O., 'The red dragon and red flag: the cases of Jim Griffiths and Aneurin Bevan', *Modern Wales: Politics, Places and People* (Cardiff: University of Wales Press, 1995).

Morgan, Kenneth O., *Callaghan: a Life* (Oxford: Oxford University Press, 1997).

Morgan, Kevin and Geoff Mungham, *Redesigning Democracy: the Welsh Labour Party and Devolution* (Bridgend: Seren, 2000).

Morgan, Kevin and Geoff Mungham, 'Unfinished business: Labour's devolution policy', in J. Barry Jones and Denis Balsom (eds), *The Road to the National Assembly for Wales* (Cardiff: University of Wales Press, 2000), pp. 28–49.

Morgan, Rhodri, *Variable Geometry UK* (Cardiff: Institute of Welsh Affairs, 2000).

Osmond, John, *Creative Conflict: the Politics of Welsh Devolution* (Llandysul and London: Gomer and Routledge and Kegan Paul, 1978).

Osmond, John (ed.), *Parliament for Wales* (Llandysul: Gomer, 1994).

Osmond, John, *Welsh Europeans* (Bridgend: Seren, 1996).

Osmond, John, 'A constitutional convention by other means: the first year of the National Assembly for Wales', in Robert Hazell (ed.), *The State and the Nations: the First Year of Devolution in the United Kingdom* (Exeter: Imprint, 2001), pp. 37–77.

Osmond, John, *Crossing the Rubicon: Coalition Politics Welsh Style* (Cardiff: Institute of Welsh Affairs, 2007).

Pammett, Jon H. and Lawrence LeDuc, 'Sovereignty, leadership and voting in the Quebec referendums', *Electoral Studies*, 20 (2001), 265–80.

Paterson, Lindsay and Richard Wyn Jones, 'Does civil society drive constitutional change? The cases of Scotland and Wales', in B. Taylor and K. Thomson (eds), *Scotland and Wales: Nations Again?* (Cardiff: University of Wales Press, 1999), pp. 169–97.

Pempel, T. J. (ed.), *Uncommon Democracies: the One-Party Dominant Regimes* (Ithaca, NY: Cornell University Press, 1990).

Pierce, Roy, Henry Valen and Ola Listhaug, 'Referendum voting behavior: the Norwegian and British referenda on membership in the European Community', *American Journal of Political Science*, 27 (1983), 43–63.

Prescott, John and Tom Pendry, *Alternative Regional Strategy: a Framework for Discussion* (London: Labour Party, 1982).

Price, Emyr, *Yr Arglwydd Cledwyn o Benrhos* (Penygroes: Cyhoeddiadau Mei, 1990).

Prys Davies, Gwilym, *A Central Welsh Council* (Aberystwyth: Undeb Cymru Fydd/New Wales Union, 1963).

Prys Davies, Gwilym, *Llafur y Blynyddoedd* (Dinbych: Gwasg Gee, 1991).

Prys Davies, Gwilym, *Cynhaeaf Hanner Canrif: Gwleidyddiaeth Gymreig 1945–2005* (Llandysul: Gomer, 2008).

Rawlings, Richard, *Three Faces of the National Assembly for Wales* (Swansea: University of Wales Swansea, 2002).

Rawlings, Richard, *Delineating Wales: Constitutional, Legal and Administrative Aspects of National Devolution* (Cardiff: University of Wales Press, 2003).

Rose, Richard, 'The United Kingdom as a multi-national state', *University of Strathclyde Occasional Paper* (1970), no. 6.

Rowlands, Ted, 'Whitehall's last stand: the establishment of the Welsh Office, 1964', *Contemporary Wales*, 16 (2004), 39–52.

Sanders, David, Harold D. Clarke, Marianne C. Stewart and Paul Whiteley, 'Does mode matter for modeling political choice? Evidence from the 2005 British Election Study', *Political Analysis*, 15 (2007), 257–85.

Sarlvik, Bo, Ivor Crewe, James Alt and Anthony Fox, 'Britain's membership of the EEC: a profile of electoral opinions in the spring of 1974 – with a postscript on the referendum', *European Journal of Political Research*, 4 (1976), 83–113.

Scottish Constitutional Convention, *Towards Scotland's Parliament* (Edinburgh: Scottish Constitutional Convention, 1990).

Scottish Constitutional Convention, *Scotland's Parliament; Scotland's Right* (Edinburgh: Scottish Constitutional Convention, 1995).

Scully, Roger, 'Has devolution made the people of Wales more Welsh?', paper presented to the Department of Politics and International Relations, Swansea University, February 2010.

Scully, Roger and Anwen Elias, 'The 2007 Welsh Assembly election', *Regional and Federal Studies*, 18 (2008), 103–9.

Scully, Roger and Richard Wyn Jones, 'The legitimacy of devolved government in Scotland and Wales', paper presented to the Annual Conference of the American Political Science Association, Boston (2008).

Shipton, Martin, *Poor Man's Parliament? Ten Years of the Welsh Assembly* (Bridgend: Seren, 2011).

Smith, J. Beverley (ed.), *James Griffiths and his Times* (Labour Party Wales and the Llanelli Constituency Labour Party, 1978).

Tam Cho, Wendy K. and Charles F. Manski, 'Cross-level/ecological inference', in Janet M. Box-Steffensmeier, Henry E. Brady and David Collier (eds), *The Oxford Handbook of Political Methodology* (Oxford: Oxford University Press, 2008).

Tanner, Duncan, 'Richard Crossman, Harold Wilson and devolution, 1966–70: the making of government policy', *Twentieth Century British History*, 17 (2006), 545–78.

Trench, Alan, 'Rhodri's retreat', *Agenda: the Journal of the Institute of Welsh Affairs* (summer 2004), 40–1.

Trench, Alan, 'Introduction: the dynamics of devolution', in A. Trench (ed.), *The Dynamics of Devolution: State of the Nations 2005* (Exeter: Imprint Academic, 2005), pp. 1–22.

Vowles, Jack, 'The politics of electoral reform in New Zealand', *International Political Science Review*, (1995), 95–115.

Weill, Rivka, 'Dicey was not a Diceyan', *Cambridge Law Journal*, 62 (2003), 474–94.

Williams, Gwyn A., *When Was Wales: a History of the Welsh* (London: Penguin, 1985).

Williams, Tim, 'Yes, we have no bananas', *Western Mail*, 12 August 2002.

Wyn Jones, Richard, 'Route map to power', interview with the Right Hon. Peter Hain, Secretary of State for Wales, *Agenda: the Journal of the Institute of Welsh Affairs* (winter 2005/2006), 24–8.

Wyn Jones, Richard, *Rhoi Cymru'n Gyntaf: Syniadaeth Plaid Cymru. Cyfrol 1* (Caerdydd: University of Wales Press, 2007).

Wyn Jones, Richard, 'In the shadow of 1979', *Planet: the Welsh Internationalist*, 194 (spring 2009), 8–15.

Wyn Jones, Richard, 'Seiliau cyfansoddiadol y ddeddfwrfa Gymreig', darlith flynyddol y Coleg Cymraeg Cenedlaethol, Eisteddfod Genedlaethol Wrecsam a'r Fro 2011 (Caerfyrddin: Y Coleg Cymraeg Cenedlaethol, 2011).

Wyn Jones, Richard and Bethan Lewis, 'The Wales Labour Party and Welsh civil society: aspects of the constitutional debate in Wales', paper presented to the 1998 Annual Conference of the Political Studies Association.

Wyn Jones, Richard and Bethan Lewis, 'The 1997 Welsh devolution referendum', *Politics*, 19 (1999), 37–46.

Wyn Jones, Richard and Dafydd Trystan, 'The 1997 Welsh referendum vote', in B. Taylor and K. Thomson (eds) *Scotland and Wales: Nations Again?* (Cardiff: University of Wales Press, 1999), pp. 65–93.

Wyn Jones, Richard and Roger Scully, 'A settling will? Wales and devolution, five years on', *British Elections and Parties Review*, 13 (2003), 86–106.

Wyn Jones, Richard and Roger Scully, 'Devolution in Wales: what does the public think?', *Briefing Paper 7, ESRC Programme on Devolution and Constitutional Change* (2004), available at *http://www.devolution.ac.uk/Briefing_papers.htm.*

Wyn Jones, Richard and Roger Scully, 'Minor tremor but several casualties: the 2003 Welsh election', *British Elections and Parties Review*, 14 (2004), 191–210.

Wyn Jones, Richard and Roger Scully, 'Devolution and electoral politics in Scotland and Wales', *Publius*, 36 (2006), 115–34.

Wyn Jones, Richard and Roger Scully, 'What happened in the 2010 election? Why?', paper presented to Public Seminar on the 2010 General Election, Cardiff (2010).

Young, Hugo, *This Blessed Plot: Britain and Europe from Churchill to Blair* (London: MacMillan, 1998).

Internet sources

Constitution Unit, Wales Monitoring Reports, March 2004, June 2004, September 2004, December 2004, April 2005 and January 2006, *www.ucl.ac.uk/constitution-unit*.

Electoral Reform Society, *The Electoral Commission's Response* (Cardiff: Electoral Reform Society Wales, 2005).

Electoral Reform Society, *Much Better Governance for Wales* (Cardiff: Electoral Reform Society Wales, 2005).

Hain, Peter and Rhodri Morgan, 'Memorandum to the House of Commons Select Committee on Welsh Affairs, 10 November 2005', *Government of Wales Act: Explanatory Notes* (2005), *www.legislation.gov.uk/ukpga/2006/32/pdfs/ukpgaen_20060032_en.pdf*.

Ieuan Wyn Jones interviewed in the *Guardian*, 25 February 2003, *http://www.guardian.co.uk/politics/2003/feb/25/wales.comment*.

Labour Party general election manifesto (1970), *http://www.psr.keele.ac.uk/area/uk/man/lab70.htm#dem*.

Index